THE VOYAGE OF THE *SCOTIA*

Scotland to Coats Land

TRACK CHART OF THE "SCOTIA," 1902-1904, BY WILLIAM S. BRUCE, LL.D.

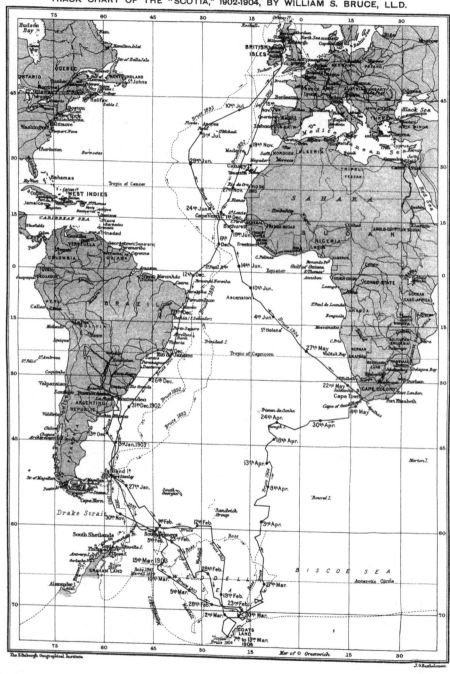

The Edinburgh Geographical Institute

J. G. Bartholomew.

THE VOYAGE OF THE *SCOTIA*

Being the
Record of a Voyage of Exploration
in Antarctic Seas

R.C. MOSSMAN
J.H. HARVEY PIRIE
R.N. RUDMOSE BROWN

With a new Foreword by
DR DAVID MUNRO
Director of the Royal Scottish Geographical Society

mercatpress
www.mercatpress.com

First published in 1906 by Blackwood, Edinburgh
Simultaneously published by C.Hurst and Company in London
This edition published 2002 by Mercat Press Ltd.
10 Coates Crescent, Edinburgh EH3 7AL

© Mercat Press Ltd., 2002

Foreword © David Munro, 2002

All photographs are from the collection of the Royal Scottish Geographical
Society, Glasgow, and appear courtesy of the Society

Set in Minion 10.5 pt at Mercat Press

Printed and bound in Great Britain by Bell & Bain Ltd.

CONTENTS

CHAPTER VIII
SLEDGE AND BOAT JOURNEYS
J.H. Harvey Pirie

CHAPTER IX
TO BUENOS AIRES AND BACK
R.N. Rudmose Brown

CHAPTER X
THE SUMMER PARTY ON THE SOUTH ORKNEYS
J.H. Harvey Pirie

CHAPTER XI
SECOND CRUISE IN THE WEDDELL SEA
J.H. Harvey Pirie

CHAPTER XII
GOUGH ISLAND AND SOUTH AFRICA
R.N. Rudmose Brown

A forgotten island—Anticipations—A beauteous land—Difficult landing —Plants and birds—Ruined huts—Geology—Better weather— Trawling—Sounding mishaps—Nearing civilisation—Phosphorescence —A break-down—Table Bay—A disappointing town—A hapless colony —Along the coast—Saldanha Bay —Boer villages—The veldt ......

CHAPTER XIII
THE HOMEWARD VOYAGE
R.N. Rudmose Brown

Quick runs—Pleasant times—St Helena—Napoleonic relics—Excursions— Prickly pears—An extinct flora—Swarms of fish—Birds on board—Ascension—A ship on shore—Turtles—Wideawakes—A desert land—Green mountain—Water-supply—Rollers—Tropical heat—Flying-fish—Pelagic animals—The Doldrums —Looking for the trade-wind—Cape Verdes again—Gulf weed—Another effigy —The Princess Alice Bank—Fayal—A smiling land—More temperate climes— A breeze in the bay—Tuskar Light again—A wild morning—Kingstown Harbour —Ireland's welcome—In the Clyde—Home at last ...

CHAPTER XIV
THE SECOND WINTER
R.C. Mossman

Departure of *Scotia*—House improvements—South-east gale—Building a breakwater—Capture of cuttle-fish—Another south-east gale—House in danger —Damage done—Building of new store-room—Independence day—Optical and atmospheric phenomena—Winter routine—A cold snap—A remarkable iceberg —Scientific work in winter .....

CHAPTER XV
RETURNING SPRING
R.C. Mossman

Weddell seals—A long excursion—A blizzard—An unpleasant month—Return of penguins—A long-continued snow-storm—Penguins' eggs obtained—A sun-bath—Fantastic bergs—Excursion to caves—A young Ross seal—Boldness of skuas—A boating trip—A busy naturalist—A dull Christmas—Arrival of relief ship ....

CHAPTER XVI
THE VOYAGE OF THE *URUGUAY*
R.C. Mossman

Note: for this edition, the publishers have re-titled the original Chapter I as Introduction, renumbering subsequent chapters accordingly.

ILLUSTRATIONS

Frontispiece: Track chart of the *Scotia*, 1902-1904

Between pages 48 and 49:

Between pages 112 and 113:

FOREWORD TO THE 2002 EDITION
Dr David Munro, Director of the Royal Scottish Geographical Society

WILLIAM Speirs Bruce (1867-1921), leader of the Scottish National Antarctic Expedition of 1902-04, was without doubt one of the most experienced and respected polar scientists of his time, participating in eleven expeditions to the Arctic as well as two to the Antarctic. He not only made a substantial contribution to our knowledge of polar regions in the fields of geography, meteorology, zoology and oceanography, but also can be said to have been, in the words of Sir Patrick Geddes, 'the initiator of this now world-wide movement of Antarctic Exploration.'

New perspectives on the life of William Bruce, who worked tirelessly for polar research for nearly three decades, have been revealed through the recent study of a wealth of manuscripts, photographs and press cuttings, and at last his place in the 'Heroic Age of Polar Exploration' has been established. As so often happens, History re-evaluates its famous men and women and some who had little recognition in their day are given their dues many years later.

The *Report on the Scientific Results of the Voyage of SY Scotia*, painstakingly edited by Bruce, was published in six volumes between 1907 and 1920 under the imprint of the Scottish Oceanographical Laboratory that he founded in Edinburgh in 1907. Only shortage of funds prevented all of the projected volumes from being published: the major omission, the *Log of the Scotia*, eventually being edited by Dr Peter Speak of the Scott Polar Research Institute and published as Volume I of the series in 1992 with a foreword by Sir Vivian Fuchs.

Crammed with matter-of-fact scientific data and analysis, Bruce's reports rarely indicate what it must have been like to travel from Scotland to the Antarctic and back at the beginning of the 20th century in what was described fifty years later by one of the ship's scientists, Robert Rudmose Brown, as 'one of the last of the old-time efforts with a wooden ship, with auxiliary steam, no radio, no mechanical transport, and no sonic sounding.' *The Voyage of the Scotia*, on the other hand, provides a first hand account that is both readable and gripping.

Penned by the scientists Robert N. Rudmose Brown, John H. Harvey Pirie and Robert C. Mossman and first published by William Blackwood & Sons in 1906, *The Voyage of the Scotia* has all the elements of a tale of high adventure, describing as it does the rigours of life at sea, the trials of overwintering in Antarctica and the highs and lows of morale ebbing and flowing with the icy waters of the South Atlantic.

It is appropriate that this edition of *The Voyage of the Scotia* coincides with celebrations marking the 100th anniversary of the Scottish National Antarctic Expedition of 1902-04, one of a series of celebrations highlighting the achievements of those who went south to Antarctica during the 'Heroic Age'. In the summer of 2002 the Royal Scottish Geographical Society, in collaboration with individuals and organisations such as the National Museums of Scotland, the National Youth Orchestras of Scotland, the Royal Scottish Country Dance Society and the universities of Scotland, embarked upon a substantial and imaginative Centenary Programme under the joint patronage of HRH The Princess Royal and HSH Prince Albert of Monaco.

This centenary is not only an opportunity to celebrate the outstanding contribution made to scientific exploration by Scots, both past and present, but also a chance to highlight the importance of geographical teaching and research in advancing our understanding of the world we live in. Each element of the Scotia Centenary Programme is designed to create something lasting that will benefit society in the long term. The creation of music and art, the promotion of educational material and the advancement of scientific studies in Antarctica are all part of this centenary celebration.

In his Prefatory Note to *The Voyage of the Scotia*, Bruce unashamedly stated that 'While "Science" was the talisman of the Expedition, "Scotland" was emblazoned on its flag'. By rekindling the 'spirit of the Scotia' a hundred years on, Scotland has an opportunity to demonstrate that it continues to take pride in advancing educational excellence and its role in exploring the wider world. Like Bruce and his men we will, in the process, hopefully be able 'to serve humanity by adding another link to the golden chain of science'.

Dr David M. Munro
Director and Secretary
Royal Scottish Geographical Society

PREFARATORY NOTE
William S. Bruce

A SINGLE line to introduce the reader to three of my *Scotia* comrades—the authors of this volume—who, during all the vicissitudes of a difficult and adventurous voyage, staunchly supported me in endeavouring to carry out the work to a successful issue.

Within these pages will be found a faithful account of the life and work of the Scottish National Antarctic Expedition, which I had the honour to lead. Those perusing this book will find much that is interesting and instructive, for the authors, besides endeavouring to give a popular account of the voyage, have by their thoroughness and enthusiasm in the cause of science brought together many facts of scientific interest and importance that cannot fail to be of value in giving the public a true account of one of the least known parts of the South Polar regions.

The volume is especially for Scots throughout the world. It has been suggested that the despatch of the Scottish Expedition was superfluous and unnecessary; but I venture to state that there is at least no biologist or oceanographer of note who will agree with that opinion. While "Science" was the talisman of the Expedition, "Scotland" was emblazoned on its flag; and it may be that, in endeavouring to serve humanity by adding another link to the golden chain of science, we have also shown that the nationality of Scotland is a power that must be reckoned with.

SCOTTISH OCEANOGRAPHICAL LABORATORY,
SURGEONS' HALL, EDINBURGH,
September 1906

PREFACE

RECENT years have witnessed a notable revival of interest in the Antarctic regions, the outcome of the great international campaign directed against these ten million square miles of the globe's surface which, despite the efforts of a few daring navigators at infrequent intervals during the last two centuries, still remained an almost unknown region. This great international campaign of scientific discovery is now at an end, and the five participating countries—Germany, Sweden, France, England, and Scotland—can fairly claim that, though much remains to be accomplished, yet their attempts have one and all been crowned by success each in its own particular area of work and its own special branches of science. It was a peaceful and unobtruding campaign, devoid of glamour and thrilling glory, but still a campaign that merited, in virtue of its objects and aims, more attention than the public have paid to it. But the world of science knows well what rich additions it has received from these five expeditions, and what stores of facts, as well as light upon debated problems, it is still to acquire as collections and observations are carefully worked over, correlated, and allotted to their places in the scheme of knowledge.

But it is in the hope of bringing before a larger public the aims and the work, as well as the results, of one of the expeditions—the Scottish—that the authors have ventured to add another volume to the crowded book-shelves of to-day. There is still a lurking tendency to judge an expedition of exploration largely by the sensational character of its adventures, and to crown with plaudits of approval men who can lay claim to have escaped half a dozen times from a near and overshadowing death. Every expedition—particularly those to such unknown and inhospitable regions as the Antarctic—must of course meet with its full quota of adventure, but Polar seas are not the place to court it, and to play with death at such close quarters is but a fool's game. Fully prepared to meet all eventualities are the men who go to thread their way through the ice of uncharted seas and over the snow of trackless lands; but yet the fewer adventures the more content must a really earnest explorer be, and it may be very truly said that the less sensation a traveller has to recount the better and more far-seen were his preparations. And this is the only apology that the authors would offer should the reader regret that they were not more frequently at death's door during the two years of the *Scotia's* voyage.

But if there is one note the authors would more gladly dwell on than another, it is the truly Scottish nature of this expedition. Germany, Sweden, and England,

and later France, each had its own expedition, several of them largely aided by Government support. It remained for Scotland to show that as a nation her old spirit was still alive, and that she could stand beside the other nations and worthily take her place in this campaign of peace. It was in this spirit that the Scottish National Antarctic Expedition was planned, organised, and carried through by its indefatigable leader, Mr William S. Bruce.

While it is impossible here to name all those to whom the authors are in various ways indebted, they feel that any record of the Scottish National Antarctic Expedition would be very incomplete without the most grateful mention of Mr James G. Ferrier, the erstwhile Secretary of the Expedition, who bore a great part of the burden of sending off the *Scotia,* and who remained, the years the *Scotia* was absent, the true friend of the Expedition, ever zealously working in its interests through times of difficulties such as only the authors can fully appreciate.

To Mr Ferrier, and no less to Mr T. B. Whitson, who held the arduous position of honorary accountant of the Expedition's funds, the authors desire to record their sincerest thanks.

R.N. RUDMOSE BROWN.
R.C. MOSSMAN.
J.H. HARVEY PIRIE.

INTRODUCTION

Brief Summary of Antarctic Exploration

NOTWITHSTANDING the length of time during which the Arctic regions had engaged the attention and interest of navigators, it was not until comparatively recent years that any serious attempt was made to lift the veil overhanging the frozen regions of the South. The cause of this apathy was not far to seek. In the North the advantages that would accrue to commerce from the discovery of the North-West Passage were such that numerous expeditions having this object in view were despatched. These led directly to the discovery of the prosperous seal and whale fisheries, which gave rise to the British, Dutch, and Norwegian whaling and sealing trade, so actively carried on and combined with scientific research and exploration. The Antarctic regions, on the contrary, offered few attractions from a commercial point of view; the terrors of these inhospitable areas, so graphically described by Cook, acting as a deterrent to all but the most intrepid navigators.

The history of Antarctic discovery dates from 1567, when the Governor of Peru sent out an expedition under the command of his nephew, Alvaro Mendaña, to explore "Terra Australis Incognita." In 1605-06 a second Peruvian expedition sailed under the command of Quiros, and discovered Pitcairn's Island and an island of the New Hebrides Group. In the interval Dirk Gerritsz, in 1598, had set sail from Amsterdam with a small fleet. A storm near the Straits of Magellan, separating him from his companions, drove his vessel south, when he was said to have sighted some mountainous land now known as the South Shetlands. Considerable doubt, however, is attached to this discovery, and it is now believed that he did not visit this region.

In 1675 a French expedition under Antony La Roche sighted the island of South Georgia; and in 1772 a Breton sailor, Kerguelen, discovered the desolate island named after him, which was annexed by France so recently as 1892.

The first navigator who is known to have actually crossed the Antarctic circle is Captain Cook in the year 1773. Repeating this in 1774 he attained the high latitude of 71° 10′ S. No land south of 60° having been discovered by him in a second voyage, during which he circumnavigated the globe in high southern latitudes, the Terra Australis was eliminated from our maps. It is worthy of note, as showing the apathy with which Antarctic exploration is viewed, that we know practically no more about the islands called the Sandwich Group than at the time of their discovery by Captain Cook in 1775. In 1819 the South Shetland Islands, most of which are volcanic, were discovered by Mr William Smith of Blyth in the brig *Williams*, when on a voyage from Buenos Aires to Valparaiso. They were examined by Captain Bransfield in 1820, who also sighted Bransfield Land. In the same year the Russian navigator, Bellingshausen, crossed the Antarctic circle, attaining the latitude of 70° 15′ S. in 1° 30′ W. He also sighted Peter and Alexander Islands, at that time the most southerly land known. About this time Sheffield, an American engaged in the seal trade, visited the South Shetland Islands with such profitable results that during the next summer no less than fifty American and English sealers were prosecuting this industry in these waters. Little is known regarding them; but one or two, notably Palmer and Pendleton, made important geographical discoveries.

In 1821 the South Orkney Islands were discovered by Captain Powell in the sloop *Dove*. In 1823 Captain James Weddell of Leith eclipsed all former records, sailing as far south as 74° 15′ S in 84° 17′ W. Here, on the 20th February, there was an open sea, and only three ice-islands in sight. Viewed in the light of recent experiences in the same regions, this was a remarkable achievement, and reflects great credit on this intrepid and distinguished explorer. His craft, consisting of the brig *Jane* of 160 tons, accompanied by the cutter *Beaufoy* of 65 tons, were but ill calculated to withstand the dangers incidental to navigation in these ice-strewn waters, but Weddell's characteristic courage and determination overcame them all. In 1831 and 1832 John Biscoe, in the service of Messrs Enderby of London, on two occasions effected a landing, and had the distinction of being the first to set foot on land within the Antarctic circle. In 1837 the French Government despatched some vessels to the austral regions under the command of Dumont d'Urville, who explored the coast of Louis Philippe Land. In 1838 Balleny discovered some islands in 66° 44′ S., 163° 11′ E., as well as a coast near 116° E. long., which was designated Sabrina Land. In 1839 Wilkes, commanding an expedition from the United States of North America, made several discoveries.

By far the most important of all the expeditions sent out was that under Captain (afterwards Rear-Admiral) Sir James Clark Ross, between the years 1839 and 1843. With two stout ships, the *Erebus* and *Terror*, Ross crossed the Antarctic circle in three successive years, attaining far higher latitudes than any of his predecessors. On the 11th January 1841 he discovered land near 70° 41′ S., 172° 36′ E., which he traced for 8°, his progress farther south being prevented by an ice-barrier 300 miles long, which presented a perpendicular face of from 100 to 150 feet, marking the termination of the ice-cap of this portion of the Antarctic continent so suitably named Victoria Land. An active volcano, Mount Erebus, over 12,000 feet high, was discovered, and east of this an extinct crater, Mount Terror.

In 1842-43 the region lying to the south and east of Cape Horn was visited, but unfavourable ice conditions were met with, effectually preventing a southern advance. Pushing farther eastward, a latitude of 71° 30′ S. was attained, and here the ships were beset and had much difficulty in effecting a retreat. Much to Ross's regret, he was unable, during any of his voyages, to find a safe place in which to winter. On one occasion an inlet which it was hoped might afford a secure refuge during the winter was observed, but, owing to fifteen miles of unbroken ice, land could not be approached.

Among other minor Antarctic expeditions, principally engaged in whaling and sealing enterprise, might be mentioned those of Kemp in 1833, Smiley in 1842, and Dallman in 1873-74. The first vessel to cross the Antarctic circle under steam was the well-known research ship, H.M.S. *Challenger*, under Captain Sir George Nares, which in 1874 reached 66° 40′ S. in long. 78° 30′ E. In 1892-93 the Dundee whaling fleet, four in number, visited Erebus and Terror Gulf, Louis Philippe Land. These vessels were sent down south to try the resources of the Antarctic seas for whaling and sealing, as for several years the Arctic fisheries had proved unremunerative. Accompanying these vessels were Mr W. S. Bruce and Dr Donald, who contributed valuable scientific observations, especially in the domains of meteorology and zoology. Captain Thomas Robertson, the able commander of the *Scotia*, was on this occasion captain of the *Active*, and was so fortunate as to make several interesting geographical discoveries.

Concurrently with the visit of the Dundee fleet in these waters, a Norwegian whaler, under the command of Captain C. A. Larsen, was at work in the same region. To Captain Larsen belongs the honour of having found on Seymour Island the first fossils ever discovered in the Antarctic regions. Returning in 1893, he penetrated as far south as 68° 10′ S. in long. 59° 59′ W. on the east coast of Graham Land, and discovered, on December 1, a mountainous land which received the name of King Oscar II Land. In 1893-94, Evensen in the *Hertha*, and Pedersen in the *Castor*, sailed along the west side of Graham Land, the former reaching 69° 10′ S. in 76° 12′ W. In 1894-95 Leonard Kristensen, in the Norwegian whaler *Antarctic*, revisited Victoria Land, and landed at Cape Adare and on Possession Island. Between the years 1897-99 Adrien de Gerlache, in the *Belgica*, discovered and surveyed Belgica (now called Gerlache) Strait, and, being caught in the ice, drifted for a year to the west of Graham Land, reaching 71° 36′ S. in 87° 39′ W., and spending the first winter in the Antarctic regions. The scientific results of this expedition are most important, and through the aid of the Belgian Government a magnificent series of memoirs dealing with oceanography, biology, and meteorology have been published. Altogether, the results of this expedition reflect the greatest credit on the scientific staff. In 1898-99 Carl Chun, on the *Valdivia*, rediscovered Bouvet Island, and did some valuable work in the departments of oceanography and marine zoology. Although in an unprotected steel vessel, a latitude of 64° 15′ was attained. The last expedition preceding the great Antarctic campaign of 1901-04 was that financed by Sir George Newnes, and organised by C. E. Borchgrevink, who in the *Southern Cross*, between the years 1898-1900, landed and wintered at Cape Adare. Mr Borchgrevink was the first to land on the southern ice-barrier discovered by Ross, and in a short sledge-trip over it reached 78° 50′ S. in 165° W.

For many years before the departure of the English, German, and Swedish expeditions in 1901, the pressing necessities of Antarctic research on a large scale had been prominently brought before the scientific world by such eminent authorities as Sir John Murray, K.C.B., Dr Neumayer, and others, more particularly in relation to magnetism. As the outcome of these efforts, two great international expeditions left England and Germany in the summer of 1901, followed in the autumn of the same year by the Swedish expedition. The English expedition, under Captain Scott, spent two winters in the south of Victoria Land in latitude 77° 50′ S.; and in a sledge journey Captain Scott, Lieut. Shackleton, and Dr Wilson reached the high latitude of 82° 17′. The German expedition, under Professor Erich von Drygalski, spent the winter of 1902 in latitude 66° 2′ S., long. 89° 48′ E., close to newly discovered land named Kaiser Wilhelm II Land. The Swedish expedition, commanded by Dr Otto G. Nordenskjöld, established a wintering station at Snow Hill, on the east side of Graham Land, in latitude 64° 22′ 5.; while the *Antarctic*, after landing a party, proceeded north and did some valuable work at South Georgia, Tierra del Fuego, and in the South Atlantic. The good ship was crushed in the ice in Erebus and Terror Gulf on February 13, 1903, when proceeding to the relief of the land-party under Nordenskjöld. After hazardous experiences the crew reached Paulet Island, where they wintered in a small hut built of stones and moss. A small party of three men, in making an effort to reach Snow Hill over the ice, were unable to proceed, and were forced to winter in Hope Bay, enduring great privations. The arrival of these two parties at Snow Hill within a few hours of each other, and their timely rescue by the Argentine sloop of war *Uruguay*, under Captain Irizar, on 8th November 1903, form one of the most remarkable chapters in Polar history.

To complete this brief and necessarily somewhat incomplete summary of Antarctic exploration, one must refer in a word to the recent expedition of Dr Charcot, in the *Français*, to the west coast of Graham Land during the years 1904-05.

While the Antarctic seas are now free of expeditions properly so called, scientific research in the austral regions has received a fresh impetus, through the praiseworthy efforts of the Argentine Government in equipping and maintaining the meteorological and magnetical station at the South Orkneys, since the departure of the Scottish National Antarctic Expedition in February 1904. At the present time the sphere of operations has been still further extended by the establishment of new stations in Graham Land and South Georgia. Meteorologists and magnetists throughout the world are under a deep debt of gratitude to Mr

Walter G. Davis, Director of the Argentine Meteorological Office, for the energy and initiative displayed by him in his efforts to extend our knowledge of the climatic and magnetic conditions in that portion of the austral zone lying to the south and east of Cape Horn; and one must congratulate him on having behind him a Government so keenly alive to the importance and utility of this work.

CHAPTER I

PREPARATIONS

PURCHASE OF HEKLA—ALTERATIONS AND REPAIRS—SERVICES OF G. L. WATSON—DESCRIPTION OF SHIP—EQUIPMENT— APPOINTMENT OF CAPTAIN AND STAFF—FINANCIAL DIFFICULTIES—GENEROSITY OF THE MESSRS COATS.

IMMEDIATELY after Mr Bruce's return from his Antarctic cruise in the Dundee whaler *Balœna* in 1893, he began drawing up plans for an Antarctic expedition on a large scale. Notwithstanding the interest taken in this proposed expedition by a large number of scientists and the public generally, it was not until the close of 1901 that sufficient support was obtained in the form of subscriptions to justify the organisation of the Scottish National Antarctic Expedition. In the interval Mr Bruce had availed himself of every opportunity that presented itself for the furthering of his enterprise. From 1894 to 1896 he was in charge of the Ben Nevis high-level meteorological observatory, gaining there much valuable experience in meteorology. In 1896-97 he was Naturalist with the Jackson-Harmsworth Arctic Expedition to Franz-Josef Land, and also took part in subsequent expeditions to the Arctic with Mr (now Major) Andrew Coats, D.S.O., and H.S.H. the Prince of Monaco. In the late autumn of 1901 Mr Bruce went to Norway, and there purchased the whaler *Hekla*, which early in the spring of 1902, arrived at Troon for alterations and repairs. These were executed at the Ailsa Shipbuilding Company's yard, under the able guidance of that eminent naval architect and yacht designer, the late G. L. Watson, who generously gave his services free of charge to the Expedition. The magnitude of these alterations and repairs was such that when the work was finished very little of the old *Hekla* was left. She was then renamed the *Scotia*; and after new engines and boilers had been put in, she was a ship of which her skipper might well be proud. Her original lines were retained, and she presented an extremely graceful and beautiful appearance. The vessel was a barque-rigged auxiliary screw-steamer of about 400 tons, having a length of 140 feet, and drawing about 15 feet of water. With her new engines and boiler a speed of fully 8 knots was attained; but in order to economise coal the average speed when under steam was 6 knots. Needless to say, the vessel, in spite of her lines, was of immense strength. At her stem there were no less than 9 feet of solid timber, while her "wooden walls" at their thinnest part amidships were 25 inches thick, being there composed of three layers of timbers supported by massive wooden knees, while huge cross-beams, situated at frequent intervals, looked as if they could hold the sides against the greatest ice-pressure imaginable. That part of the outer hull likely to receive the assaults of the thick-ribbed ice was protected by a sheathing of "green-heart," a timber possessing special resistance to the grinding to which whalers are sorely subjected. Between decks and forward were the crew's quarters, well lighted and ventilated. The fo'c'sle was a very comfortable and commodious apartment, containing sixteen bunks, each man being provided with a couple of lockers. The ship's officers were quartered in a cabin amidships, which was not the least luxurious part of the ship. Aft was the saloon, round which were eight cabins, the captain's room (which was also the chart-room), a bathroom, a pantry, and a store-room. Most of the scientific work was carried on in a deck-house amidships, the after part of which formed the galley. This deck-house was well lighted, so as to facilitate the execution of the delicate microscopical and other examinations to be made there. A second laboratory, mainly for zoology, was located almost underneath the upper one: close to this was the photographic dark-room, fitted up in the most complete and modern fashion. For the preservation of the zoological specimens, a tank containing 1000 gallons of methylated spirits was placed in close proximity to the lower laboratory. On the same deck were situated two great drums, each carrying 6000 fathoms of cable, for use during the deep-sea dredging operations. This cable was led up on deck to a specially constructed 40-horse power steam-winch, from which it was carried over the side of the ship by means of a derrick for the purpose of deep-sea trawling. For work near the surface, special tow-nets were employed.

The tow-nets used for collecting *plankton*—a collective name for the minute and generally microscopic surface organisms—were of various types, both as regards dimensions and material. The coarser ones were made of muslin or coarse butter-cloth, but the finer ones were made of different meshed silk gauzes: the finest of these, and one most in daily use, was No. 20 miller's gauze, which has 5926 meshes to a square centimetre, with the side of each mesh 0.05 mm. long. It is very regularly made and extremely strong, while the fineness of the mesh ensures that hardly anything can pass through; but it naturally becomes choked very soon, particularly where diatoms are abundant, and has often to be renewed. As the greater part of the tow-netting had to be done without slowing down the ship, it was essential that the net used should have a small diameter to offer as little resistance as possible to the water. With this in view, Brown devised a form of net 4 to 5 feet long, with a mouth 4 inches in diameter, and the tail-end narrowing to 2 inches. To overcome the difficulty, particularly in Antarctic weather, of turning such a narrow net inside out to remove the catch, there was a device by which the terminal six inches, clamped into a brass ring, could be unscrewed from the body of the net, which ended in a similar brass ring. The catch could then be carried into the laboratory and quickly preserved. These nets proved quite serviceable with speeds up to 10 or 11 knots an hour. Other nets of a similar shape, but with a 6-inch mouth, were also used, as well as larger nets (8 inches to 12 inches across) for slow speeds or for boat work. The larger the net the coarser the mesh, was naturally the case; and on occasions, with a view to catching large jelly-fish and the like, we used a huge net with an 8-foot mouth made of inch herring-net, lined at the terminal end with very coarse butter-cloth. Curiously enough, a fine meshed net, even with a large mouth, will not as a rule catch large organisms,—the small wave of water which such a net must naturally push before it seems to wash them aside.

The arrangement by which the nets were trailed was as follows. Amidships a 10-foot boom projected over the ship's side with a pulley at its outer end, and over this pulley the tow-net line ran, while a short tripping-line was paid out to keep the net just below the water's surface, unless the object was particularly to skim the top. This arrangement kept the net clear of the ship's side, and prevented any refuse or greasy water from entering it. The boom was always on the weather side; and every sailor knows that it is a grave offence to throw anything overboard to windward.

On the roof of the scientific deck-house was placed the Lucas automatic sounding-machine for depths up to 6000 fathoms. Instead of the usual ordinary single-strand piano wire, a triple stranded wire was employed, which stood the wear and tear much better. A small quick-working steam-winch was connected with the sounding-machine, and wound the wire in at the rate of 100 fathoms per minute. For getting a sample of the deposit at the bottom of the sea, the sounding-tube invented by Mr J. Y. Buchanan was employed, while special thermometers to withstand great pressure were clamped to the wire so as to give the temperature of the sea at various depths. Samples of seawater were brought up by the Pettersen-Nansen water-bottle. On the top of this deck-house was also placed the Barr & Stroud range-finder so much employed for survey work. A special feature of the scientific programme on the *Scotia* voyage was in the domain of meteorology. The exposure of meteorological instruments on board ship is, as might be expected, associated with many difficulties which do not present themselves at land stations. This applies more particularly to thermometric observations, which are liable to be vitiated by heat from the engines and air currents from the galley and cabins of the vessel. On the *Scotia* special attention was given to this matter, in order that the best possible results might be obtained, duplicate methods of observation being employed in many cases. The form of thermometer screen adopted was the small single-louvred pattern, recommended and supplied by the Meteorological Council, who, by the loan of instruments and in other ways, rendered valuable help to the Expedition. Two of the screens referred to above were in use, each containing a dry- and wet-bulb thermometer. They were secured to posts which projected clear of the ship's side to the extent of eighteen inches. One was placed on the starboard and the other on the port side, well aft on the poop. Both boxes were read at each observation, and the indications of the instruments exposed on the weather side were entered in the log as giving the closest approximation to the true thermal condition of the surrounding atmosphere. A further check was afforded by the records of three Richard thermographs, which give continuous records of temperature, on charts coiled around brass cylinders actuated by a clock movement. Some little trouble was at first experienced with the wet-bulb thermometers. This was found to be due to saline accretions on the muslin and bulb of the instrument, such as are formed on every exposed part of a vessel at sea. The result was that in the course of a week or so a coating of salt formed round the bulb, which could with difficulty be removed by scraping with a knife, or even be dissolved by placing the thermometer in tepid water. By changing the water in the reservoir frequently, and placing a fresh piece of muslin on about once a-week, thoroughly satisfactory results were obtained, the wet bulb being further syringed daily with distilled water. A Richard hair hygrograph was employed as a check, so that any serious discrepancy between the two instruments was at once apparent. For the measurement of the intensity of solar radiation, a black-bulb thermometer *in vacuo* was employed. This was fixed in a stand secured to the bridge, in such a position that the sun could shine on it at, as nearly as possible, all hours of the day.

Two barometers of the Kew marine pattern were in use,—one being placed in the deck laboratory at a height of seven feet above the sea, while the other was a spare instrument, kept aft in the cabin. Three self-recording Richard barographs gave continuous tracings of barometric pressure.

One of Dr Black's marine rain-gauges was placed aft on the poop, well clear of the deck. Its position was changed occasionally as circumstances arose, in order that it might always be on the weather side. The exposure—taking into account the various difficulties attending rainfall observations at sea—was a very good one, as the gauge was never sheltered by the sails. The thickness of the rain-band in the spectrum of sunlight was taken daily at noon, and the temperature of the sea surface was observed every four hours, and at more frequent intervals when rapid changes were in progress. For ascertaining the height of ocean waves a Richard statoscope was employed. This is really an extremely delicate aneroid barometer, in which changes of pressure are magnified twenty-five times. A chart actuated by clockwork receives a tracing of the pressure fluctuations due to the rise and fall of the waves the height of which can thus be readily determined. Aft on the poop was a small machine for reeling n the piano wire attached to box-shaped kites of the Blue Hill pattern. Specially constructed meteorographs made of aluminium were carried up by the kites, and a record of the vertical distribution of pressure, temperature, and humidity was thus graphically recorded. The Expedition was well equipped with sunshine recorders and other special instruments for use in high latitudes at any winter station which might be established. Observations four times daily were commenced immediately after leaving Kingstown, but on reaching latitude 30° S. hourly observations were initiated, and these continued until the termination of the Expedition.

The magnetic instruments taken for use during the Expedition were a Kew portable unifilar magnetometer for determining the absolute horizontal force and declination, and a Barrows' dip-circle for ascertaining the absolute dip or inclination. Our magnetic programme was on a much more restricted scale than on either the *Discovery* or the *Gauss,* where many sacrifices were made to ensure that there was no iron or steel within thirty feet of the magnetic instruments. This considerably increased the cost of these vessels, as large quantities of brass had to be used instead of iron.

Much attention was given by Dr Pirie to bacteriological investigations, and accordingly special apparatus was on board to facilitate this work. Unfortunately for complete success there is on deep-sea expeditions much trouble, due to the presence of mould, the spores of which are everywhere present about the ship. These often find their way into the cultures, and make further investigation of their growth impossible. In the way of equipment for land-journeys there were on board sledges of the improved Nansen pattern, two Esquimaux kayaks or canvas canoes, very light and seaworthy, Norwegian ski or snow-shoes, and stockings of goat hair and human hair to be worn with them. All manner of fur garments were also provided, and deerskin sleeping-bags to accommodate one, two, or three persons; also aluminium "cookers" and other utensils for use on sledging excursions. Needless to say, all these preparations were not made without the expenditure of a vast amount of thought, labour, and correspondence. Early in the summer of 1902 the captain, ship's officers, and staff had been appointed, and they rendered valuable aid in the preparations. The captain of the *Scotia* was Captain Thomas Robertson of Peterhead, who had had over twenty years' experience in Arctic navigation, and who had also made a voyage ten years previously to the Antarctic regions. The ship's officers, Messrs Fitchie, Davidson, and MacDougall, had all previous experience in navigation. The scientific staff consisted of six—four senior and two junior men. Along with Mr Bruce, the zoological work was undertake by Mr Wilton, who also tested the specific gravities of the water-samples obtained. Mr Wilton had an extensive experience of Arctic life and work, having lived for some years in the North of Russia, where he became an expert ski runner, and an adept in all that pertains to sledging. In 1896 and

1897 he took part in the Jackson-Harmsworth expedition to Franz-Josef Land. Thereafter he returned to Edinburgh, studying at the University and Royal Colleges, attaining distinction in zoology and botany. He also gained a sound knowledge of meteorology at the Observatory on the summit of Ben Nevis, and had taken part in an expedition to Turkestan and Western China.

Mr R. N. Rudmose Brown was botanist. Mr Brown, who was a graduate in science of Aberdeen University, held the post of chief assistant to the Professor of Botany, University College, Dundee. He had also had extensive experience at Kew and in the British Museum, under Mr George Murray.

Dr J. H. Harvey Pirie was geologist, bacteriologist, and medical officer. He was a graduate in science and medicine of Edinburgh University, and had experience in the study of deep-sea deposits in the Challenger Office under Sir John Murray, K.C.B. He was also trained in field work with the members of the Geological Survey of Scotland.

The taxidermist to the Expedition was Alastair Ross, a student of medicine in Edinburgh University; while William Cuthbertson, who had studied in the schools of Edinburgh and Paris, was artist.

Mr R. C. Mossman directed the meteorological and magnetic work, being ably assisted in the former by Mr Bruce, Captain Robertson, and the other members of the staff.

To fully acknowledge the help rendered the Expedition, both in money and in kind would require a chapter in itself, but special mention should be made of the handsome donations of food and clothing, which enabled a very material saving to be effected. As the work of the equipment proceeded, it was found that the first estimate was insufficient,—a result largely due to the expenses incurred in the reconstruction of the ship. Through the magnificent generosity of Mr James Coats, jun., of Paisley, who, along with his brother, Major Andrew Coats, D.S.O., of Ayr, had already subscribed very largely to the Expedition, the financial difficulties were overcome. It was through Mr James Coats' liberality that the Expedition was able to engage in the second season's campaign; and a further benefaction received from the same source after the expedition returned enabled the rich collections and other scientific data to be examined, and the results prepared for publication.

Among public bodies who officially lent their support to the Expedition were the Royal Society of Edinburgh, the Royal Scottish Geographical Society, and the Perthshire Society of Natural Science. Valuable instruments were lent by the Admiralty and the Meteorological Office, while Mr John Anderson gave most of the equipment for the exploration of the air by means of kites. There being no committees, we were much indebted to various home and Continental experts in different branches of science for their advice and criticism. Each member of the staff was made responsible for the efficiency of the scientific equipment pertaining to his department, while Mr Bruce exercised a general supervision over the whole. This arrangement worked well, as it greatly facilitated the ordering of instruments and other gear.

CHAPTER II

SCOTLAND TO THE FALKLAND ISLANDS

DEPARTURE FROM THE CLYDE—KINGSTOWN—IN THE CHOPS OF THE CHANNEL—WARMER WEATHER—MADEIRA—GEOLOGY— BEGGARS—AIRING OUR PORTUGUESE—OBSERVATIONS STARTED—CAPE VERDE ISLANDS—FISHING—ST PAUL'S ROCKS— IN THE DOG-WATCH—TRAWLING—SUN-FISH—PORT STANLEY.

THE voyage of the *Scotia* commenced on the 2nd November 1902. For the two months previous to our departure, the vexations of spirit we endured are too vivid, even now, to put down in cold-blooded print. The unpacking of stores and stowing them on board, the humping of boxes along the quays of Troon, and, over all, hanging the hideous nightmare, "Would we get away at all?" Ugh! all, or nearly all, our troubles were due to the insufficiency of funds, which caused grievous delay in the equipment of the vessel. But at length, through Mr Bruce's tireless energy, the difficulties were overcome; so suffice it to say that we did get off, late in the season though it was. Our official departure took place on the 25th of October, when we were depicted by the illustrated papers as steaming majestically down the Clyde, surrounded by a fleet of gaily-bedecked yachts and other craft. But truth will out. On that date I find, on referring to my diary, this statement: "Ten more waggon-loads of 'stuff' arrived to-day; that and more has to be stowed on board, even though coal has to come out of the hold to make room for it." The coal came out and the "stuff" came on board, with the result that the ship was like a midshipman's bag, everything on top and nothing handy. A week later, however, everything was ship-shape and Bristol fashion, or at least as much in order as most ships are when they first put to sea. The day of our departure being a Sunday, we got away fairly quietly,—a proceeding much to our taste; for of a surety one's feelings on the occasion of leaving the home country for an indefinite period, and to face unknown dangers, do not harmonise altogether with the concomitants of what is ordinarily called *a hearty send-off*, though it is perhaps only natural that spectators and friends should wish to give vent to their feelings in some tangible and readily perceived manner.

As it was, we were not allowed simply to slip our cable and vanish, for even the kirks "scaled" to see us off,—a proceeding which may have been responsible for a local paper's condemnation and lament, "Stands Scotland where she did, when a ship can sail on the Sabbath with pipes playing and people singing, not psalms, but profane songs, such as 'Auld Lang Syne'?" Ah, well, it *may* have been wrong, but it was very human!

Once outside the harbour, the ship was swung to have her compasses adjusted, the accompanying tug cast off, and the 7000 miles' voyage to our destination had commenced. In the offing were Mr James Coats' yachts, the *Gleniffer* and the *Triton,* which were to accompany us a little way.

Going down the Clyde we had a lovely sunset view of Arran, our last glimpse of Scotland for many a day.

Early on the 3rd we put into Kingstown Harbour, Ireland. To some on board the unveiling of the unknown had already begun, and the opportunity of catching a glimpse of dear, dirty Dublin was eagerly grasped. There was time for a little sight-seeing and pleasure in the four days spent here, although our call was really a business one. Of the hundred and one things necessary for the complete furnishing of our little world-to-be "down under," the hundred were safely stored on board, but the one was still amissing. It comprised numerous little odds and ends, not perhaps essential, but still highly desirable, and which, if not obtained here, could certainly not be had in the outposts of civilisation, which still lay between us and our goal.

Amongst other things the chief officer wanted some holy-stones for polishing decks: these are commonly known to sailors as "Bibles." On inquiry at our Irish boatman whether any were to be had in Kingstown, the reply came pat, "Sure, Mr Mate, an' don't you know there are no Bibles in Ireland." And there were not.

We received on board many of the scientists of Dublin, and in return visited some of their haunts. Not the least interesting was the Chemical and Bacteriological Laboratory of Messrs Guinness,—probably the finest of its kind in the United Kingdom, and one which amply repays the outlay spent upon it in the excellence which it ensures in the quality of their products. Guinness' quays, piled high with barrels, are one of the sights of Dublin, and their works appeared to be the only place in the city that hustled (to use an Americanism). Such, at least, was the impression given by one or two hurried visits to it.

Leaving Kingstown on the 8th, Mr Coats convoyed us out for a few miles; then our last link with home was parted midst firing of salutes, dipping of flags, cheering and waving, and, rising above all, the skirl of the pipes as our piper marched gallantly up and down the foc's'le-head, blowing a stirring march to cheer our drooping spirits.

The next few days I find my diary, if not witty, at least possessing the soul of wit, and having a certain pithiness more expressive than detailed. Here are two specimen entries:—

Sunday, Nov. 9.—"Sick and miserable."

Monday, Nov. 10.—"Very sick and very miserable."

Head-winds made the sea very choppy, and forced us considerably to the westward off our course. Father Neptune claimed toll of several who were becoming new citizens of his realm: some of the old salts even found things a bit lively, but not even the worst on board reached the second stage of *mal-de-mer*, when things are so bad that one is afraid the ship is *never* going down. The one advantage of this tossing was that the fastenings of the various instruments and glassware in the laboratory were well tested and their weak points exposed; and, however well stowed things may appear on an even keel, it is curious how they can shift about with a roll of 30° or 40° from the vertical. By the time the Bay was crossed, life once more seemed worth living, and we could take an intelligent interest in what was happening on the surface of the sea, instead of sighing for the bottom of it.

Regular observations were not begun on board before Madeira, but there was much to be done in the way of getting instruments into working order, and everything arranged in the laboratory in the most convenient fashion.

Monday, Nov. 17.—Lat. 39° 36′ N., long. 17° 50′ W.

"Mist and fog are all behind us, we have sailed into summer; the wind has died down into mere cat's-paw puffs, and the sails are flapping against the masts. Our thoughts have turned from the gloom and mirk of the North to the fairyland of the South. The sea has lost its dull slaty hue, and is now a lovely transparent blue that defies description, and is the despair of our artist when he tries to reproduce it on canvas: however brilliant his tints may seem, they pale into insignificance when compared with the liquid azure that is seen on looking down the rudder well. At night our wake is a trail of light. Every turn of the propeller brings up thousands of minute forms of life which give out phosphorescent gleams. Most are too small to be seen individually, but the general effect is that of a shimmering veil of light, with every here and there a bright blot where some larger organism has been churned up by the screw."

On the 19th, at 10 p.m.,—or, to use the nautical phrase, at four bells in the first watch,—the light of Porto Santo was visible ahead.

Next morning every one was up early. Madeira could be seen on the starboard side, and, well astern now, Porto Santo, the small most northerly island of this group, well known to geologists from the occurrence of fossiliferous limestones which give the clue to the age of the islands, showing that they form part of the great volcanic outpouring which took place along the western coasts of

Europe in Miocene times, extending from Franz-Joseph Land in the Arctic seas through Iceland, the Faroe Islands, west of Scotland and north of Ireland, at least as far south as the Azores and Madeira.

To port lay the Desertas, high rocky islets famous as the breeding-place of rare sea-birds, and off which lie some of the finest fishing-banks in the world, even now tempting trawlers from Europe to visit them.

In the clear cool dawn of the morning there lay a picture which, as our first impression of a sub-tropical island, can never be forgotten,—the steep rising hillsides deeply trenched by ravines, clad in the upper parts with pine-forests and culminating in serrated peaks, the like of which one hardly thought existed except in pictures; the lower stretches of the hills of a lighter green, and highly terraced for cultivation by the industrious peasantry, whose little whitewashed cabins could be seen dotted over the hillsides, perched, some of them, like eyries, in most inaccessible places, but led up to by long, winding, zigzag mule tracks or footpaths.

Between the green land and the blue sea were the high coastal cliffs, with their alternating layers of black lava rock and red and yellow bands or volcanic ashes.

On arrival at Funchal, the port of Madeira, the first business was the visit from the port medical officer. After giving us free pratique to land, he informed us we might haul down our quarantine flag. "What quarantine flag?" I asked. "Why, that yellow flag up there," came the reply. On looking up, there was a yellow flag sure enough, draped against the crow's-nest on the mainmast. It was the Scottish Standard, only there was nothing visible of the red lion rampant. On being informed it was not a cholera flag, but our national emblem, he was apologetic as only a "Dago" can be, and the incident passed in mutual amusement.

The first sensation on landing at Madeira is one of annoyance at the numerous beggars and "bums," who swarm like flies round sugar, and turn this otherwise peaceful paradise into a howling *inferno*. The beggars are chiefly children, who render life hideous with their perpetual "Penny, penny." Should you meet any particularly interesting-looking one, and show signs of wishing to photograph it (him or her),—oh no! you must hand over your penny first, otherwise you can only get a back view. Such is the effect of civilisation of the tourist variety. Curiously enough, British money is preferred to the local *milreis*,—even the post-office accepting cash sterling without demur. Of these *milreis* some 6000 go to the pound sterling. Should you not know this, and a little bill of, say, 30,000 *milreis* is presented, do not file a petition for bankruptcy straight away: it is only for a "flyer" after all.

The "bums," of assorted ages and degrees of cleanliness, will show you anywhere, sell you anything, do any little thing in fact, to earn an honest but lazy penny. In this lotus land of the *mañana*, why should they work hard when they can scrape along very comfortably, and get enough to eat and a sufficiency of *cigarillos* to smoke, by doing very little? The only way of escape from these pests (and pests they were from our point of view) is to enrol one as your protector, guide, and friend: he will blithely keep off the others for a consideration. We secured the services of a genial ruffian who answered docilely to the name of Ferguson. With or without him we visited most of the sights of the town, which, after all, are not very numerous, and need hardly be enumerated in guide-book fashion. There is a nice hotel at the head of the funicular railway, where a very pleasant *al fresco* meal may be had in the gardens; and the right thing to do, of course, is to come down by a *carro do monte* toboggan. These cars slip on their smoothly polished wooden runners over the finely cobbled streets and paths which stretch up the steep hillside on which Funchal stands, and are guided by two men running alongside and holding on by ropes attached to the front of the runners. As a means of getting downhill this method of transit is passable; but as a sport it is feeble,—the pace is too slow and not at all exciting, though there is always the chance of a collision with a bullock-sledge or wayfarer, despite the warning shouts of the guides as a corner or crossing is approached. Perchance you may meet on the way a long string of *borrocheiros*, or "wine mens" as they are called on the English-as-she-is-spoke picture-postcards. Each bears on his back a goatskin full of wine, with which they have trudged from some vineyard in the country.

I would advise any one anxious—as we were—to try the produce of the land, to shun the local wine as sold in the cafés of Funchal. When thirsty—and this is a thirsty place—we always asked at first for "wine Madeira," but soon desisted, for it was sour pain-giving stuff. Madeira is a wine that is not in fashion at present, and most of what is made now is not of good quality,—although the right article is to be had; only, you have first to find out where to get it.

The second day of our stay we paid a visit to the fish-market, which is famous almost the world over, at least amongst zoologists, for the variety of fish which occur. Rare species are frequently brought in by the fishermen, amongst others weird fishy denizens of the deep—the real deep, that is,—fish whose habitat is two miles or more below the surface. They seem to float up not infrequently in this neighbourhood, and are caught in the fishermen's nets. The commonest fish is a large species of tunny, a fine fellow, who looks as if he would give excellent sport on a rod. Some of the staff also made an excursion along the shore in a launch, kindly lent by Messrs Blandy Bros., to see the geological sections exposed along the cliffs, and to make collections in the shore pools.

Among the rocks small lizards are very common basking in the sunshine. On attempting to catch one which looks rather sleepier than its fellows, it generally happens that it is very much awake, and all that you capture is the tip of its tail, which it kindly leaves in your hand on its retirement into a crevice of the rock. It is very annoying, this sort of thing,—not to the lizard, which promptly grows a new tail, and probably enjoys the sport, but to the enthusiastic collector who is thus baulked of his "specimen."

In the evening a party of the staff and officers had dinner ashore: on coming out we were surrounded by the usual crowd of loafers, and, in the absence of Ferguson, we thought to get rid of them by airing some of our more forcible Portuguese expressions. The effect was remarkable, but not what we had expected: a troop of horses appeared, springing apparently from nowhere, one for each member of the party, and each with an attendant groom. Much amused, but nothing loath, we mounted, and enjoyed a good gallop round the environs of the town.

It was late on the third day when we had finished taking coal and water and the various little odds and ends on board, and had the last picture-postcard mailed for home, so that we did not up-anchor till daybreak of the 23rd; and then we were once more off on the out trail, sorry to leave an interesting spot where one might well spend a month sight-seeing and collecting, but yet glad, since we were out on a definite quest, and its locale was not here, but still far afield.

After leaving Madeira the weather became warmer, and at night most of us shifted our quarters up on deck. In addition to being comfortably cool, this ensured an early morning, for the bo'sun came round to wash down decks at 6 A.M., and though a shower-bath under the hose was, like a well-known cocoa, grateful and comforting, there was a certain disagreeable clamminess about it when still in swathed blankets. We were not often caught napping, though.

The only cases of illness resulting from bad food that I had to treat during the whole voyage occurred now. Any tin of meat that was the least suspicious was invariably rejected On this occasion a tin of preserved fish, which to all appearance was quite good, must have contained some ptomaines. Captain Robertson, the second steward, and one of the crew were the unfortunate sufferers; but after three or four days they luckily recovered completely.

Before reaching the Cape Verde Islands most of the routine work that had to be gone through in the south was under way for practice. The chief, as Mr Bruce was called by common consent, saw to the sounding machines, water-bottles, traps, &c., and generally directed and encouraged. Mossman had his thermometers, barometers, and various other meters set agoing—each one having a neat little house to itself, or "louvred screen" as he called it. When he tired of reading an 'ometer, it was always possible to count the number of dust particles in the air, and, so far as we could observe, this consisted in sitting on the poop in the most comfortable deck-chair and promptly going asleep,—but of course that was only our ignorance of matters meteorological. Brown started daily *plankton* hauls. *Plankton* is the collective term applied to all the life—animal and vegetable —living in the surface waters of the open sea. It was obtained as follows. A short boom was let out on the weather-side of the ship; from the outer end ran a long rope, and attached to this was a tow-net composed of strong miller's silk of any desired size of mesh. Being on the weather-side there was no risk of contamination from the ship, for any refuse is always flung over on the lee-side. By using nets only four inches wide at the mouth, and tapering in their four feet of length to almost two inches, it was found that they could be used even when going ten knots without risk of tearing. This department certainly had most to show at present: five or ten minutes' dragging produced a cupful or so of a gelatinous-looking mass that resolved itself, when examined under the microscope, into a great multitude of living beings,—strings of diatoms, a lowly form of plant life, but possessed of marvelously beautiful siliceous skeletons; minute foraminifera, unicellular animals, little globules of protoplasm surrounded by a calcareous shell, through whose interstices or foramina are protruded the pseudopodia or so-called feet, really projections of the protoplasia, which come forth in search of food to ingest.

Even thus far down in the scale of life the terrible struggle for existence goes on, quietly but none the less surely: the motto of the sea is "Eat!" with its awful corollary "Or be Eaten!" There were also delicate swimming-bells, scarcely visible save by their rhythmical contractions, tiny cuttles, and, lashing blindly through the others, minute crustacea clad in coats of shining armour. But belay there! a full account of even one haul might more than fill this book. At night the catch was even greater, for during the day many of the organisms seem to sink a few fathoms out of the bright sunlight: when emptied into a dish, it was as if we had a glass of liquid fire, so phosphorescent are all these tiny creatures. Just on the tropic of Cancer the first species of *Halobates* was captured. This animal is interesting as being really an insect closely related to the bug family: it has deserted the land and adopted a pelagic existence, one of the very few insects that live in the open sea. The same day there was a cinder in the catch,—could it have been a product of the volcanic outburst at Mount Pelée? It is hardly likely, as, at the lowest reckoning, it would take a year to come here, *via* the southern branch of the Gulf Stream. It may only have been from a steamer: the fragment was too small to be certain of its nature.

Wilton worried over the density and salinity of the sea, which was taken by reading the depth to which a glass hydrometer was immersed, by a gradually increased load, in a tall cylinder full of sea-water. This work was carried out on a swing-table in the laboratory, and required much patience, especially when there was any sea on. Dry work, but none the less important for a proper understanding of the ocean circulation; for it is all a question of temperature and salinity —nothing more—which way the currents will flow.

Ross, so far, had very little to do. The open tropical seas are strangely poor in bird life,—so much so, that it was quite an event to see a solitary petrel, almost as exciting as sighting a sail. For Cuthbertson there was never any lack of subjects to draw and paint,—scenes on deck, and nature in all her varying moods, particularly the angry lurid sunrises with lowering green and purple clouds shading a coppery sun, which seemed to betoken stormy weather that never came. Having no patients and no geology, I had to content myself with preparing media on which to cultivate bacteria in innocent-looking test tubes, one of which might, under certain circumstances, contain virulent germs sufficient to bring death to a whole army.

For the crew there was always work and to spare, for if one thing more than any other in this world is never complete, it is a ship. There are always old sails to mend, and new sails to bend, and rigging and ropes to keep in proper order. I call them "ropes" as a convenient generic term. Nautically speaking, very few of them are "ropes": they are "stays," "shrouds," "sheets," "lines," "braces," "halliards," &c. Such apparent complication is really necessary to give clearness to any given order.

On December 1 we put into St Vincent, the chief port-of-call in the Cape Verde Islands. What a contrast to Madeira! Instead of hill-sides covered with vines, bamboos, and flowers, there is a bare, burnt, arid waste of sand and dust, rocks and ashes, with scarcely a shrub, and such as there are so dry that they crumble to powder when pulled. The harbour is an extinct volcanic crater, one side of which has been breached by the sea; otherwise it is surrounded by high cliffs formed of stratified volcanic rocks everywhere dipping outwards from the centre, and traversed by many vertical dykes, often showing a well-marked columnar structure. These—the product of a later phase of volcanic activity, when a liquid magma welled up from below in the cracks which were rent in the original volcanic cone—run sheer up and down the cliffs, and being harder than the surrounding rock, weather more slowly, and stand out like massive walls that might have been raised by some prehistoric cyclopean builders.

Twelve hours was the limit of our stay here, sufficient to fill up water-tanks and coal-bunkers,—the coaling being expeditiously, if noisily, carried on by a horde of grinning, jabbering niggers. The population is mainly a negro one, brought over from the adjacent African coast. The white population consists of Portuguese officials, British shipping-office clerks, and a large staff of telegraph operators,—for this is a relay station on both the South African and South American cables, and all messages have to be retransmitted. It is a miserable hole of a place to be condemned to live in: when we were there no rain had fallen for about a year; later, we learned they had rain about a week after we left. It brought in its wake the usual outbreak of fever, to which four of the cable operators succumbed.

A short run ashore was all there was time for, to get a few chips of rock, fish, and fresh fruit, which is brought here from the adjacent islands of St Antonio and St Jago, where there are some fertile valleys. Then off once more in the heel of the North-East Trades, as Kipling has it. The trade-winds were rather disappointing, but feeble as they were, they kept the temperature comparatively moderate till they failed us a few degrees north of the Line. With them came occasional heavy showers, mostly at night: pools of water would collect on the awning over the poop till a gust of wind swished the lot off, usually on to some unsuspecting sleeper below. Such little incidents give some variety to life.

Flying fish were here numerous, coming out of nearly every wave, and skimming along forty or fifty yards before falling back into the water. Although closely watched through a glass, opinions were divided over the vexed question, "Do they move their long pectoral fins in a manner analogous to the flapping of a bird's wings, or is their flight merely due to the momentum with which they start off, aided by the æroplane action of their fins?" Most of us inclined to the latter view, though they seemed undoubtedly able to swerve or travel on a curved course by tilting one fin or moving the tail like a rudder. Several flopped over on to the deck; to clear the bulwarks they must have been at least nine to ten feet above the surface. The flying habit has, no doubt, been acquired partly to escape their common enemy, the bonito; but so many may be seen skimming the waves in different directions that it must, I think, be partly also a means of letting off steam or method of expressing their *joie de vivre*.

The bonito, which belongs to the mackerel tribe, has a habit of piloting a ship much in the same manner as porpoises do. By getting out on the bowsprit, one can get quite good sport with them: we found a simple hook, with a piece of white rag, more effective than either flies or spinners. A 20-lb. fish gives some trouble to haul in; it also yields passable steaks. Sharks were occasionally caught when the ship was stopped for any purpose. No skill is required, merely a strong hook baited with a juicy morsel of pork, with a strong rope to haul up the victim. But keep at arm's-length once he is on deck. Shark cutlets are tender enough, but just a trifle strong flavoured: if you don't know what is being served up, it is all right.

On December 10 there came a break in the long run from St Vincent to Port Stanley at St Paul's Rocks. These isolated rocks rise up in mid-Atlantic just a few miles north of the equator. They are only about a half mile in circumference and some sixty feet above sea-level. They have been visited and described by Darwin, Sir James Ross, and the naturalists of the *Challenger*; but, geologically speaking, they are still a puzzle and of great interest. The rock is of a variety not met with anywhere else in the world, and it is an open question whether it is of volcanic or of deep-seated plutonic origin. If the former, then the presence of these tiny rocks sticking almost sheer up like a needle from water close on 2000 fathoms deep, though still remarkable, is understandable. If the latter—*i.e.*, if the rock is of a kind that has solidified at some distance below the crust of the earth under considerable pressure—then how comes it to occupy this isolated position? Is it the wreck of some lost Atlantis, and if so, how has it been reduced to this sharp pinnacle towering up 10,000 feet from its narrow base at the bottom of the Atlantic? We were very anxious to secure some rock specimens, but our hopes of effecting a landing were frustrated by a heavy swell which intensified the strong westerly equatorial current; there was a rise and fall of about ten feet, and every now and again waves breaking in spray almost right over the summit of the rocks. As geologist I was given the honour of first attempt at a landing: the whale-boat was backed in as close as was possible and I jumped—but just a fraction of a second too late: the boat had begun to fall with the swell, the take-off was bad, and instead of getting a firm footing, I fell down, down into the water literally swarming with sharks which had followed the boat up to the rocks. The men were pushing them off with oars and boat-hooks when I came up, luckily, right underneath the boat, and was hauled in by the scruff of the neck by Davidson ere the boat was dashed on the rocks by the succeeding rise, but it was a narrow squeak for all concerned. With care and more skilful jumping, no doubt, a landing might have been made, but the chief considered it inadvisable to risk another attempt, so we had to depart contented with some specimens of the boobys and noddies which nest on St Paul's, and fragments of the rat's-tail like seaweed (*Caulerpa*) which grows around it. From St Paul's to the latitude of Monte Video all days were much alike—hot blue sky overhead and hot blue sea underneath; and a ship built to withstand polar cold is not altogether a floating palace of comfort in the tropics.

We had no ceremony crossing the Line,—none of the old-timers had initiative enough to get up one. Our track lay inside Fernando Noronha, and down the Brazilian coast in full sight of Parahiba and Pernambuco. At this time there was quite an outbreak of colds on board—a most unusual thing at sea. Apparently the infection had been caught (from the birds?) at St Paul's.

Off Pernambuco we saw a number of catamarans, on which the natives come out fishing four or five miles off shore. Frail little crafts they were,—merely two parallel logs with some cross pieces, and a primitive tiny mast and sail.

The pleasantest recollections, perhaps, of this part of the voyage are those of the dog-watches.

In the cool of the evening, the day's work done, almost all on board would be gathered on deck. Here would be one group listening to a thrilling yarn of adventure "up North" among the ice-floes of Davis Straits; there another to a blood-curdling story whose scene was laid in 'Frisco; or it might be a brush with pirates in the China Sea, for every corner of the globe yielded its tale.

Then would come a lull filled in by a pibroch or reel from the piper, or a song in some plaintive minor key; though it must be confessed that the good old sea-chanteys were not so much in evidence as the more modern music-hall products.

Then all is an uproar; some wag—usually one of the cooks—has doused an unsuspecting fellow-man with a bucket of water, and there is no peace till the victim has "got square," midst the cheers and laughter of the onlookers. It is curious how these little incidents remain sharp and clear on one's memory, while the big important events seem to grow vague and shadowy!

Before leaving the tropics, we had a trial trawl in the shallow water over the Abrolhos bank. Everything worked well, but the catch was almost nil, the trawl-bag being so torn by the sharp coral rock. The attached swabs yielded a few "beasties," the most interesting being a small crab, with sponges and seaweed growing all over its back and legs: probably it had planted them there for protective purposes; certainly it would have required a smart enemy to detect the crab under its wealth of foliage.

Christmas Day was much like the other days. We merely worked a little less, and ate and drank a little more than usual. There was a sense of unreality about sitting down to a Christmas plum-pudding in blazing sunshine, especially when the fiddles were on the table and the dishes careering here, there, and everywhere. At midnight on the 25th the hourly meteorological observations commenced. We were close on 30° S. lat., south of which lay the area of the globe at this time receiving special meteorological attention.

On the 28th, in 83° 51′ S., 48° 48′ W., we crossed a great yellow band of gelatinous scum stretching from horizon to horizon. It proved to consist of microscopic algae (*Desmideæ*) closely allied to the diatoms, and in the scum were numbers of Portuguese men-of-war (*Physalia*), Jelly-fish (*Aurefia*), Ctenophores, and other organisms.

The following two days we met in with the tail-end of a "pampero," and the ship received her first regular baptism as she shipped it green over the poop and in at the cabin skylight as we sat at dinner below.

New Year's Day, 1903.—"About 150 miles off the mouth of the River Plate. A tropically warm day, but the sea temperature has dropped considerably, and the water is now green,—changed quite suddenly from the deep blue we have had so long. Had a trial sounding, with very bad luck, losing 1800 fathoms of wire and a sounding tube; using a spliced wire, and one of the splices drew. To make up for this had a 'big catch,' the first of the year, in which we hope to get so much that is new."

This catch consisted of a large sun-fish (*Orthagoriscus*), weighing about three-quarters of a ton. Some half-dozen of these huge fish were seen during the day basking on the surface, the largest being about the size of a small haystack. The one captured was really quite tiny, but it was all we could do to hoist it on board. Its stupidity was amazing: unable to swim faster than a boat could row, all it had to do to escape was to sink,—and this they can do quite well,—but although struck by a harpoon a dozen times before one held, it made no attempt to escape. Davidson, an expert harpooner, ultimately managed to insert a harpoon into the gill cleft, then the beast allowed itself to be towed to the ship,—apparently dying of disgust, for no other reason was evident.

When cut up it was easily seen why the first harpoons would not hold, as under the skin was a layer two or three inches thick of a hard cartilaginous material. The dissection was performed mainly with axes. The central nervous system was very interesting on account of its minute size relative to the body, the spinal cord being only about half an inch long and barely coming outside the cranial cavity.

This degeneracy is doubtless correlated with the feeble musculature and swimming powers. Intelligence and mobility have become superfluous, the size and thick hide being sufficient protection against most enemies; but as usual it has had to pay a price—in this case by becoming the host of numerous parasites both internally and externally.

The following day or two there were great and rapid variations in the temperature, colour, and salinity of the sea water. This is apparently due to the mixing of the cold Cape Horn current with the warmer water of the South Atlantic. On the 3rd we had our record run so far, 215 miles in the twenty-four hours, but as we had stopped an hour and a half over a sounding, it worked out at a little over 9½ knots per hour,—not quite the speed of an ocean greyhound, but very fair for a craft of the wind-jamming, blubber-basket type.

Early on the 6th January we sighted the Falklands. In the cold grey dawn the low, bleak, treeless, but grassy land looked very like some parts of the North of Scotland, and this home-feeling was intensified a few hours later when we passed through the Narrows into the fine land-locked harbour of Port Stanley, and saw the peat-stacks crowning the heights behind the town, and smelt the peat-reek mingled with the fresh odour of land which is so evident after a long spell of the briny ocean.

Port Stanley lies on the south side of the harbour, and consists of one main street along the water front, and a couple of small streets behind. Most of the older houses are simple white wooden structures, but the newer ones are built of sandstone, the most conspicuous buildings being the cathedral, with its spire still unfinished, the Falkland Island Company's store, and Government House, a somewhat rambling structure, at the extreme west end, and isolated from the rest of the town. Of greater interest than the buildings ashore are the old hulks moored in the harbour and used as stores; amongst others are the *Great Britain*, famous in her day as the first iron steamer, and the *Snow Squall*, which took refuge here from the *Alabama* in the days of the American Civil War, and found a permanent home in this last resting-place of so many "lame ducks" from the Cape Horn seas.

Our first visitor was one of the Falkland Island Company's men with some letters from home; then Lieutenant Beckwith of H.M.S. *Basilisk*, which was anchored a little farther up the harbour. These calls over, we got into our shore-going garb, and a few minutes later were once again standing on good solid British ground.

CHAPTER III

FIRST ANTARCTIC VOYAGE

DEPARTURE FROM PORT STANLEY—A HEAVY GALE—FIRST ICEBERG—ENTERING THE PACK—THE SOUTH ORKNEYS— BATTLING WITH THE ICE—SOUTHWARD HO—BESET— FORMATION OF SEA-ICE—AN OUTBREAK OF FIRE—OUR FARTHEST SOUTH—SLOW PROGRESS—TRAWLING AND SOUNDING—SEEKING A HARBOUR—A CLOSE SHAVE— DAMAGE TO RUDDER—ANCHORED.

IN the early morning of January 26 we got under weigh after a stay in port of nearly three weeks. During this time we had been very busy. Several excursions of scientific interest had been engaged in, and at Cape Pembroke Lighthouse, which was to serve as a base meteorological station during our Antarctic campaign, we had fitted up several instruments to complete the equipment already there. Mr Pearce, the principal lighthouse-keeper, was to make the observations, and as he had considerable experience, there was no question about this part of the work being well done.

Much of my own time had been taken up in making, under many difficulties, a series of magnetic observations at Navy Point. The ship's officers and crew were fully occupied in stowing provisions and coal, of which necessary commodity we had nearly 200 tons on board. As we had to be provisioned for two years, we were under the necessity of carrying a deck cargo of various foodstuffs, which completely filled the deck from the after-deck house to the fo'cs'le head. The summer was now getting very late, and we were anxious to begin work. Before finally taking our departure we steamed round H.M.S. *Cambrian*, whose crew gave us three hearty cheers, whilst the band played "Stars and Stripes for Ever," "Weel may the Keel Row," "The Bonnets o' Bonnie Dundee," finishing up with "A Life on the Ocean Wave." There was plenty of enthusiasm on both sides. The *Cambrian* then signalled "Luck," and "Wish you a Pleasant Voyage," while Captain Green, of the *Sorata,* who kindly took the last of our home letters, wished us success. After stopping in the Narrows to hoist a fish-trap, we resumed our voyage. A little after 2 P.M. we passed Cape Pembroke Lighthouse, where we dipped our ensign in response to their good wishes, and then steered south-east. Soon after we got into rough water; the ship rolled a good deal, and things banged about generally, but no seas were shipped. Next day the rolling continued, the clinometer registering 40°, so that sleep was almost impossible owing to the constant row occasioned by rattling dishes, the coal-scuttle, &c. The weather continued dry and fair, but a heavy cross swell from west and north was experienced. "The deck cargo, as expected, is proving a nuisance; the lead lining on the boxes cuts one's rubber sea-boots like a knife, and is further a source of danger in the dark. Began hourly meteorological observations at midnight. These hourly observations were commenced on December 25, but were interrupted during our stay at Stanley. I have the night-watch, remaining on duty till 4 A.M., when I am relieved by the chief until 1 P.M., when my spell again begins."

On January 28 the barometer fell steadily with a generally overcast sky and a misty haze, which restricted our view to a short distance. We were now in a region frequented by icebergs, so that a sharp look-out was kept for those unwelcome neighbours, so soon to become our almost constant companions. The temperature was now falling, so opportunity was taken in the evening to distribute a welcome gift of worsted jerseys, mitts, mufflers, and gloves, the work of the inhabitants of Fair Isle, and thoughtfully provided by Mr James Coats, jun., for the use of the Expedition. In the evening the wind increased considerably a force with a rising sea, so that at 10 P.M. sail was reduced. Next day we encountered a heavy gale which blew with hurricane strength, testing for the first time the sea-going qualities of the *Scotia*. After 9 P.M. we were hove to under lower main-topsail with three oil-bags out, one at the "cat-head," the second well forward on the starboard side, and a third amidships. The oil used being whale-oil, which is both heavy and thick, was most effectual in modifying the action of breaking seas, although its effect was somewhat reduced owing to the low temperature of the sea, which caused it to thicken too much and thus to spread unevenly. As it was, only one heavy sea came on board, the *Scotia* "taking it green." The weather bulwarks were stove in, and two of the crew washed into the lee scuppers, while some of the deck cargo went overboard. This must have been the time when the cabin was flooded. It was rather novel seeing one's boots, &c., floating about in the water. Our harmonium, which had already developed a few dyspeptic notes, did not have its tone improved by the Neptunian invasion. Several icebergs were passed, the most characteristic being those of the tabular form, with perfectly smooth sides, as though they had been chiselled out of masses of beautiful alabaster. Others again, that had been exposed for some time to the action of the sea, were beautifully excavated into a series of lofty arches and deep caverns which sparkled in bright sunshine with many-coloured tints; while ever and anon the swell rushed in, burying the sides in masses of foam, while their presence at night could be distinguished by the roar of the surf as it dashed against their weather sides.

On January 30 we resumed our Antarctic progression under pretty favourable conditions, the sea being moderate till about 5 P.M., when it went down. Passed several bergs, one at 11.45 P.M.,—too near to be pleasant. At this time I was startled by a cry of "Hard-a-port!" and on rushing on deck was just in time to see the ghostly outline of a huge berg on our weather quarter. It had loomed suddenly out of the misty haze right ahead of us, but vigilant eyes were on the look-out. At noon we were in lat. 56° 25′ 8., long. 47° 52′ W. On the following day we took our first Antarctic sounding in lat. 58° 22′ S., when bottom was touched at a depth of 169 fathoms. A sample of the bottom deposit was brought up and found to consist of diatom ooze, among which Pirie found hornblende, felspar, augite, and other minerals. Wind was light from N. W. most of the day, falling calm in evening, and at 10 P.M. changing to the south, with a failing temperature and sleet. The atmosphere continued very misty, so that a sharp look-out was kept for bergs. Two men for this purpose were on the fo'c'sle-head, and one on the forward bridge. The mist lifted towards evening, but the driving sleet obscured the view and made things rather unpleasant. Passed several bergs during the day, including a large one several hundred feet long and at least 200 feet in height, with its summit capped with mist.

On February 1 it was snowing heavily at 1 A.M., when we passed a berg at a distance of nearly 300 yards. About 3 A.M. it cleared up to windward, and a band of dull red could be seen stretching from about E.S.E. to S.S.W. As the sun rose the effect was very fine, there being five bergs on the horizon which were brilliantly illuminated in the morning light. At 10 A.M. a sounding was taken—depth 2307 fathoms: deposit, diatom ooze, with particles of mica, felspar, quartz, and hornblende. Passed a number of bergs during the day, there being as many as twenty-five visible at one time. This was a very fine day, temperature round about 30° and brilliant sunshine.

At twenty minutes past midnight on February 2 we reached the edge of the pack, having previously encountered several stray pieces of ice. As we proceeded the *Scotia* got more and more surrounded, but did not get her baptism till 1 A.M., when she struck a fairish sized lump of ice that sent a thrill through her timbers. At 2 A.M. we had put about, as the pack became very heavy and compact. Thumps now became frequent, as in the dim light one could not get a clear idea of the best course to steer. At 6 A.M. we were coasting along the edge of the ice, and did not enter the pack again till noon. A sounding was attempted at 2 P.M. when in lat. 60° 28′ S., long. 43° 40′ W., but it did not prove successful owing to the ship drifting away from the wire. In the evening Wilton and Pirie left in the dinghy and shot a seal and several birds. After their return we resumed our former course until 9.40, when we lay to till daylight. There is no doubt that we had made the pack much farther north than usual. Ross, in 1843, in this longitude did not encounter it till about lat. 65°; d'Urville, in 1838, in about 63° 30'; while Powell, in 1821, also came across it several degrees south of our position. Evidently conditions over the Weddell Sea had been abnormal during the past winter, which was exceptionally severe in Stanley, with south and south-east winds instead of the usual air currents from west and north-west. The unusual cold prevailed into October, and there had been no time for the ice to get broken up and scattered over the ocean. We later learned that the Swedes under Nordenskjöld had experienced a very hard winter at Snow Hill, near Cape Seymour. Doubtless the ice conditions in this region vary from year to year as in the North, and although the causes of these variations are at present unknown, yet they will be found to coincide with anomalies in the distribution of barometric pressure over a wide area, and the prevailing winds resulting from the abnormal pressure conditions. On February 3 the pack-ice closed in round the ship in early morning, and at 9 o'clock the *Scotia* was steaming north, as very heavy ice lay to the south. The South Orkneys were visible at 3 A.M., distant twenty-five miles, and bearing W.S.W. We got outside the pack at 1 P.M., and steamed along its edge for several hours, entering it again late in the afternoon and lying to for the night in an open pool of water about half a mile in diameter. Next day the staff paid a visit to Saddle Island, South Orkneys, which had only been visited twice before, and that not since 1838, when Dumont d'Urville, in the French corvette *Astrolabe*, trod its shores. The *Scotia's* naturalists, along with Mr Bruce and three seamen, effected a landing in a little rock-surrounded bay on the north side of the island. On landing, large numbers of ringed penguins were met with, as well as many interesting birds, such as Cape pigeons, sheath-bills, skuas, giant petrels, and shags, 11 of which were nesting in the vicinity. Walking was difficult, owing to loose stones intermingled with ice and guano, the odour of which was far from pleasant. An interesting little lake, owing its origin to the melted snow in the vicinity, was discovered, and from a crest near it an excellent view was obtained to the south. The party returned about 11 o'clock with a boat-load of penguins, eggs, rocks, and botanical specimens. Two living penguins were brought on board, but somehow they managed to disappear, having been worried by men and dogs past endurance. After noon we started to steam S.E. through the pack, and were favoured with several leads of open water. The outlook at 9 P.M., when we stopped for the night, was, however, far from promising, very heavy ice surrounding us on all sides.

February 5 was a disappointing day to us all. The pack during the night became very close, and Captain Robertson, at 7 A.M., put the *Scotia* about, and the ship's course was N.W. and W. for some time. It was hard lines to have to turn back at this early stage of our southern advance, but heavy ice lay all around except to the N.W. and N., and a strong ice-blink sweeping nearly all round the horizon was anything but an encouraging prospect. In forcing her way out of the pack the *Scotia* received some severe blows, and I did not get much sleep in consequence, after turning in at 11 A.M. By 8 P.M. we were practically clear of the pack and in open water, having since the morning steamed through eighty miles of ice, which was a very creditable performance, as it seemed impossible at times for the vessel to find a path, so compact and dense was it. During most of the day the bo'sun was on the quarterdeck keeping a sharp look-out to see that none of the tongues of ice struck the propeller when she was going astern. It was with much satisfaction that we saw how well suited our vessel was for the work undertaken. In the skilful hands of Captain Robertson she threaded her way with ease through a seeming labyrinth of real polar pack-ice, some of which was from fifteen to twenty feet thick. In the course of the day numerous seals and penguins were seen lying on the ice or sporting in the lanes of water, imparting an air of life and animation to the surroundings. Our course was now to be about 250 or 300 miles to the east, in which direction previous explorers in this region have been able to turn the pack edge and get south. Position at noon, lat. 61° 05′ S., long. 43° 40′ W.

In the early morning of February 6 we passed several large bergs on the port bow. On a loose piece of ice near one of them were resting a large number of penguins, who were much startled by our sudden appearance, jumping into the water with loud cries. At 2 A.M. we hauled to the north-west to clear a point of ice, but during the day a course was steered that was approximately due east through much slack ice, and for a short time we were in quite open water. The barometer continuing high the weather was fine, although dull, with light variable winds, chiefly northerly. There was a perceptible swell on the water for a short interval, showing that we were quite under the influence of open sea to the north.

The sun shone dimly for a sufficient time to enable our position to be determined. From the observations our latitude at noon was 60° 10′ S., long. 42° 38′ W. Early in the morning Pirie shot a Ross seal, the rarest of the four species known to inhabit Antarctic waters. At 10 P.M. the engines were stopped for the night, and we proceeded very slowly under easy sail; the ice continued fairly heavy, but there were fine leads in the vicinity. Quite a perceptible reduction in our deck cargo was now observable, one or two boxes of provisions being consumed daily.

The 7th February, like so many days in the Antarctic summer, was dull, with dense mist and showers of snow, sleet, and rain. Our view was thus restricted to a small area, and as we were navigating through much ice the ship's course was seldom the same for two minutes together. The manoeuvres of one of the mates while on bridge-duty were very entertaining. The navigation among the ice-blocks was so intricate that he sometimes gave three or four orders in one breath, so that the two men at the wheel had a lively time of it with "Port—steady—starboard—steady," following one another in rapid succession. It was very amusing to watch him running up and down the bridge as we approached heavy pieces of ice, and the joke of it all was that in spite of his great caution he usually did the wrong thing, but the blocks we struck did no damage. One of his stock injunctions to the helmsmen was, "Watch my hand!" and it required a lot of watching.

February 13.—"For some days we have steered a course sometimes to the north, at other times to the south of the sixtieth parallel of latitude, keeping the pack edge, which has all the time presented a thick and impenetrable appearance, on our starboard hand. The weather continues very dull and misty, except for a short time on the 10th, when the sun shone brilliantly for a few hours. Temperature varies but little; sometimes it goes up to or a little higher than freezing-point, but usually the thermometer shows two or three degrees of frost. Bergs are our constant companions, and a sharp look-out has to be maintained. A sounding was taken at noon on the 9th when in lat. 59° 52′ S., long. 34° 12′ W., depth 1325 fathoms; and another on the 10th, when in lat. 60° 03′ S., long. 32° 10′ W.,—bottom was found in 590 fathoms. On the 10th we were to all appearance thoroughly beset, but in the course of the day the ice opened up a little under the influence of a north-east gale, and we made some progress."

On February 14 we seemed to have turned the main pack, as our course for the day was due south. Occasional streams of ice driven off the main body were met with. A considerable number of large pieces of ice were passed, shaped like mushrooms, with a wide base of solid blue ice surmounted by a cone of snow and ice, rising well out of the water. These lumps, when worn flush with the surface, are a menace to navigation, as they cannot readily be perceived. About 10 o'clock the moon came out, and the prospect was very fine. At 11.45, without any warning, we went bang into a "growler," which is the name applied to the stumps of weather-worn pack-ice referred to above. The *Scotia* took it stem on; and although a most violent shock was experienced, no material damage was done. A large number of bergs were seen, but, with a single exception, they proved small insignificant affairs.

Excellent progress was made to-day, there being a fresh north-west wind till about 6 P.M. A sounding was taken at 8 P.M., depth 2250 fathoms. Between 6 and 7 P.M. there was a fine display of mock suns, which were formed on a partial halo of 22° radius. So far, optical phenomena have been scarce, owing to the continuance of cloudy skies. At nightfall we proceeded under easy sail close-hauled to the wind. Many whales and a sea leopard were seen.

Next day, the sea remaining almost clear of pack-ice, good progress was again made. Bergs were numerous until 9 P.M., by which time we had just cleared a long chain of them. It is curious how they are met with in clusters, sometimes as many as a dozen within the radius of a mile, while the rest of the sea shows only an isolated specimen here and there. About 2 o'clock an "appearance of land" to the west was reported, and the ship was put about for a little. The land, however, turned out to be a "Cape Flyaway." Such mistakes are very common in the Antarctic, a wreath of snow-like clouds, or an iceberg with earthy matter in it, being very liable to be mistaken for land. A few seals were seen among some loose ice, also numerous whales, which have been plentiful for some days past. We were sailing midway between Weddell's and Ross's tracks over unexplored seas, and at noon were in lat. 62°.

February 17—"A fine forenoon, but, being on night duty, missed it. The quiet weather continued till the evening, when wind and sea rose, making things very unpleasant. A sounding was taken at noon, depth 2729 fathoms. The deck cargo was stowed down the main hold, the space formerly occupied by the coal we have consumed having made room for it. Every one is glad to see it thus safely housed, as it has been a nuisance to all, and a positive danger in heavy weather to those engaged in working the ship. The decks are now nice and clean, and everything is ready for a blow. We are scudding along at seven knots under sail, which is very good speed for us. Position at noon, lat. 64° 18′ S., long. 23° 09′ W."

Next morning we had a moderate gale from the E.S.E., with a fairly heavy sea. Having been so long in the "small waters" among the ice, many of us had again to find our sea-legs. In the evening we crossed the Antarctic circle with all sails set, and in a sea clear of ice. "Our hopes of a rapid run south are now strong: it is Wednesday, but by Sunday we expect to have passed Weddell's farthest, and are beginning to experience that excitement which is inevitably associated with the advent of unexplored lands and seas."

The early morning of February 19 was fine, but after 6 A.M. the sky became overcast. A sounding was taken at noon, depth 2651 fathoms. Few bergs were to be seen, but a good deal of ice was met with in the evening, there being a strong ice-blink to south-west and south. A water sky was, however, visible to the south-east and east.

We made little southing next day, owing to the increasing tightness of the pack, which Captain Robertson did not consider expedient to negotiate. Any mistake now would finish our work for the season, and we had no wish to repeat the experiences of the *Belgica* and drift helplessly about all winter, frozen up in a sea of shifting ice. The pack continued heavy, and young ice had commenced to form.

The formation of "young ice," as met with in the polar seas, is an interesting process. The first stage, which takes place when the cold is very intense, is the ascent of large quantities of vapour from the sea, so dense that it looks as if a veil had been spread over the surface of the ocean. If there are spaces of water and portions covered with ice, the water spaces look like boiling caldrons, so dense are the masses of vapour that ascend. This, however, is of brief duration. Owing to the lowering of the temperature through evaporation, heat is removed from

31

the water, thus assisting the cold of the air in producing a covering of young ice. Soon a thickening is observed on the surface of the water, and threads like the web of a spider radiate in all directions. This covering, which is at first thin and pasty, becomes thick, less vapour is produced, and finally it disappears. The salt-water ice is now a pasty mass, so elastic that every movement of the water on which it floats is clearly discernible. The ice, however, is quite different from that formed on fresh water; for although it becomes tougher with very intense cold, it will not support the weight of a man with safety until after thirty or thirty-six hours. Even after twelve hours, with a temperature of 40° below zero, the new ice is still so soft that, in spite of its thickness, a stick can be easily pushed through it. After three days it is still in no way brittle, and bends under the weight of a man without breaking. The impression it gives is as if one were walking on well-stretched leather; and this characteristic it retains for a considerable time. After a fortnight, when over a foot and a half thick, the young ice looks as if the water had been surprised by the cold and every wave turned suddenly into ice.

This persistent viscosity is due to the large quantity of salt remaining in the surface-layers of the ice congealed by intense cold, and of the moisture attracted by it. The salt is quite eliminated in the process involved in the formation of each ice-crystal. If a very low temperature prevails, then the formation of ice takes place very rapidly, so that a large number of ice-crystals are formed in a very short time, and among them is entangled a good deal of the salter brine. As the cold increases, more ice is produced out of the brine, but no matter how great the cold, the surface-layers of sea-water ice are never so hard as, nor do they acquire the appearance of, fresh-water ice. The pastiness of the surface of the ice is due to the presence of a very concentrated briny solution, principally chloride of calcium, which in the course of time is absorbed into the ice. Until snow falls this ice is very difficult to ski over, as the snow-shoes will not slide over the surface, so that the foot has to be raised at each step, as in walking through heather. In spite of the low temperature, one is astonished to find that every step one takes leaves an impression on the surface, which appears in a semi-liquid condition, giving the impression that the ice is in a state of thaw, although the temperature may be 70° or more below the freezing-point.

During the day we dodged along to the east under easy sail to economise coal. A sounding was taken at 6 P.M., depth 2540 fathoms. It was eighty years ago on this date that Weddell reached his farthest south, a little to the west of us. The conditions must have been very exceptional, as he saw no ice when he turned north in lat. 74° 15′ S. The temperature remained low, averaging ten degrees of frost, and no bergs were seen.

February 21 was quite the finest day since leaving Stanley, the sky keeping bright and clear, with hard frost and a calm atmosphere. Slow progress was made, young ice continuing to form in considerable quantities. In the afternoon we passed the seventieth degree of south latitude. We saw a large number of emperor penguins (*Aptenodytes fosteri*), and one over four feet was shot in the afternoon. An accident happened to-day that might have had very serious consequences. On entering the deck laboratory at 1 P.M. to read the barometer, I was astonished to find the stove one sheet of flame: shouting for assistance, Murray and Florence, who were at work in the galley adjacent, promptly responded and smothered the flames. The fire was due to a quantity of sealing-wax having been left simmering in a pan on the top of the stove. The bottom of the pan had been burnt out, thus igniting the wax, which spluttered all over the stove and floor. As there was a large quantity of benzine, alcohol, and other highly inflammable substances in the laboratory, not to mention the methylated spirit tank right underneath, an extension of the fire would have resulted in a series of explosions that would in all probability have caused serious damage to, if not the total loss of, the ship. No bergs were seen even from the mast-head, although we could see for a great distance owing to the transparency of the atmosphere. The mean temperature was 21°.5, the highest being 23°.0, and the lowest 18°.6; yesterday's mean was 22°.2.

February 22.—"Only one berg was to be seen from the mast-head, although we had an extensive view, owing to the clear air. Unfortunately for our progress the frost became very keen, the mean temperature being only 19°.3 and the lowest 13°.5 at 5 A.M. Some curious mirage effects were seen about 3 A.M., just before I turned in. There was a bank of fog to the S. and S.E. in front of which was a sort of thin bluish vapour. Pieces of ice a foot or two high were drawn out to several times their natural dimensions, while here and there through the fog could be seen castellated towers and battlements rising above it. We reached our farthest south, lat. 70° 25′, long. 17° 12′ W., at about 8 A.M. Here young ice had formed to a considerable extent, cementing the pack together. As we were to all appearance thoroughly beset, the captain decided to go north if he got the chance, and try again farther to the eastward. We made slow progress in a northerly direction until 9 P.M., when the engines were stopped for the night. An emperor penguin was caught on the ice and brought on board alive. He seems to have settled down to his strange surroundings with remarkable equanimity, and walks up and down the deck, every now and again giving utterance to a musical cadence. We have named him Amaswagla, which, in Esquimaux, means 'plenty.' The day turned out very clear, enabling a wide and extensive view to be obtained from the mast-head. No sign of land; there is certainly none within a radius of seventy miles. A sounding was taken at noon, depth 2543 fathoms."

February 28.—"During the past six days we have had a hard battle with the ice, which on many occasions threatened to hold us fast for the winter. In this time we have only made about half a degree of northing, but have gone about ten degrees to the west, taking the course which offered the least resistance. On the 23rd we started butting the new ice at 5 A.M., but stopped at 2 P.M., as hardly any progress was being made. On the 24th we were again closely beset, and made little northing until the afternoon of the 25th, when several fine leads made their appearance. The weather being clear, one could form some idea of the best route to take. On the 26th there was a decided rise in the temperature, which during the preceding six days had ranged from 24°.3 to 13°.4. A marked northerly swell helped to ease the ice a little, and on the 27th we traversed a considerable expanse of bay ice nine inches thick with occasional areas of open water. To-day we have been lying to, Mr Bruce being engaged in taking an elaborate series of deep-sea temperatures, &c., with the Pettersen-Nansen water-bottle, from the surface to a depth of 2587 fathoms. The general outlook to-day was much as usual—i.e., considerable leads of open water, with new ice and some old pack."

We were now into the month of March, and the question arose, Where were we to winter? In a few weeks the seas, kept open at present by ocean swell, would permanently freeze over. The nights were getting long and dark, and it was unpleasant work navigating among bergs and pack. After mature deliberation the chief decided to winter the ship at the South Orkneys, where it was expected we should get released early in October. From a meteorological point of view observations there would be of extreme interest, and our previous visit showed how rich the islands were in bird life. Before getting there, however, every effort had to be made to sound, trawl, and make other physical observations, more especially as we hoped to shape our course over entirely unexplored seas.

Just before turning in at 4 A.M. on March 1, I had an excellent view of a grampus (a cetacean, the largest of the *Deiphinidæ)* passing under the stern of the ship. This creature is remarkable for its great strength and ferocity, and is the only cetacean which regularly preys on its warm-blooded kindred, systematically attacking whales, while it is also very partial to seals. Our course was about W.N.W., and we passed through considerable streams of loose pancake ice, with here and there a portion of an old broken-up floe. About 6 P.M. we crossed Weddell's track, but under very different conditions from those experienced by him; for while he was favoured with open sea, we had the impenetrable pack under our lees. On the 4th we lay to all day in order to replenish our water-supply from a low berg. Two boats were employed, each containing half a dozen men armed with pickaxes. On getting alongside they climbed on the berg and hacked enough ice to fill the boat, which was then rowed back to the *Scotia*, where the ice was put into a barrel on deck communicating with the steam pipe of the boiler, and there melted and conveyed to the water-tanks.

March 19.—"During the past fortnight we have continued to sail or steam in a N.N.W. direction, stopping nearly every day to take a sounding or trawling. On the 8th, at 11.40 P.M., when driving before a heavy easterly gale, the *Scotia* struck a large piece of ice amidships, which made her quiver from stem to stern, but no damage was done. On the 11th we recrossed the Antarctic circle, and again remarked how few bergs were to be seen in this region. On the 12th we were busy taking a series of observations with the Pettersen-Nansen water-bottle, which was anything but pleasant work. There being 15 degrees of frost, the sounding platform, workers, and the water-bottle itself were soon a mass of ice. The 13th was even colder, the average for the day showing over 22 degrees of frost. Large numbers of bergs were seen on the 14th, but, fortunately, we had the moon with us, otherwise navigation among these masses of ice would have been extremely difficult, not to say dangerous. This morning we tried to go west in order to investigate the 'appearance of land' reported by Ross in 1843, some seventy miles away, but there was too much heavy ice about, so that our course had to be altered to north-east. Between 10 P.M. and midnight we passed close to some very large bergs of the usual flat-topped variety. On the 17th we got into open water after passing through some heavy broken-up pack, which made great de-mands on the vigilance and activity of Captain Robertson and the ship's officers. On the 18th we reached comparatively shallow water, three soundings taken rang-ing from 545 to 210 fathoms, showing that we were over the shelf of rock running out from the Orkneys. During the day good progress was made, but towards evening we came into some exceptionally heavy broken-up pack. Fortunately there was no swell, and about 9 P.M. we lay to for the night in a small pool of water."

March 20.—"The morning broke dull and hazy, and a start was not made till 10 o'clock. We passed through some very heavy ice, and a swell having arisen during the night, the navigation gave a good deal of trouble. After a time we got into the open ocean clear of the ice; and then the sea began to rise. In the evening there was a general collapse of the scientific staff, only the Captain and Mr Bruce being about at 8 P.M. The wind increased to a gale from the N.N.W. in the late evening when the outlook was far from promising, all hands on deck having an anxious time looking out for bergs."

March 21.—"The Orkneys were sighted about 6 A.M., and about noon we were quite close to Cape Dundas, the eastern extremity of the islands. Heavy pack-ice was found to be lying along the south side of the islands, blocking the way in a westerly direction. We were thus unable to get into Leathwaite Strait to have a look at Spence Harbour. Heading for the open with much reluctance, we got into a tremendous swell, the wind blowing a gale from the N.W., with thick snow. It was a disappointment, as we were looking forward to a quiet night in a harbour of some sort."

March 22.—"At 9 A.M. we were steaming past Saddle Island under most un-favourable conditions for finding Spence Harbour. The whole prospect was gloomy and forbidding in the extreme, the land being enveloped in a dense pall of cloud. Heavy snow-squalls blew off the land, laden with tons of snow-drift, so that our view was restricted at times to a radius of fifty yards. We had some rather exciting experiences in the afternoon, being surrounded by icebergs; and more than once we nearly ran on rocks. About noon, when in the vicinity of Cape Bennett, the wind suddenly fell, and the sea, with equal rapidity, became quite smooth. We could not see half a cable's length ahead for the driving snow. The skipper instantly rang 'full speed astern,' and before the vessel had lost way the spectral figure of a huge berg loomed out right ahead. It was really awful weather to be near uncharted land, so at 6 P.M., darkness coming on, we headed again for the open, the weather having now become tolerably quiet. Later on it again blew very hard, but before 9 o'clock we cleared a large cluster of bergs aground near the land. Fortunately the night became fine and the horizon cleared."

March 23.—"In the early morning it blew a living gale, but the sky continuing fairly clear, bergs could be seen before getting into too close proximity to them. About 5 A.M. we began to steam back to the Orkneys, and about noon were in Leathwaite Strait. The weather turned out very fine, and we had magnificent views of superb glacial and mountain scenery. Spence Harbour turned out a fraud, being ridiculously exposed, with very deep water. Indeed it was more of an indentation or bight than a harbour. Ellison Harbour also proved quite unsuitable, being too small, and not adapted to a vessel of the *Scotia's* size. As it is eighty years since these harbours have been used, changes may have taken place in the location of the glaciers which surround them. In the evening we had again to head for the open, and as the night was very dark, with thick snow-drift, our position till day broke was again an unpleasant one."

March 24.—"In the middle watch it was fairly clear, and light to moderate N.E. breezes continued to prevail most of the day. At 6 P.M. the wind veered to the W., with snow and mist, and soon increased to a full gale. We were lying comfortably in the pack on the lee-side of the islands, and but for the proximity of bergs would have felt in clover. There must have been a heavy sea running outside, as a considerable swell was perceptible at times."

March 25.—"The gale continued through the early morning hours, accompanied with snow and slight fog. Was wakened at 4.15 A.M. by a noise overhead. On investigation, found that the rudder had torn two of the blocks out of the deck, and was hanging by only one pintle. At and a little previous to the time of the occurrence we were beyond the shelter of the Orkneys, so that the heavy pack was being smashed up by the northerly swell. Some heavy pieces must have been driven against the rudder with much violence. Owing to the difficulty of steering with the temporary arrangements rigged up for that purpose, we were badly thumped and squeezed by the ice, but coming into open water about 10 A.M., were soon in a more comfortable position. The weather by this time had improved, displaying an extensive prospect of bergs to leeward. We reached the Orkneys about 1 P.M., after which the Captain and several others left in the gig to look for a harbour, but without success. Fortunately, continuing our course up a large bay on the south side of Laurie Island, we found a suitable and well-protected anchorage near its head, with ten fathoms of water. Needless to say, the prospect of a quiet night after such a trying week as we had experienced was much appreciated, and there were few on board who did not sleep the sleep of the just on this occasion."

CHAPTER IV

THE SOUTH ORKNEYS—A GENERAL SURVEY

THEIR DISCOVERY—FORMER VISITORS—ADVANTAGES AS A WINTER STATION—PECULIARITIES OF THE GROUP—THE GLOOM AND BEAUTY OF THE ANTARCTIC—A QUESTION OF OWNERSHIP.

DESPITE their relative nearness to civilised lands and their position on the verge of the Antarctic Ocean, the South Orkneys were practically unknown from a scientific point of view until the visit of the *Scotia.* In the beginning of the nineteenth century, subsequent to the discovery of the South Shetland Islands, the seas in these parts of the Antarctic regions were visited yearly by large fleets of American and British sealing schooners in search of the rich harvest of fur seals (*Arctocephalus australis*) then to be found there. It was one of these sealers—an Englishman, Captain Powell of the sloop *Dove*—who in 1821 discovered the South Orkneys, which are still occasionally referred to as Powell's Islands. He seems to have made a short stay and a rough survey of the islands, for it is Powell's work which is incorporated in the first Admiralty chart of the South Shetlands and South Orkneys. In the two following years Captain James Weddell of Leith, in the brigs *Jane* and *Beaufoy*, visited the South Orkneys, and on his later visit spent some time in roughly surveying the islands. But his search for fur seals proved very unremunerative, and since then, apparently, no sealer has thought these islands worthy of his attention, unless it be perhaps some of the little Canadian sealers who still, to the number of over a dozen, frequent these southern seas, making the Falkland Islands their headquarters. Some of them have as likely as not been to the South Orkneys: I have it from their own lips that they know the South Sandwich Group and the South Shetlands, but a canny northern discretion forbids them to say much of what they found there. Southern fur seals are very scarce now, and the less said about their haunts the better,—that is

38

what the sealers feel. Weddell gave the name South Orkneys to the islands, and called the two main islands Pomona or Mainland and Melville Island, but these names are generally supplanted now by Powell's earlier, but later published, Coronation and Laurie Islands,—the former named in honour of the coronation of George IV. These two islands are separated by Leathwaite and Washington Straits and Powell and Dibdin Islands. It was in Leathwaite Strait that we had looked in vain for the enticing Spence Harbour,—I fear but a fabrication of Powell or some of his men. To the north of Washington Strait lie the little islands of Saddle and Weddell, which are the most northerly outliers of the group, and were our constant companions all winter on the northern horizon.

After Weddell, the next explorer to touch at the South Orkneys was the French admiral, Dumont d'Urville, in the corvette *Astrolabe,* who in 1888 landed on Saddle Island and Weddell Island, and cruised along the coasts of Laurie and Coronation Islands. He has something to say about his experiences, but his general description is more verbose than explicit, though it must be said that his scientific observations, scanty though they were, have since proved very accurate in respect to botany and geology. Then for a long period the South Orkneys were neglected. Antarctic explorers were few and far between, and those that were pushed onwards in search of the great continent in the south, and left alone these little outlying islands, and neglected their wealth of unexplored scientific treasure lying on the very threshold of the unknown. At length, in 1893, the veil was again lifted, this time by Captain Larsen of the Norwegian whaler *Jason*— the same Larsen who was in command of the ill-starred *Antarctic* of Otto Nordenskjöld's Swedish South Polar Expedition, which sunk off Louis Philippe Island early in 1903, but, thanks largely to the energetic resourcefulness of Larsen, with no loss of life. In 1893 Larsen recounts having visited the islands, and his brief story is chiefly remarkable for the wonderful new species of penguin which he reported, but, with singular misfortune, lost the specimens of on his way home.

We never quite gave up hope of finding this penguin, "with a yellow patch under each eye and a red supraciliary crest extending backwards on each side," until Mossman returned in 1905, and even after his two-year sojourn had seen nothing of it. Then we sorrowfully relegated it to the realm of travellers' tales or sailors' imagination.

With such an unknown land around us we felt that the Scottish Expedition could hardly have chosen a better spot in which to pass the winter. Not that the islands are large, for they certainly do not altogether cover more than some 800 square-miles, but Mr Bruce's objects had ever been devote our time to biological and meteorological work rather than mere map-making when he could not do the oceanographical work for which the *Scotia* was specially planned and fitted out. For meteorology the place was well adapted,—on the verge of the winter ice-bound sea, and only some 800 miles from Cape Horn, two circumstances which made it a spot whence observations would be of great importance. Biologically, its position on the border of, and still within, the polar ice, promised collections of peculiar interest both in seals, birds, and marine fauna—a promise that was richly fulfilled.

The islands are really but a chain of submerged mountains whose peaks alone rise above the waters of the ocean. The land merely consists of a series of lofty snow-clad ridges meeting the sea in precipitous cliffs and bold headlands. The ridges run seaward to north and south in narrow peninsulas, cutting off deep bays whose heads are bounded by steep ice-cliffs, the seaward end of broad glaciers, which fill every valley despite the relatively small gathering-ground on the heights above. Many of the glaciers are very small,—barely a mile in length, and perhaps not a few hundred yards in breadth,—while very few are more than a few (two) miles long, but are often half a mile to a mile along their ice-cliff. It took us very little time to find that travelling any distance overland was almost out of the question; for it is only at the eastern end of Laurie Island, on Ferrier Peninsula, that there is really any land approaching to level, or indeed at all fit for sledging over. At sea-level I think Laurie Island has only one beach of any size, which is at the head of Scotia Bay, between it and Uruguay Cove. That is The Beach on which we built Omond House and Copeland Observatory. Here and there along the coast, especially in Scotia Bay and Fitchie Bay, are a few narrow strips of beach,—enough to afford a camping-ground, but certainly no more. In consequence of this we were not surprised to find, on sounding, that the water rapidly shelved down to over fifty fathoms and more, while on our departure from the islands at the end of the year we found 1746 fathoms within a distance of some fifteen miles.

Few of the Laurie Island peaks are very lofty, but their precipitous character lends height to their appearance. The most imposing is Mount Ramsay, in which the name of our chief engineer is perpetuated. From its snow-capped 1500 feet avalanches were of constant occurrence, rushing over with a dull roar into the waters of Jestie Bay. Coronation Island we landed on but once, and then for only some ten minutes during the search for a winter harbour; but from the ship it seemed very similar in physical conditions to Laurie Island, though it is larger, and has loftier peaks and wider glaciers.

All early records of these islands mention the bleak and forbidding appearance they have; Weddell even speaks of their "terrific appearance," comparing them unfavourably to other Antarctic islands. But polar scenery is always forbidding in the usual grey weather which seems to predominate in these regions; though in fine sunny days, which we sometimes had, I can imagine nothing more perfectly beautiful than the glittering snow-tipped ranges rising in a sea of peaks into the blue sky, perhaps with its veil of soft fleecy clouds, while around one on the sea-level runs a line of bright azure-blue ice-cliffs, clear cut or crumbling into fairy caverns, or on the verge of tumbling in huge titanic blocks on to the undulating plain of sea-ice stretching to the horizon. Far out to sea that plain is broken here and there with monster icebergs, firm prisoners until the gales and waves of spring release them.

Little rock was to be seen at most seasons but in sheer precipices. It was only in summer that all along the shore-line, where glaciers did not meet the sea, rocks made their appearance,—some greeny grey with lichen, and others brilliant orange. Too often all was shadowed in the gloom of grey skies or mist or snow,—a weary and depressing landscape, it is true, and one that made me often long for some colour—any colour—to rest my eyes upon; then the black hull of the ship was a delightful relief, or still better, the bright red of Copeland Observatory. The evening and early morning colours are not for a pen to describe: it requires the magic touch of an artist's brush to paint those deep violets on the ice-floe at evening, or the delicate blush o'erspreading the snowy ranges at sunset, or still more, those amazing skies which, tinged with every colour of the rainbow, are one of the greatest wonders of the Antarctic,—itself a world of wonders,—and of which it is so difficult to convince the unseeing and unimaginative of the reality. There is, I feel sure, no region in the world more grand in its scenery than the Antarctic, and no place more transcendent in its beauty. It is a vast wonderland laid out on a giant scale, in which littleness has no place; but its very vastness, no less than its beauty, while it quickens the traveller's daily wonder and deepens his reverence, forces him to feel that it is a world he can never conquer, a world in which the forces of nature are too tremendous to overcome, and must resignedly be bowed before in the hope that they will suffer him to come and pass again unscathed.

Often, among the varied topics brought forward in the cabin in the long winter evenings, arose the question of the ownership of the South Orkneys. And after many long discussions we arrived at the pleasing conclusion that even in this age of imperialism the South Orkneys had escaped the grasp of any country, and that we enjoyed the privilege of living in No-man's Land. But I fear that is no longer so. Not that we claimed them for Britain,—for even had we been seized with a desire to widen the confines of our empire, we could not lay claim to new territory in our country's name without a Government mandate,—and as for claiming them for Scotland, I fear that still less would have been recognised, though in Mossman they certainly had a Scotsman for their first governor. However, when the *Scotia* returned to the islands in February 1904, with an Argentine staff to take over the meteorological observatory at Omond House under the auspices of the Argentine Government, the Argentine naval flag was hoisted on the cairn where formerly the Scottish Lion flew; and I presume the South Orkneys are looked upon as a possession of that power,—the nucleus of an empire, perhaps, they may even seem to ambitious Argentine expansionists.

The South Orkneys are certainly the only spot in the Antarctic regions that have been inhabited without a break for a period of over three years, and they bid fair to become a permanently inhabited. meteorological observing-station of the Argentine Government; for that country has, for the present at least, agreed to keep a staff of six men there, to be relieved annually.

Fitchie always insisted that the real use for the South Orkneys would be as a penal settlement. For that purpose, he said, they were almost ideal. In summer the convicts would be imployed in house-building, and in winter he would keep them busy shovelling snow off the glaciers. It is an excellent plan, with much to recommend it.

CHAPTER V

IN WINTER QUARTERS

SCOTIA BAY—POLAR ICE—PREPARATIONS FOR WINTER—THE
DAY'S WORK—DREDGING AND TRAPPING—A RICH FAUNA—
FILLING THE LARDER—VITALITY OF SEALS AND PENGUINS—
BOTANISING—THE HOURLY OBSERVATIONS—EVENING
RELAXATIONS—WHAT WE ATE—PENGUIN AS FOOD—WINTER
CLOTHING—RUSS'S ESCAPADES.

IN the Antarctic regions the summer is very brief, and little more than summer in name; but for the longer days and higher sun it differs little from winter. From the end of November to the end of February is the extreme limit of what one could reasonably call summer. But of course as we were, in the South Orkneys, near the northern limit of the regions of ice, it was only to be expected that the spell of winter would be mollified and delay its advent for a few weeks. However, it was very soon evident that we had found winter quarters only just in time. For three days after our arrival, Scotia Bay (as our winter harbour has since been named) was open,—that is to say, the pack-ice to the south drifted in and out as the wind held southerly or northerly, until a colder and more lasting southerly wind drove it in, and tightly jammed a couple of miles of the bay. Before the wind changed it had begun to freeze together enough to prevent its floating away.

It was all old pack, much of it fifteen to twenty feet in thickness, and often crushed or crumpled into hummocks up to twenty feet or more in height, with even here and there small stranded icebergs, though, where the *Scotia* lay, the depth of water—some ten fathoms—acted as an effectual barrier to these in their progress up the bay. The pack being of old and very irregular ice, many lanes of water and open pools were left between the contiguous floes, and, until these had permanently frozen up, a walk over the ice demanded care. The larger pools entailed some little difficulty, as they could only be negotiated safely by ferrying oneself across on a floating block of ice. A thick fall of snow, which soon came, not only delayed the solidification of the pack, but, by obscuring these traps, made the floe very treacherous, and more than one partial ducking was the outcome. However, within a week a secure and solid covering of ice stretched from the head of the bay for about two miles southward, and, as the winter progressed, the still open water beyond was transformed into floe, until in time nothing but ice could be seen to the south. Doubtlessly had there not been a vast stretch of pack arriving from the south, drifting with wind and current, the ice in Scotia Bay might again have broken up and floated away before it finally froze together, as it had been previously doing; and that is, in fact, what we had hoped would be the case until at least much later in the winter.

One reason, and by no means the least potent one, for selecting the South Orkneys as a winter station was the hope that the ship would be late in being frozen in, and so would be at liberty to make trawling and dredging excursions in the vicinity of the islands in fine weather during the late autumn and early winter. Nothing whatever was known, by direct observation, of the climate or ice conditions of the South Orkneys; but by inference from the position of the islands this hope seemed a very reasonable one. Much, therefore, was our surprise when we found the *Scotia* firmly beset in the first week of April, and all plans of trawling excursions had to be deferred until the spring, when we expected an early release highly probable,—with what result the reader will in time hear.

On all sides of the ship lay a rugged and uneven plain of snow and ice, over which travelling was at first somewhat difficult; but in the course of the winter the successive and heavy falls of snow most effectively smoothed down the irregularities by filling up the little valleys and glens, and before many months had elapsed the floe was, in the head of Scotia Bay at least, almost monotonous in its level surface—at least, so I occasionally thought until the spring sledge-journeys began, and then I devoutly wished that all the ice around the islands was as smooth as that in Scotia anchorage, or even smoother.

The use of the term "ice" in this connection, of course, conveys to most the idea of a hard glistening surface such as one is used to on a loch in winter. But polar ice bears little resemblance to such fresh-water ice. When sea-water freezes, a large proportion of the salts it contains in solution are precipitated, and remain on the top of the ice. These salts produce the same effect on the surface as the addition of a handful of salt does to ice or snow, as one commonly sees done with slippery pavements on frosty days. The salt and ice in these proportions form a mixture with a lower freezing-point than water, or, as is popularly said, the salt melts the ice. In consequence of this the surface of new sea-ice remains invariably slushy. While a light fall of snow accentuates that state, a heavy snowfall effectively overcomes the slush and covers the ice with a soft coating of perhaps a foot in depth. This is added to almost daily throughout the winter, and though it does of course to some extent harden under foot, particularly if frost follows a thaw, the normal condition of the floe is one in which, on foot, one sinks a certain distance, varying from ankle-deep to waist-deep. I have, it is true, seen the floe in Scotia Bay quite hard and smooth in places, but that was due to a hard frost following upon several unusually mild days in autumn, and, what was more extraordinary, a total absence of snow-fall all that time. The occasional small pieces of hard dry ice one comes on are the lower surfaces of small overturned pieces of pack, for the lower surfaces being free from salt, keep hard and dry when exposed to the air, and in a windswept position on a floe-berg such a piece might keep clear of snow all winter. Polar ice, therefore, in the best of conditions is not smooth; but as it is almost invariably deeply covered with snow, it will, I hope, be readily understood why members of polar expeditions do not indulge in skating.

As soon as the floe was solid around the ship we lived to all intents and purposes on land, although there were sixty feet of water below us. The *Scotia* lay with her head almost due south, with The Beach a quarter of a mile astern; but low land such as that showed little difference from the sea in winter. The passage from one to another was almost imperceptible except for the slight uphill towards the land and the tide-crack; which of course were kept open all the winter by the whole floe rising and falling some six feet twice every day.

The ship was now at once prepared for the winter, and a new routine established for all hands. To begin with, all sails were unbent and stored away, and quarter-boats were lowered on the floe, and then, to lessen the resistance to the wind, the top-gallant yards were sent down. The engine fires were of course let out and the boiler emptied, whereupon Gravill eagerly set about taking "the job" to bits and putting it together again,—a task which engineers apparently dearly love. Companionways were fixed over either side of the ship on to the floe, and a canvas porch was constructed covering a part of the deck. Everything was done to make life as comfortable as possible under the circumstances. The same care was no longer required in stowing away everything to prevent breakage as was necessary at sea. In consequence, work in the laboratory was both simplified and hindered: simplified, as one could work at ease with as much apparatus as was required; and hindered, because, when need no longer demanded it, jars, basins, bottles, and odds and ends tended to be left about, until at times the tiny little laboratory was truly a chaos. Snow was allowed to accumulate on deck, with the double purpose of protecting the deck from frost and of keeping the ship warm. When the temperature of the after end of the cabin had been down once or twice to freezing-point, all hands were employed for several days in building a snow-bank around the ship as high as the top of the deck-house. This, when completed, was a most effective protection against cold, acting, in virtue of its poor conducting power, as a blanket, which produced of course no heat, but kept the internal heat of the ship from escaping. I must not omit to mention that almost the first thing done on the floe forming around the ship was to cut a fire-hole, and keep it continually free of ice to ensure a plentiful supply of water in case of fire.

It has always proved a difficult matter to winter a ship in the polar regions with a large crew; and consequently the plan of sending away the ship and crew, after landing only the scientific staff, is generally adopted. This is probably the most satisfactory plan under many circumstances; but we were wintering in a latitude where we would escape the long polar night and its ever attendant inertia, and, moreover, being well equipped with a supply of collecting apparatus of all sorts, and having in view the project of building a house, the only question that troubled Mr Bruce and the Captain was how to get all the work done with only thirty-three men. There was, all the winter, a continual demand for helpers on every side. They were wanted for house-building or to repair the snow-bank. Wilton wanted help in skeleton-cleaning, Ross in bird-skinning, Pirie perhaps in surveying, while I wanted men to help with the traps. Davidson was often in despair as to how to allocate all the hands without unduly hindering any particular piece of work. Certainly no one had any idle time during the working hours of that winter. By 7.30 A.M. all hands were at work except in mid-winter, when it was yet too dark at that hour. The first duty was to quarry the water. That may sound a somewhat confused expression at first hearing, but it was literally the case. Convenient hummocks not too far from the ship were selected, and large pieces broken off with picks and drills and sledged up to the ship, where a day or two's store was always kept stacked on the main hatch. The ice was melted down in a large copper standing on the galley stove, and so a splendid supply of most perfect water was obtainable. The ice that was used for this purpose was largely sea-water ice, but had not the faintest brackishness about it, owing to the reason I have before explained of the salts being precipitated on the water solidifying.

At 8 A.M. breakfast was served for all hands, and directly after, on the mate's cry of "Trawl O!" all on board not otherwise occupied attended to the daily haul of the dredge. When the ice had last come into the bay, a narrow lane of water almost 100 yards long had been left crossing the bows of the ship to east and west. As long as this remained open it was a simple matter to drag a small dredge along it. But it was vain to hope that we could possibly continue in this way, for as winter progressed the frost would conquer all our efforts. Therefore a long whale-line of about 600 feet was lowered along the crack, with its ends above the ice. Two holes were kept open at the extremities of the crack, and the dredge could thus be shackled on to the whale-line at one hole, dragged along the bottom and up the other hole, and emptied. It was then unshackled and carried across to the first hole. After the line had been hauled back till the shackle came to the surface at the same hole, the whole process could be repeated. Nightly the holes froze over and had every morning to be broken out afresh—but that was a relatively easy matter; what gave far more difficulty was the filling up of the holes with slush after a night's blizzard. This did not freeze, and in consequence proved almost impossible to effectually remove. One could scoop out enough to reduce it to the consistency of thin soup, but even that amount left behind proved a great nuisance in choking up the dredge. To obviate this difficulty, the bo'sun, who was in charge of this operation, built a small snow-hut over the hole, and thereafter there was a marked improvement in that worthy's language during the daily dredge. Two hauls were thus taken on practically every day we were in Scotia Bay; and despite the fact that the dredge must of course have covered, in each of the 400 or so hauls, almost identically the same ground, it continued several times a-week all the while to bring up new animals. This alone would show the teeming mass of life that exists in those shallow Antarctic waters. Large isopods, and small ones strangely resembling the long-extinct trilobites; myriads of small sea-spiders or pycnogons (*Nymphon sp.*), including a few of the extraordinary and previously unknown ten-legged kind (*Pentanymphon antarcticum*), and many of a big scarlet species (*Decalopoda australis*), also with ten legs, and apparently new until zoologists at home found a long-kept record of it from the adjacent South Shetland; hundreds of bright crimson cushion-stars, some sea-urchins, and many sea-cucumbers of divers kinds; curious spiny sea-squirts and occasional little fish; large ugly nemertean worms, and dainty glistening polychæts, allies of the beautiful sea-mouse,—all these and many more animals were among our Scotia Bay collections. We neglected nothing, and bottled even the apparent refuse, knowing well that it swarmed with numbers of minute crustacea. After dredging, crew and scientists separated for different work that might be on hand. Most of the men were engaged in house-building, of which I shall have more to say later on, and by 10 A.M. I generally found myself, with half a dozen men, setting out towards the mouth of the bay, on a visit to the various traps that we had set. We took a sledge with us to carry the ice-drills and shovels required to clear the holes, and also to carry back the catch on—for we always looked for a good haul, and generally not in vain. The position of these traps varied, for we shifted them often, but they were generally in deeper water than the dredge—as a rule, from twenty to fifty fathoms. The traps used were a species of lobster-pot, which the Prince of Monaco had found to work with great success in some of his cruises. The smaller ones took the shape of a skeleton box, covered with 1-inch herring netting, with a funnel at either end and an opening door above to extract the catch: one to two feet in height, and two to four in length were the dimensions of this shape. A larger and very successful one was constructed, with the two sides meeting along the top, and with, consequently, triangular-shaped ends,—the funnels and door being similar to those of the other shape. The traps were all built on board by MacDougall, whose previous experience on North Sea trawlers stood us in splendid stead on every occasion when fishing and trawling were to the fore. We baited the traps with penguin carcases thrown in the bottom or hung from the top, and a daily examination of them resulted in large though not varied catches of fish and other animals. There were two species (both probably allied to *Notothenia*), one rare and the other very common. Of this latter the large trap had some fifty, and I have taken out at one time as many as ninety-nine,—neither a fisherman's nor a sailor's imagination shall tempt me to add one. They were dull green in colour, from six to eighteen inches in length. The first ones, of course, went to the laboratory; but even the greed of the zoologist found satisfaction, and when the cook asked for a supply of fish for breakfast, the zoologist showed himself open to human temptations after all, and several days a-week we all committed the sacrilege of feeding on what was an animal probably new to science. The crimson cushion-stars were the commonest animals in the trap: I have taken over 200 from a single one. It was a curious fact that in working with the traps one frequently found that to warm one's hands (and very cold they often were) the best plan was to plunge them into the water, though woe to him who recklessly exposed them to the air afterwards, without carefully drying and covering them. The reason of this seeming paradox was that the water temperature was seldom below 28° F., while the air temperature was rarely as high as that. Examining the traps took some time, as all the broken out ice and snow of the previous night had to be carted some fifty yards away to prevent the formation of snow-drifts round the hole itself, and so render the daily work still more arduous. As often as not, before I returned to the ship with this party of men we visited several "skeleton holes"—that is to say, places where we had cut a hole in the ice and lowered to the bottom a roughly cleaned seal skeleton with the object of allowing the little sea-lice (or amphipoda) to complete the work. These sea-lice swarmed in myriads in parts of the bay, and ate voraciously off any carcase lowered amongst them, thus very obligingly preparing beautiful skeletons for us in a week or thereabout.

It was generally lunch-time (12.30 p.m.) before we regained the ship. In the afternoon the crew were probably house-building again, and often the scientists assisted. If the weather was very inviting—a rare occurrence after the month of April—or if one required exercise after being employed on the ship in the morning, excursions for collecting or exploration on a minor scale were planned. There was still an occasional Weddell seal (*Leptonychotes weddelli*) to be observed, and it was generally killed for its skin and skeleton. Penguins were almost daily passing northward across the bay, during April, on their way from the frozen regions to the open water beyond, where they pass the winter months. Many of these fell victims as they passed the *Scotia,* and served for skins or for food. On the 28th April, during the first long spell of severe cold we experienced, vast droves of penguins passed towards the north. There were several thousands of them, chiefly gentoo (*Pygoscelis papua*), with a few black-throated, or adelia (*Pygoscelis adeliæ*),

1. *Antarctic research ship* Scotia

2. *Captain Robertson and First Mate Jack Fitchie fixing the* Scotia's *position*

3. *Three of the scientists in the laboratory aboard the* Scotia. *From left to right: Robert Rudmose Brown, botanist; David Wilton, zoologist; and John Harvey Pirie, ship's doctor and geologist*

4. *Operating the Lucas Auto-matic Sounding Machine from the deckhouse roof of the* Scotia

5. *Launching the weather kite from the* Scotia

6. *Dr John Harvey Pirie measures a Ross seal on board the* Scotia

7. *Mending sails on the* Scotia

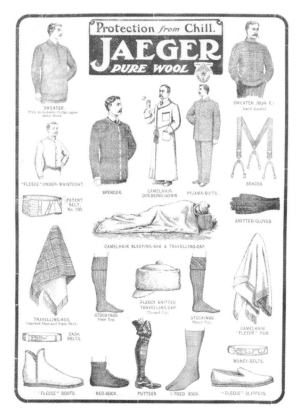

8. *Advertisement for Jaeger clothing, as worn by the crew and staff of the* Scotia *expedition*

9. *Exploring Laurie Island*

10. *Scotia Bay, Laurie Island*

11. *The* Scotia *icebound in Scotia Bay*

and a sprinkling of ringed or bridled penguins (*Pygoscelis antarctica*). No doubt the increased cold had driven to migration all the dilatory birds, but many never lived to see the open water. Over a hundred were hunted down and killed with a blow on the head: these were stowed away under the boats and on the forward deck-house to serve as the winter's supply of fresh food, for the frost acts in the Antarctic as the best preservative, and meat is yet quite fresh, if perhaps a little dry, after six months. The primal hunter's passion came very near the surface as we chose a good prosperous-looking bird, and brought down a club with a mur-derous smash on its head. The most depraved sportsman could find no sport in that. It was sheer cold-blooded unskilled murder, whose only excuse was that we were hungry, and needed fresh food to keep us alive and healthy. And so it was in the killing of seals but another case of murder. Very seldom does a seal (except the huge sea leopard) make any show of defence against man: it never fights, and lies in ignorance of man's cruelty until the blow is struck. We found that it was useless to expend ammunition on shooting seals except at the pupping season. It was a simple matter to walk up to them as they lie, in their favourite position, on the side of the back, and stab them to the heart with a large deer-knife. Antarctic animals, particularly penguins and seals, are wonderfully tenacious of life. I have seen a Weddell seal, with a six-inch blade and the hilt of the knife as well, buried right in its side, live for forty minutes, and for part of that time travel quickly over the floe. As for penguins, they are even harder to kill. A favourite method of killing them was to pierce the skull with a sharp instrument. That generally had instantaneous effect, but by no means always: even under such treatment a bird occasionally refused to die. Later in the year, when we collected them at the rook-eries for food, we caught them by gripping them round the throat, then, seizing their legs, dashed their heads against a rock. They had all the appearance of dead penguins after that, and as such were loaded on the sledge and dragged back to the cook. But on the way—and I have seen it happen more than once—two or three apparently quite dead birds quietly got up, dropped off the sledge, and walked off.

Botanical excursions in the Antarctic are fraught with certain disadvantages not met with in a more temperate land, leaving out of account the scarcity of plants that there are to be collected. It means rather working in the dark, as the moss-clothed rocks are seldom visible through the snow except in summer, while the visible lichens are all on precipices until spring reveals some more accessible localities. In winter I had to arm myself, not with a trowel, but with a hammer and cold chisel, and thus equipped, I sometimes set out in the afternoon to hew off "chunks" of moss, if by chance I came on any exposed to view.

Pirie likewise had many difficulties to contend with in geology, but he tri-umphed over all in his discovery of fossils in the rocks near Cape Dundas.

After the evening dinner all hands were free for the rest of the day with the exception of the watchman and the meteorological observer. The hourly

observations we had begun when we left the Falklands were of course continued. Mossman was busy most of the day ashore with his magnetic observations,
so the meteorological work fell largely to the rest of us, including the Captain.
During the day the watches were variable in length, and depended on the daily
work on hand. The night-watch began with the 10 P.M. observation and finished
with the 3 A.M. one. This watch was taken for a week in turn by Wilton, Pirie, and
myself, while at 4 A.M. Mr Bruce came on and went off at 8 A.M. The night-
watchman, needless to say, had a lonely life during his week of duty. There was
seldom any one awake after 10, and he only rose the following day in time for
lunch, after which he always spent the afternoon in outdoor exercise. In consequence, the week was largely spent in a solitude which often was far from
unacceptable. Not that we tired of our fellow-creatures, for we all lived on the
most amicable of terms, but the occasional solitude which every one requires
was seldom obtainable in life on so small a ship as the *Scotia*. We were practically
always in sight and hearing of one another. That, I may say incidentally, is one of
the greatest hardships of polar exploration—the impossibility of escaping for an
hour at a time from one's fellow-creatures. Moreover, the night-watchman had
the greater part of his time on his hands, for the observations rarely required his
attention more than some ten minutes every hour. For the remainder of the
hour he could do what he chose, whether it was reading, mending clothes, print-
ing photographs, or anything else he wished. Some ingenious observers even
contracted the habit of dozing peacefully before the cabin fire, and waking regularly in time for the observation. Sometimes it was wild work to go on deck
fighting one's way in the fury of a blizzard; and after a silver thaw, when huge
10-lb. blocks of ice crashed from the rigging to the deck, which itself was a veritable glacier, the observer was not altogether free from risk: but on the whole it
was pleasant work, and except in the depths of winter, when night-watch involved so serious a curtailment of one's hours of daylight, no one felt annoyed
when their week came round again.

The watchman forward had duties no more arduous than the meteorologist
aft. He had to keep a general eye on the safety of the ship in the remote eventu-
ality of the floe moving suddenly: in addition he looked after the fo'c'sle and
galley fires. His only other duty was to take the half-hourly readings of the tide
gauge; the hourly ones were attended to by the meteorologist on his rounds. It
was a seaman who kept watch until midnight, Martin and Anderson by turn,
when he was relieved by the second or third mate, Fitchie or MacDougall. Many
a pleasant hour of my watch have I spent with these men in the galley, when the
talk ran merrily over all things; and the watch was far too short when Fitchie was
in a reminiscent mood, and recalled his strange tales and stirring adventures
during the thirty years he had sailed all the seas of the world.

The winter evenings, after the day's work was done and we gathered together,
whether in cabin or fo'c'sle, are in many ways among the pleasantest memories

of life in the Antarctic. There can be few subjects that did not at some time or another come under discussion, and occasionally we speculated on the course that events in the world would have taken, but never, I must say, very accurately, in the light of later knowledge. The absence of newspapers was not, as some more "civilised" people might think, a great drawback. If an old one turned up among any odds and ends it was read, but no one seemed to miss a daily record of the world's events. With letters, it was perhaps different; old ones were often re-read, but yet we expected no new ones, and so seldom troubled about the absence of a mail. We lived in a little world of our own, indifferent to wars and rival policies, ignorant of international intrigue and hatred. The temperature, the state of the ice, the health of the dogs—such were the most important events to us, and were eagerly discussed every morning. Thanks to the kind generosity of various publishers, we had books in plenty, from the ponderous scientific tomes of the *Challenger* to the lightest of light novels. There were sufficient books to keep us all employed in reading for several years, and our scientific library was well stocked with results of former deep-sea expeditions,—'Valdivia,' Prince of Monaco's, 'Ingolf,' 'Belgica,' as well as the 'Challenger.' Polar travels north and south, and geographical and other scientific treatises, were plentifully distributed through the various cabins.

Amusements had their fashions in the ship, and when chess ceased to be in vogue in the cabin, poker was the rage for weeks, and matches, or with a rash player candles, were the stakes, for both these were very valuable,—matches being dealt out at the rate of so many boxes a-month and candles one a-week. The Captain had with great forethought provided himself, before we left Scotland, with a calendar which daily recorded at least two anniversaries. These he announced each day at breakfast, but only if the occasion, by general consensus of opinion, merited it, did we have the smoker he aimed at. I fear the description of one of our *Scotia* smokers will seem tame to those accustomed to the luxurious entertainment of a similar feast at home, and yet perhaps no merrier evenings were ever spent than those winter evenings in the South Orkneys. We had little musical talent in the cabin, but we managed very well in the absence of a critical audience. The Captain gave us rollicking songs of the sea, Pirie contributed with a few Scottish student songs, Mossman never exhausted his music-hall *repertoire,* and Wilton, we always will gratefully remember, gave us his one Russian song. What it meant he never deigned to explain, but the song was just as sure to come when enthusiasm ran high as it was always welcome: nor must I forget Mr Bruce's inimitable rendering of "Two Blue Bottles," or Davidson's "Just one Girl," whom we never failed to hear about.

We had in addition a small harmonium in the cabin, but it lacked efficient players, and moreover a wave that had the year before washed into the cabin still seriously affected it, despite the repairs which Ramsay and I had carried out. But the great acquisition for our "concerts" was a small phonograph, whose forty or

51

fifty records were faithfully ground out on these occasions, and seldom failed to arouse applause. It may seem strange that we so often cared for sounds which are so discordant to our ears to-day, but it was a pleasure to listen to voices we were not familiar with, and hear accents that did not daily fall on our ears: that, I think, is why the phonograph was so popular.

Birthdays were, of course, duly celebrated in like fashion: and sometimes in honour of these events the cook was prevailed upon to exercise his skill in the making of cakes, and I am sure no cook could have succeeded better. We also had concerts in the fo'c'sle, where there was a first-rate singer, in the person of Low; and many a strong deep-voiced chorus rang from the ship on such nights. The sailors too had their arguments, and very bitter the discussions were at times. Murray was a prime mover in many of these, slipping down from the galley to start a discussion, and then retreating when pandemonium reigned supreme. At other times he would carefully read up facts in 'Whitaker's Almanac,' start an argument, say, as to the tonnage of the largest ship, and when the fo'c'sle was at boiling-point produce his facts and his authority, and so make matters worse.

Sailors are proverbially handy, and on the *Scotia* this was certainly the case. In Johnny Smith, a Shetlander, we had a most efficient boot-repairer; and several, notably Martin and Anderson, were good tailors, while the latter was also our chief hairdresser. Others used to busy themselves in the long evenings in making rag mats, or in modelling grotesque little ships inside bottles—two occupations extraordinarily dear to the heart of a sailor. On my part, I had to devote much time to sewing tow-nets for next summer's work, and I found it a particularly tedious task.

It was surprising how often conversation at meals turned towards food: each man had his especial delicacy which he associated with the return to civilisation, and which was unobtainable in our wilderness. Whether it was a Vienna steak or a cream bun, his highest ambition seemed to be centred in it. And yet we certainly suffered in no way from bad or insufficient food; but however good it may be, preserved meat is never appetising after any length of time. Exploration now is not what it used to be when the daily fare of salt-beef or pork brought with it its daily fear of scurvy. We had an ample supply of tinned meats (many with tempting labels which we learnt to avoid), tinned and dried fruits and vegetables of all sorts, tinned butter and milk, but, best of all, an almost inexhaustible stock of oatmeal and flour. Penguin was a staple article of meat diet. At first the crew showed some objection to it, but in the course of the winter they learned to like it as well as we did, and asked for nothing better. Some Antarctic expeditions have found penguin utterly unpalatable. Dr Cook of the *Belgica* compares it to a mixture of "a piece of beef, and odoriferous cod-fish, and a canvas-backed duck roasted in a pot, with blood and cod-liver oil for sauce." I must really protest against this caricature; and while I admit its dark red-black appearance is unusual, and that it cannot be compared in taste to anything I know, I yet must bear testimony to its excellence as a food. When we no longer could get it we sorely missed it, and drew comparisons between it and mutton far from favourable to the latter. I think it would be well worth while to establish penguin rookeries on many of the barren rocks off the western isles of Scotland, and so introduce a new and delicious food to the inhabitants of this country. The *Belgica's* cook cannot have understood the art of cooking penguin, which Florence certainly did. Only the breasts were used, and were cut into thin pieces, first browned in the frying-pan and then stewed, and finally served with fried onions. The cook also used it frequently for soup, with great success, while it made most excellent curry. There is a difference in the flesh of the various species of penguins, and we found by experience that the black-throated penguin was most satisfactory.

The gentoo flesh is somewhat tougher and more stringy, and that of the emperor, while very eatable, is rather dry. Some idea of the size of the pectoral muscles of the birds may be gained from the fact that the breasts of only two black-throated penguins were required to feed twelve to fifteen hungry men. Seal we took less kindly to, for the meat is apt to be tough, rather like very indifferent beef; but the seal's heart stuffed with sage and onions was a great delicacy.

It is a very common fallacy to picture polar explorers going about their daily work clothed from head to foot in furs. Picturesque though this illusion may be, it is one which I must dispel. Furs are so clumsy, and, as they admit of no ventilation, so unhealthy, that they are barely ever used to work in. On sledging journeys furs are, of course, required to sleep in, but on the march thick woollen clothing is worn, while for everyday work about the vicinity of the ship we wore simply warm tweed clothes, with a sufficiency of woollen under-clothing. Fair Isle jerseys were universally worn, of which, by the generosity of Mr James Coats, jun., we had a large supply on board. They are thick jerseys, handknitted in wool of every brilliant hue,—red, green, and yellow side by side in endless, different, and all extraordinary and apparently meaningless designs. We also had caps and mufflers of the same material and make, and all proved of wonderful wearing quality. Caps were of many different kinds, and provided they covered the ears, almost any description did equally well.

A much-used kind was a soft woollen cap of Jaeger make, with a protective covering for neck and face rolled up around the brim, and able to be let down in severe weather, leaving then only an open space for the face. Fingerless woollen mitts were almost always worn—often two pairs at a time. Fur mitts of Esquimo make are very comfortable over woollen ones if one is only going for a walk, but if snow and ice have to be handled the heat of the body melting the snow makes the mitts very uncomfortable and unusable for the time. Foot-gear was, however, the most serious consideration. We generally wore rough leather ski-boots of Norwegian make. These boots are always chosen a size or so too large, to admit at least two pairs of thick socks and a handful of senna grass in the toe. Such protection for the feet is required in even ordinary weather, but in colder days, when the temperature was 20 degrees or more below zero, felt or fur boots were almost necessary, unless one was continually on the move. Leather froze, at these temperatures, as hard as a rock. Soft leather moccasins, or "slush boots" as they are technically spoken of, were much worn, and proved very comfortable in cold weather, and had the especial advantage of very seldom freezing. The outer pair of socks was always one of goat's hair, or a mixture of goat's and human hair, which proved very warm.

Long before the winter was over most of the clothing on board had been patched again and again, and a most extraordinary set of beings we must have appeared had we not gradually become accustomed to one another's garb, and almost failed to notice it unless with critical appreciation. Patches of all colours adorned coat and trousers, and long lines of herring-bone stitches in white thread marked seams and rents in many a jacket. Socks and mittens were darned and patched in various ways, but often with extreme care and neatness,—for I can honestly say that when a sailor darns well, he far out-rivals any feminine hand.

The winter wrought a considerable change in every one's personal appearance. With hardly a single exception we all became stouter, but plenty of vigorous outdoor exercise prevented any correlated lowering of health. After leaving civilisation behind with the Falkland Islands, we all became bearded, and the winds and snow did their work in tanning faces, with the result that almost all looked older and maturer than at the outset of the Expedition. There was one very decided disadvantage in having hair on the face, which, at times during the winter, induced a wave of fashion in shaving. On very cold days the moisture of the breath, congealed in the air, firmly fixed together beard and moustaches, with the result that many a time a hungry man returning to dinner had to thaw out the ice from his face before he could open his mouth sufficiently to eat; and when, as often occurred, the beard froze to cap or hood, it was even more uncomfortable.

Of all the ship's company I think it was our Siberian sledge-dog, Russ, who enjoyed the winter most. The Antarctic regions were like home to him, and he really revelled in the snow and ice. The restraint of his life at sea, when his territory was, of course, very limited, had proved, no doubt, irksome to so high-spirited a dog, and two days after we had anchored in Scotia Bay, Russ disappeared over the glacier to the north. As day after day elapsed and there was no sign of him despite our careful search, we concluded he had met with an accident and come to his end. Much, therefore, was our surprise when, eleven days after his departure, Russ appeared alongside the ship none the worse for his adventures, but ravenously hungry. Where he had spent those eleven days we could not tell, but probably he had for days been cut off from the shore by shifting ice, and so been an enforced prisoner until it closed again, for he was not fond of jumping into the sea. By his appetite he must have starved for several days, but the cold had affected him not at all, for he refused the privilege of sleeping in the cabin, and spent the night, as was his wont all winter long whatever the weather, curled up on the floe. The other dogs, mongrel collies from the Falkland Islands, never ventured farther than required from the ship, and dearly loved to sleep at the head of the fo'c'sle companion or in the shelter of the deck-house.

All accounts of winter life among the Polar ice, be it in the north or in the south, must present a certain sameness to one another, so that a too detailed recital of those relatively monotonous months could prove of little interest to the general reader; while those who themselves have had the good fortune to count a Polar winter among their personal experiences, will need little to re-awaken its remembrance.

These days in the far-off Antarctic were very happy, and now seen down the long vista of memory seem happier still. They were days of peaceful uneventful-ness to think of amid the turmoil of life in crowded cities, days the mind loves to dwell upon until they weave a spell that almost irresistibly tempts one back again to taste the charm of these great solitudes. For, despite the many things one obviously lacked, despite too the faces one could but conjure up in dreams, we were never lonely. Isolation among the fastnesses of nature does not bring lone-liness: that can perhaps be only felt in its full extreme among the busy haunts of men.

CHAPTER VI

MID-WINTER

AN ANTARCTIC COLONY—HOUSE-BUILDING AND ITS DIFFICULTIES—"VIVENDO DISCIMUS"—GLACIER OBSERVATORY —MAGNETIC HUT—BAD WEATHER—VICISSITUDES OF TEMPERATURE—ANTARCTIC DISCOMFORTS—KITE-FLYING—A WILD-GOOSE CHASE—OUR BIRD COMPANIONS—FLOE BREAKING UP—SKI AND SKI-RUNNING.

A VERY few days after Scotia Bay had frozen, Mr Bruce fixed on The Beach sites on which to build the central cairn for starting our prospective survey from, the wooden magnetic hut we had brought with us, and a larger stone house.

The sites of these three buildings were all practically in a line along the highest part of the southern beach. The house was within fifty yards of the cliffs of Mossman Peninsula, a position which, in the light of after experience, proved a little unfortunate, as the snow seemed to always drift deepest thereabout. About 100 yards along, farther to the eastward, was the cairn. In two weeks' time this was completed, and stood twelve feet high, surmounted by a flagstaff, from which, by the way, the Scottish Lion flew, on great occasions, during our stay. A little beyond the cairn was the magnetic hut, which was placed in this position to be as far as possible from any disturbing influences in the vicinity. With the same end in view it was an unwritten law to always give it a wide berth when Mossman was at work inside. The carpenter erected the hut in a few days, and after it had been painted a brilliant scarlet, it served as a very pleasing landmark in a wilderness as yet with hardly a sign of man's handiwork. The observatory was very appropriately named Copeland Observatory by Mr Bruce, in honour of that veteran astronomer, the late Professor Ralph Copeland of Edinburgh, who from the first had taken a most lively interest in the plans for a Scottish Antarctic Expedition.

The primary object in building a house was to accommodate a party of scientists during the following spring months, when the *Scotia* of necessity would have to return to the Falklands to refit, and for some slight repairs. By leaving several men behind, the real Antarctic work would therefore not be interrupted, and the meteorological observations would continue without a break—a most important consideration; while it would doubtlessly also be possible to secure many rare eggs and young birds in spring and early summer, for the position of these islands gave promise that they were the haunts of many birds in the breeding season.

But beyond these plans in the immediate future, Bruce, as usual, had others more ambitious and with great possibilities. The South Orkneys are particularly well situated for a meteorological observatory, while their relative nearness to South America, and the great likelihood of the ice in the vicinity admitting of easy access to Scotia Bay every summer, prompted Mr Bruce to hope that it would be possible to persuade the Argentine Government to take over and maintain in future an observatory if we built it,—a hope which was fully realised.

The many moraines and screes near by afforded an ample supply of stones, but some little difficulty was experienced in obtaining them, as generally each stone had to be literally quarried, for the ice which bound them together was as hard as rock, and most effectually disabled what picks and drills we had suitable for the purpose. As long, however, as the adjacent screes afforded a good supply of stones, little difficulty in transport was experienced; but after a time, when they were despoiled of all the suitable and, at the same time, obtainable stones, resource had to be had to digging a pit through the snow in various places on the beach, and sledging the stones to the site of operations. In the same way a supply of fine gravel for filling in crevices was obtained; for it must be noted that we had no cement with us, in fact no building materials or masons' tools of any description, as we had little expected to winter in a latitude where it would have been practicable to build and set agoing such an observatory. The site was carefully cleared of snow, and the foundations of a house fourteen feet square were laid with large stones. Mr Bruce was, of course, the architect, while Fitchie and MacDougall were the principal masons; the remainder of us, scientists and crew alike, were labourers either to quarry or sledge stones, or to assist in lifting large ones into position. In a task like that, and under these circumstances, every one soon found the work he was best suited for, and skill alone meant advancement. The walls were built on the "dry dyke" principle, and, to ensure safety and per-manence, were about four to five feet thick, with buttresses at the corners. Progress at all times was naturally slow, and became still slower in bad weather, for it was impossible to build during driving snow, since any snow between successive tiers of stones would make the upper ones very liable to collapse when the tempera-ture rose sufficiently to melt the snow. This lesson we were severely taught when the S.W. corner showed signs of unsteadiness, and excavations revealed that it had partly been built on snow, which necessitated our underpinning it. By the middle of May, however, the walls were ready for the roof. But then the question which had long been debated had to be solved, Where shall we get the necessary timber? Our supply of planks was long ago exhausted, and for many weeks past every empty box had been greedily grabbed by some one or other for some work he had in hand. However, with some ingenuity, from various sources enough wood was got together, and the framework of the roof put in position. A spare yard was cut in half, and formed the cross-tree, resting on the summit of the facing gables, and from it ran rafters to the other walls. A double layer of canvas (an old sail), with an intervening layer of felt, was then stretched over, and the ends securely weighted down with stones. This roof was then well saturated with oil and grease, with the object, which was entirely successful, of making it water-tight. In both the northern and eastern walls of the house was a small window, both unopenable, for the smallest possible chink will admit driving snow during a polar blizzard. These windows, however, admitted plenty of light at most seasons of the year, though in mid-winter they were almost smothered in snow-drifts, which half hid the house.

The narrow door—an unused one taken out of the ship—was surrounded outside by a canvas porch, closed to the exterior by a hanging canvas curtain. This precaution was necessary to prevent snow from driving into the house when the door was opened. The house consisted, I need hardly mention, of but one room, about 14 feet square and 6 to 8 feet high; the walls were lined with stout canvas, which prevented any chill polar draughts from percolating through the stones; and the floor consisted of the *Scotia's* 'tween-deck hatches, which the Captain generously decided he could quite well do without. A spare fo'c'sle stove furnished the cooking-range; and the carpenter constructed from packing-cases the little furniture that was required; while two mattresses and four hammocks supplied the necessary beds. It proved altogether a most serviceable and comfortable house, and so far was it from being cold in winter that the inhabitants occasionally had cause to complain of the heat. To the west of the house we erected a substantial store-room and coal-shed, using, in place of stones for the walls, a large number of boxes of ship's biscuits which, being all of a size, were easy to work with, and also ensured the future inhabitants of the house a store of something like a ton of food in the event of emergencies. Needless to say, each box contained a hermetically sealed tin case inside its covering of wood. An old whale-boat we had on board, which, after thirty years' service in Arctic seas, had now been condemned by the Captain as unseaworthy, was utilised as a roof.

On our return to the South Orkneys in the following summer we intended to bring a plentiful supply of timber to not only roof the house, but also to build a large new store-room. The work of building and equipping was over in September, and then the last thing to be done fell to me,—that was to cut in oak upon the lintel of the door the two words "Vivendo discimus," to leave as a watchword to future explorers, as an expression of the lesson we had learnt, and still were learning day by day, in our life in these far-off wilds.

There was to have been in October an opening ceremony, celebrated by a half holiday for all hands, but unpropitious weather on two occasions chilled our enthusiasm, and, without any flourish of pipes, the name of Omond House was unostentatiously bestowed upon the building, in honour of Mr R. T. Omond of Edinburgh, the man whose enthusiasm for meteorological science was largely responsible for the establishment of the late station on the summit of Ben Nevis, and who, from its earliest inception, had shown his goodwill towards our Expedition.

Adjoining the house were the meteorological screens with their instruments, and a little farther from the cliffs, and away from their wind eddies, stood the anemometer. On November 1 the hourly observations on board the *Scotia* were transferred to Omond House, and Mossman, Bill Smith, and Martin took up their residence ashore. Pirie and Cuthbertson were at the time absent on a sledge-journey, so that for some weeks I also lived partly ashore to assist in this work. Another shore observatory was the high-level one on the glacier. There, at an elevation of about 100 feet, Pirie and I dug a six-foot pit in the glacier to place long vertical metal tubes at different depths. We then filled in the pit, and the viscous nature of ice soon healed the wound in the glacier and restored the *débris* to its former consistency. Down these tubes, projecting a few inches above the surface, thermometers were hung on chains suspended from corks, which served to plug the end of the tube and prevent the access of the cold air. Readings of glacier temperature were taken daily, and, as was expected, proved to vary far slower than the air temperature, with which, nevertheless, they showed some direct connection.

As mid-winter approached the weather did not improve on the whole. May and June were stormy months, and snow-falls were always frequent. In fact, really fine weather was rare in the South Orkneys after some perfect days in April. If snow was not actually falling, overcast skies threw an awful gloom over all, and probably nowhere in the world is gloom so depressing as amid polar ice: everything becomes a dull uniform grey, with never the relief of a shadow, and sky and ice-floe merge together into one continuous pall of ugliness. Snow-fall in such weather is even a relief, since it obscures the monotony of a wider view. Observation has shown that the mean amount of cloud was 82 per cent, and that in one year there were 180 absolutely sunless days. And yet there were occasional fine days when it was a joy to wander over the floe for hours, and when one's spirits rose to exuberance, and the Antarctic seemed the jolliest of all places. These days, generally single days amidst a week of gloom, always came with a southerly wind, and in consequence were cold. But southerly winds were usually light, and often died away to nothing before the sunshine went; and without wind 10° F. to zero is but a pleasant healthy temperature to move about in, and −50° F. or less gives no trouble if one's circulation is well maintained. Quite contrary is the case with high wind: zero then may mean frost-bites, and a lower temperature certainly will. Fortunately, however, though we had more than we considered a reasonable share of gales, they were in nine cases out of ten from the west to north-west, blowing from not far distant open ocean, and in consequence relatively warm—that is, from 20° to 35° F. With these gales squalls were very frequent, and often of such terrific force that to stand against them was all but impossible. I have more than once seen a whole party of men hurled down in a heap before a sudden squall, which had taken them unawares, but luckily one could generally hear them coming in the hills, and see the cloud of snow-drift accompanying them, and so prepare. It was this very position, near the edge of the solid polar pack, that made the climate of the South Orkneys so interesting, and at the same time so bad—I might say, trying,—had not most of us endured it and come through none the worse, if not perhaps better. A very common occurrence was this: the weather was cold, perhaps –10° or –15°, with a light southerly air, and so perhaps it remained for twelve hours or more; then a north-westerly gale arrived, and up went the temperature by leaps until it was near 30° or even over. From the one extreme to the other within twenty-four hours, which was not uncommon, made the lower degree feel far colder, and the higher far warmer, than either really was. It is the extreme of temperature one feels most, and a steady temperature, high or low though it be, one very soon becomes accustomed and adapted to. Within a day and night variations of 30 degrees occurred many times, and we have had as great a vicissitude as 63°:31° at 1 A.M., 15°.8 at 4 A.M., 30°.7 at noon, and –2°.2 at midnight

These sudden changes in temperature to some extent diminished the comfort of the cabin. In cold weather the moisture in the air within condensed in ice-crystals on the head of every iron bolt, and on every bit of metal work on the outer wall, until even a sheet of ice behind one's pillow caused no astonishment. Then came the higher temperatures, and of course the ice, unable to resist the heat of the cabin, melted, resulting in a steady drip or trickle of water down one's cabin walls. A somewhat similar occurrence used at first to worry us at meals in very cold days, when the internal moisture, coming in contact with the glass of the cabin skylight, was robbed of its heat so quickly that it fell in drops of water all day along the table. But comfort is only relative, and one's standard of luxury is largely a matter of habit; and in the Antarctic one does not expect much comfort, so that such petty annoyances were more amusing than anything else, and never seriously troubled any one.

It was a curious though quite explicable occurrence, but the highest temperature we had at any time in the Antarctic was on May 31, which is within three weeks of mid-winter. For two days during north-westerly weather a Föhn wind blew. That is purely a local phenomenon, resulting in a wind being forced down from a higher level, compressed, and consequently warmed. On each of these days the temperature rose to over 40° at midday, and as high as 46°.8 on May 31. We were even treated to the almost forgotten phenomenon of a shower of rain. The result of this warm weather was to very materially change the aspect of land and floes. The hills again showed their crags and steeper slopes bare of snow, and long hidden lichen-covered rocks came into view: the moraines loosened once more, and streams of water ran down the slopes, and the floe became soft and slushy.

The observations which I have so far spoken of gave only the temperature and pressure at sea-level, but we also made several attempts to obtain records of the weather conditions obtaining at great elevations. For this purpose we were furnished with large box kites, some 6 x 7 feet square by 2 to 3 feet deep. The framework was made of bamboo rods, lashed together with twine, and braced from corner to corner with steel wires. The upper and lower thirds of this frame-work were covered with thin white and black cloth respectively, and the middle division was left bare. The whole kite was thus extremely light, and weighed but a few pounds. Piano wire was used to fly the kite with, and was uncoiled from a small machine specially designed for this purpose. During the voyage this ma-chine was fixed on the after end of the poop-deck and connected with a small petrol motor for winding-in purposes; but the vibration that this caused was too great for the deck to be subjected to, and, in consequence, the motor was re-moved and the kite wound in by a driving rope off the steam-winch or otherwise by hand. Clamped into the wire some ten or twenty feet below the kite itself was a small instrument called a meteorograph. This contained three small self-recording instruments,—barograph, hygrograph, and thermograph,—all enclosed in a light aluminium case. The instruments ran for eight hours; and so, if it was possible to keep the kite up for that time, a good record of weather conditions at any height could be obtained.

Flights at sea, however, met with no success, partly, no doubt, owing to the difficulty of raising the kite, and largely also due to the amount of rigging on such a ship as ours, which was always in danger of fouling the wire.

In Scotia Bay the kite machine was unshipped and sledged to a convenient place on The Beach, whence several flights were attempted, but with little more success than at sea. The conditions were very adverse, for the complicated ma-chine demanded the use of fingers unencumbered by mitts, which proved a serious drawback in cold weather, while the narrow valley between the ridges on either side made the winds always squally and uncertain until once the kite had attained at least 2000 feet.

On several occasions the kite broke away and careered southward over the floe, speeding on like a lost hat in a windy street, with half a dozen men on their ski in full chase. During attempted flights several men were generally placed on the floe about a mile or more to leeward of the place of ascent, and if they saw the kite break away they could start at once in pursuit in the right direction with fair hope of making up on it.

The kite was generally stored in a large box on shore, and, despite the furious winds that whirled round it at times, appeared quite safe. However, during a severe northerly gale and blizzard in the end of September, the cook one morning reported to the mate that the kite had passed the ship not a hundred feet off, travelling at a great rate towards the south. Now Murray was well known for his love of a joke at any one's expense, and the mate considered this but another of his pranks, and consequently took no notice of it. But Murray was insistent; and when he had repeated his story to me, I felt convinced he was in earnest this time, and went ashore to look. Sure enough the kite box-lid had been smashed to bits, and the kite was gone. A strong eddy in the nature of a whirlwind must have struck the box and forced off the lid, which was not an exceptionally strong one, and then have lifted the kite. In the afternoon, the weather having moderated, the Captain ordered out all hands to search the floe for the missing kite; while Mossman, to stimulate their energies, offered a reward to the finder. In three hours all returned, but without the kite or any trace of it; still Mossman was confident it would yet be found, and doubled his reward.

Other work and unfavourable weather somewhat interrupted the search, and it was four days after the loss that late one evening, when I was looking over the floe towards the south, I saw three figures approaching with a large object, which I knew could only be the kite. MacDougall, Anderson, and Johnny Smith had been far afield in search of it, and right over in Wilton Bay they had found it, battered and broken, sticking in a snow-drift. Then, with true sailor's skill, they had climbed a hundred-foot precipice, dragging the kite with them, and so crossed Mossman Peninsula and descended to Scotia Bay. It was quite mendable, and under Fitchie's care was soon as good as ever.

Most of the multitude of birds that haunt the South Orkneys in spring and summer had left us by the end of April for a warmer clime, and the lack of animal life during the months of mid-winter added to the feeling of desolation. There were a few birds left, largely stragglers from the open water near to us on the north, but it needs myriads of birds to awaken into animation these polar wastes,—a few are but lost in the vastness. Occasionally a wandering giant petrel (*Ossifraga gigantea*), or "nelly," as the sailors call them, was to be seen scouring the sea and land for offal of any description on which to feed. In Scotia Bay these birds must have got many a good winter meal from seal carcases, or the like, which we often left to attract them. They are veritable vultures in habit, and only touch dead matter. In appearance they are far from beautiful, though often impressive with their huge spread of wing and great gaunt beaks. When any open pools appeared in the south, flocks of several score of shags (*Phalacrocorax atriceps*) were sometimes to be seen swiftly passing far overhead in their orderly formation of a long curving line on their way to fresh fishing-grounds. High up among the cliffs many snowy petrels (*Pagodroma nivea*) were to be seen flitting on any fine sunny day in winter. When they came downwards towards the floe, Russ used to delight in chasing them hither and thither, but I am glad to say he never caught one. The snowy petrel is one of the most graceful of Antarctic birds, and is pure white but for its yellowish feet and jet-black bill.

The only other bird that remained our companion in the winter was the sheath-bill or paddy (*Chionis alba*). This is another white bird with black feet and a somewhat disfiguring greenish-yellow bill. It is the only truly land bird of the Antarctic; and though they probably migrate northward, as a rule, on the approach of winter, the plentiful and tempting supply of scraps of all kinds around the ship—for paddies also live on scraps and offal—no doubt induced some to stay with us. They grew very tame, and readily came on board for food; both galley and fo'c'sle had their special tame paddies which prospered exceedingly. In June we had fewer paddies about the ship, but they returned with the spring, and only left us for the more congenial haunts of the penguin rookeries, when these latter were again inhabited. Very rarely a straggling penguin was to be seen in winter, but these visitors must be looked on as mere casuals who had lost their way, and they soon departed again if suffered to do so. It was always an under-stood law—which only Russ disobeyed—that, except in very exceptional circumstances, no bird was to be killed in the vicinity of the ship, and thus we encouraged them to come near us without fear all winter.

Seals, too, were infrequent in winter, though a sunny day occasionally tempted one to emerge from its hole in the floe to lie and bask in the sun. Most, however, and particularly the females, were away in some ampler feeding-grounds, laying on a store of blubber in preparation for their weeks of fasting after the birth of their pups in spring. The only common seal at the South Orkneys was the Weddell seal (*Leptonychotes weddelli*), a seal which a decade ago was one of the rarest of known mammals despite its extraordinary abundance in the Antarctic. The smaller and whiter species, the crab-eating seal (*Lobodon carcinophaga*), called crab-eater, doubtless, in view of the fact that its staple article of diet is a little shrimp-like crustacean (*Euphausia*) more or less distantly allied to crabs, was occasionally seen in winter. Of the other two Antarctic seals, the sea leopard (*Stenorhynchus leptonyx*) was seen a few times in late winter, but the Ross seal (*Ommatophoca rossi*) was a stranger to us until we again went south the follow-ing summer.

The gloom of June, our darkest month, was fortunately always relieved by a few hours of daylight; and even on the shortest day, the time between sunrise and sunset was over five hours: but the darkness restricted outdoor work, and was not a little depressing. Yet no one suffered any ill effect, and the lengthening days of spring found all full of hope and expectation for the release that surely would soon come.

During August continual heavy westerly and north-westerly gales began to have a distinct effect on the ice of Scotia Bay. The outer part of this, it will be remembered, was largely of one-year ice, and had consolidated much later than the rest. It was this part that, under the action of continual gales and high tem-peratures, showed signs of weakening. For many weeks before, open water could have been sighted on the southern horizon if one cared to climb high enough to look for it, and on August 11 the ice at Cape Burn Murdoch was adrift. On the 16th the water was nearly up to Point Martin, and Delta Island was cut off from Point Rae; and on the following day, as the break-up was continuing, a party was sent out to rescue the big trap which was then lying off Point Martin. It was only just in time, for on the 18th the water was within that point, and the ice was still stripping off. For two nights past a quite perceptible swell had been felt at the ship, and so imminent did the general break-up seem that all hands were set to work taking on board the ship's whale-boat, gig, and various other gear which had lain all winter on the floe.

But this alarm proved a false one, for the water came no nearer to the *Scotia* than two miles, and before long several spells of hard weather did their work, and Scotia Bay was again covered by a solid floe. But of course we were in ignorance of what was coming, and to have been so near release raised the hopes of all on board, while a south wind soon after, with a temperature no lower than 7°, assured us of open water not far to the south. The ice in Jessie Bay and Uruguay Cove behaved very differently during the winter to that in Scotia Bay, and no doubt this was due to the ocean swell running with a north-westerly wind easily gaining access to bays on the north of the island, through the narrow band of pack beyond. It was the beginning of May before the floe in Jessie Bay was sufficiently secure for long excursions, and it was only for a few weeks then that it held as far as Route Point, and, as far as we knew, there was never continuous floe from Jessie Bay around Cape Mabel into Brown's Bay. In early June the ice was again afloat in Uruguay Cove, and at mid-winter the last remnant gave way: after that Jessie Bay never froze again, but at times with a northerly wind was filled with drifting pack, to be cleared again when the wind blew from the southward. It would, therefore, not have made a safe winter harbour, for, let alone the extreme discomfort of all this and the difficulty that landing would entail, the ship would have had to be continually under steam lest she might, in northerly or north-westerly gales, drag her anchors and drift either ashore or on to the reef off Russ Point. It was fortunate, we often thought, that we had so snug a harbour as Scotia Bay. The break up of Jessie Bay was utilised for entrusting to the sea several dozen securely sealed bottles, giving news of the *Scotia's* whereabouts and future plans. There was scant hope of any of these ever meeting the eyes of man again, but in such a region one must grasp any chance of a mail, however uncertain.

As yet I have said nothing with regard to mode of locomotion over the sea-ice or glaciers, but it must not be supposed that we travelled on foot. It was very rarely that the snow-surface was hard enough to sustain a man's weight, and even on these occasions walking was relatively slow. Our almost invariable mode of locomotion was with the aid of Norwegian snow-shoes or "ski." These are long narrow strips of wood, generally ash, varying from 6 to 8 feet in length and 3 to 5 inches in breadth, with the end pointed and raised upward some 4 or 5 inches. One of these is fixed on either foot by means of a leather toe-strap near the middle of the ski, while a lashing of reindeer hide completes the fastening, the heel being free to rise up and down and only the toe being secured: a light bamboo stick for support or steering purposes completes the equipment. With the exception of Mr Bruce and Wilton, who had learnt the art in former years in Franz-Josef Land, we all found ski-ing difficult at first, and even began to doubt its advantages. But less than a month's practice proved to one and all how indispensable it was, and we seldom, all the winter through, went half a mile beyond the ship without our ski. Even over rough ice a speed of three or four miles an hour can be maintained by an unburdened man; and ski also proved of great service in crossing soft snow-drifts or treacherous ice, for in the latter case the weight of the man is distributed over a relatively wide area, thus enabling him to go over ice that would scarcely bear his weight if he were on foot.

Ski-running also provided our great source of recreation during the winter months, and was the general occupation of all on board on half-holidays and Sunday afternoons. A long sloping glacier running down on to The Beach afforded an ideal ground for this sport. You climb somewhat laboriously up the slope, zigzagging all the way where it is at all steep, until you are perhaps half a mile to a mile from the foot, and several hundred feet in altitude. The work is then over and the fun begins. Placing your ski parallel, you give yourself a slight push with your stick, and you are at once under way. Quicker and quicker grows the speed until the snow-surface rushes past at a furious pace, and the beach below is approached at some forty miles an hour; then all at once the slope ends, the level plain rapidly diminishes the speed, and in about a hundred yards you are at a standstill.

Of course every attempt is not successful. A fair degree of skill in balancing the body is required, and the slightest swerve to right or left of either ski means a collapse. Then the onlooker merely sees a cloud of snow, out of which rolls the ski-runner head over heels and anyhow down the slope until his ski catch somehow in the snow, and his downward course is stopped.

Strange though it may seem, these tumbles never hurt any one, despite the great speed of the runner when they occurred. The very worst that ever resulted was merely a scratch or a broken ski. At first one used the stick for balancing and breaking the speed, but in time that became unnecessary, and, though only some half-dozen men approached to anything like Norwegian skill in ski-running, yet most were able to do it oftener without a spill than with one. Many other glaciers and slopes around Scotia Bay could be utilised for this sport, which was in the dismal days of mid-winter a great incentive to outdoor exercise, while the daily usage of ski in the ordinary routine of work in various directions made journeying to and from traps and skeleton-holes, as well as longer excursions, quite easy instead of laborious, as they would have been on foot.

CHAPTER VII

THE COMING OF SPRING

*RETURN OF LIFE—WEDDELL SEALS—THE SCOTIA'S BABY—
PENGUINS—A FEAST OF EGGS—HUGE ROOKERIES—A PARADISE
OF BIRDS—ATTEMPTS TO RELEASE THE SHIP—A COLD SNAP—
THE SOUTH ORKNEY "JINKER"—A SUDDEN BREAK-UP—THE
SCOTIA FREE—AU REVOIR—NORTHWARD.*

IN the early spring came a period of renewed activity, for despite the fact that in a meteorological sense spring and summer in polar regions do not entail very striking changes, yet after the dead gloom of winter, with its almost entire absence of animal life, the spring, with its rapidly lengthening daylight and return of myriad birds and seals, brings with it tenfold more joy to those men who are privileged to experience it than any spring in temperate regions ever could. Preparations for sledge-journeys and outlying camps were rapidly pushed on, with a view to exploring the island in all directions and completing the detailed survey we had begun in Scotia Bay and immediate surroundings during the winter.

In the last days of August the real coming of spring was heralded by the return of the seals. Large numbers of female Weddell seals then collected in their favourite rookeries to bring forth their young. For the previous month or two no females had been seen—only a stray male now and then. These seals always pup on the floe near to land, doubtless to be able, in the event of the ice breaking up, to save their young, who at that age cannot swim. Round about Point Martin, southwards to Cape Burn Murdoch and the eastern side of Buchan Bay, were the haunt of many; and at Point Martin on August 30 the first young seal was born. MacDougall reported it in the forenoon, and that day (it was Sunday) saw more than half the ship's company leaving after dinner to see this new attraction.

The pups are at birth from two to three feet long and covered with soft grey downy hair, very unlike the coarse stiff hair of their parents. But otherwise, except for the relatively large head and disproportionately large flippers, especially the hind one, the baby is very like the adult. It moves in the same way as its parent—by drawing itself forward with the help of the fore-flippers and then dragging onward the hinder part of its body; but its movements are naturally slow, and in following its mother it has to rest every few yards.

The mothers are quite different animals at this season from the sleepy good-natured beasts we had been used to, who could hardly be provoked at all, and who resolutely refused to more than lazily open one eye to take a glance at one. The altruism of maternity transforms the seal into an alert and ferocious animal, who resents any approach to its baby, and even rushes forward to savagely snap at the aggressor. To capture a baby Weddell necessitated a vigorous annoyance of the mother to keep her attention engaged, while the little one was rapidly popped into a sack and carried from the scene.

The adult seal in this season is more noisy than usual, her hoarse rattling chuckle being varied with a loud deep roar of anger when one approaches: the young emit a curious cry, a little resembling the baa of a lamb, but strangely human at times. The mothers seem to generally treat their young with loving care, often lying to windward of them to provide shelter, and at times playing with them. We captured a young one some three days old, and brought him aboard with the hope of keeping him alive. At first he wandered round the deck searchingly, and piteously wailed for his mother, but after a day or two seemed more at ease, though I think he was still quietly continuing his search. During the day he was relatively quiet and calm, but he almost always roved about at night, generally preferring to howl dismally on the poop-deck just above the cabins. One night he transferred his attentions to the mates' quarters, and fell down their companion-way, nearly alighting in Fitchie's bunk! But it was very soon so evident that he could not live, that it was a shame to attempt to keep him any longer. We tried to feed him with tinned milk, which we put in a bottle with an indiarubber tube projecting through a seal-skin jacket to tempt him to suckle, but with little or no result. The deceit must have been very obvious. Eventually we resorted to the cruder method of pouring a pint of milk down his throat, but I fear tinned milk did not agree with him, and in two weeks' time he was seized with convulsions, and, despite Pirie's assiduous attentions, died the same day. With a second pup we had no better success. In the early days of October—that is to say, four weeks after birth—the young Weddell seals began to take to the water. The pup carefully slides off the floe into the seal-hole, and, keeping always near the surface, never leaves the vicinity of the hole. In a few minutes he clambers out again, and joyfully mother and young greet one another. Several days later the mothers finally leave the youngsters to shift for themselves. By the end of September, or even earlier, all the young were born, and by the middle of

October most had left their parents. The males, which had quite disappeared for about six or eight weeks, then began to show themselves once more.

The great event in spring was undoubtedly the return of the penguins to their rookeries. That signified surroundings full of life, a never-failing field of interest to naturalists, and last, though almost most important, a plentiful supply of eggs and fresh meat. In the second week of October they began to arrive in large numbers from the north, all of the black-throated kind (*Pygoscelis adeliæ*), and in a few days' time the large rookery at Point Martin was filled with a noisy excited crowd of birds busying themselves in settling down for nesting.

The birds came in large flocks, all moving determinedly for their chosen rookery, often in their hurry adopting their prone mode of progression—propelling themselves forward on their bellies by aid of feet and flippers. In that fashion they are able to travel over the floe considerably faster than a man on ski can follow them, as we often had reason to learn when we were bent on a penguin hunt. As soon as the birds arrive at their rookeries, the mates are chosen, and this involves much display and showing off on the part of the male. He stands erect, drawing himself up to his full height, with head thrown back and neck craned upwards, then he slowly and impressively waves his flippers several times and emits a long loud cackle; this over, he resumes his normal somewhat squat position, and looks around him to see what impression his charms and powers have had on the onlooking females. This process repeated a few times generally results in a couple being paired off, and nest-building then begins. Another very favourite demonstration of affection on the part of a couple is like this: the two stand facing one another, and stretching forward cross their beaks, and then proceed to sway from side to side in unison, uttering the while a shrill harsh cry.

Within a week after the arrival of the penguins, nest-building was in full swing on the rookeries. The first-comers choose the better positions, already clear of snow and not too far from where the water will come in time, while the late arrivals have to be content with less favourable sites. Nest material is not plentiful, and the black-throated penguin almost entirely confines itself to the use of stones. The bird walks to and fro collecting little pebbles in its beak, and carries them to the chosen spot one by one, there depositing them in a little heap. He is quite energetic over this work, and, though a penguin can walk but slowly on his feet, he often travels ten yards or more for a stone. It was very amusing to watch their cunning in acquiring stones, for I do not think a penguin ever walks far for a stone if he can steal one near by; and, since the nests are seldom more than a couple of feet apart, theft is a relatively simple matter. A penguin sets out to fetch a stone and notices a nest near by unwatched for the moment. He approaches with the obvious intention of stealing a stone, when at that moment the rightful owner, himself probably coming from a raid, returns. The intending culprit walks on with a perfectly innocent air, and, with a look as if the thought of theft never entered his head, passes on to pick up an unclaimed pebble farther on; but given a better opportunity, he will not fail to succeed next time. Often, of course, the culprit is caught, and an angry fight with beaks ensues, in which sometimes the females join, and blood may flow and feathers fly before peace is restored. In fact, the penguin seems a most pugnacious animal, and there are always several fights in progress on every rookery, while neighbours continually snarl threateningly at one another. Not uncommonly one sees an unpaired male—very probably a one-year bird whose powers had been unavailing to encharm a mate—running through the rookery in a forlorn and tattered state, pecked at by every bird it passes, and only too glad to escape to the safety of outside the confines. Penguins fight almost solely with their beaks, dealing an occasional blow with their flippers, and as every peck is accompanied by a harsh cry, it is easy to imagine that, between courtship and fighting, a rookery is anything but quiet. There is always, except in very bad weather, an incessant cackle where penguins nest; and I must confess, though of course with due reluctance, that the only hubbub at all comparable to that of a penguin rookery is the shrill musicless clatter and chatter that rises at a society "At Home" or dinner-party. There is a wonderful similarity between the two. The nest does not take long to complete, for it is merely a small heap of stones a few inches high, and scooped out in the middle into a slight hollow.

Towards the end of October the black-throated eggs were laid,—generally two in each nest, but sometimes three. The pugnaciousness of the penguins now increased, no doubt largely because, when once the eggs are laid, skuas (*Megalestris antarctica*) hover continually over the rookeries, and if they spy an unguarded egg swoop down immediately, seize and carry it off to a little distance to suck the contents. On a skua approaching, all the penguins in the vicinity combine in a terrific uproar to scare it away, but seldom with much success, and many eggs are thus destroyed during incubation.

No sooner had laying become general throughout the rookeries than all hands were sent off to collect the eggs. This presents no difficulty,—the penguin is simply pushed off its nest, and the eggs picked up; but we found it as well to be protected with long leather sea-boots, for the bite of an angry penguin is not soon forgotten.

Several thousand eggs were thus commonly collected in an afternoon, and stowed in barrels and boxes on deck for immediate use, or packed away in salt for another day. Two thousand or more were also buried in a pit in the glacier to serve the house-party during the coming winter. The penguin egg is light green, about the size of a duck's egg, with much albumen and relatively little and very light-coloured yolk; but they were indeed a luxury to all on board in whatever form they were partaken of,—boiled or fried, scrambled or in omelettes, cooked or raw. No one could be satisfied for many days, and, in some shape or other, eggs were the principal constituent of every meal, and of various irregular meals interpolated when hunger prompted. For the first fortnight that eggs were obtainable the average daily consumption of all hands was fifteen a-head, not counting various raw ones that did not pass through the cook's hands. Hundreds of carefully chosen ones were in addition blown and packed away, some day to embellish the museums of Scotland.

Two weeks after the black-throated had begun to lay, the first gentoo penguin's egg (*Fygoscelis papua*) was obtained. The gentoos, who had been about a fortnight later in arriving, inhabited the same rookeries as the black-throateds, but owing to their coming after, had the more outlying or otherwise less favourable places. They are very different in many ways to their black-throated relatives, and seldom made a stand when we approached their nests, but bolted in a body, leaving their eggs at our mercy. Hardly ever have I seen one stand firm and show fight; and on the whole they are timid and comparatively peaceful birds, who seem to be unequal to holding their own with the adelias in competition for the rookeries. They generally build fairly large nests, and use, in addition to pebbles, bones and tail-feathers; but some of the latest arrivals content themselves with laying their eggs in mere holes in the snow. In all their movements they show less activity and alertness than the black-throateds, and are altogether less interesting birds. The cry of the gentoo is often strangely like the bray of an ass,—a similarity so accentuated in the allied Falkland Island species that it goes by the name of jackass penguin. The eggs of the two species are hardly distinguishable externally from one another, but the yolk of the gentoo egg is often of a richer colour,—though there is little distinction when once the cooking-pot is passed.

A strange story of an abnormally large penguin was one day brought in by Anderson, but, though it may have been an emperor, it was never seen again. The only other penguin that was seen in spring in Scotia Bay was the bridled or ringed penguin (*Pygoscelis antarctica*), which we had seen in large numbers early in the year at Saddle Island. They arrived in the beginning of November, and settled in Scotia Bay in small numbers; but away to the north-west, at Route Point, Nigg Rock, and Eillium Isle, we afterwards found huge rookeries of them. They struck me as more pugnacious than either of the two other species; and on more than one occasion a ringed penguin has deliberately attacked me on the floe, and had to be driven off with several hard blows. But their late arrival and lesser numbers in our neighbourhood afforded little opportunity for studying this species as carefully as the other two.

For the first few weeks after their arrival the penguins seem to live on their thick coats of blubber, and to abstain altogether from fishing; but after the eggs are laid they make excursions to the nearest open water in search of food, one or other of the pair undertaking the duty of remaining to lie upon the eggs.

This coating of blubber is very characteristic of Antarctic animals, and, for that matter Arctic animals also. In penguins, when they return in spring, it is fully half an inch thick, and in seals over an inch, so it will be readily intelligible how it is that both animals can, with this reserve of food, even in the Antarctic climate, sustain life for three or four weeks without partaking of a meal.

November was a joyful month for a naturalist, and fortunately calm weather favoured most of the excursions which I daily made in various directions to watch the progress of the nesting of different birds. On the 2nd Bruce, with Wilton, Pirie, Cuthbertson, MacDougall, and Walker, set out in two boats from Uruguay Cove on a voyage of exploration along the northern coast of Laurie Island, and in consequence I remained in charge of all the biological work on board, which now principally consisted in observing birds and collecting their eggs. I also visited the little rookery at Theodolite Point daily, and dated every new-laid gentoo egg, and at the same time took away several others that I had previously dated, and so knew the age of, with the object of obtaining a complete set of embryos from one day up to the time of hatching.

At Point Davis the black-backed gulls (*Larus dominicanus*) built their nests of moss and lichen on low-lying rocks, and laid their two or three mottled brown and black eggs. This spot was also the haunt of the dainty little terns (*Sterna hirundinacea*) of scarlet beak and legs; and here, dispensing altogether with a nest, they deposited their solitary egg on bare crevices among the rocks. The terns had a curiously fateful habit of betraying the whereabouts of their eggs by hovering in mid-air above them, shrilly shrieking all the time. Would they but omit to do this, their eggs would be exceedingly difficult to find.

The opposite shores and cliffs of Scotia Bay, southward from the large penguin rookery at Point Martin, were also rich hunting-grounds for photographer and collector alike. Gulls, terns, and sheath-bills were all to be found nesting there, and on some deeply moss-covered slopes of Mossman Peninsula—a little paradise only now revealed—skuas seemed to be on the point of building. On the cliff near the house several pairs of Cape pigeons (*Daption capense*) had taken up their abode, and I eagerly kept a watch for their then unknown eggs.

For several months now we had looked for a release from our winter prison with hopes most unduly raised after our August alarm. In the end of that month the Captain decided to attempt to release the *Scotia*, by cutting a canal of over a mile in length to the open water or thin ice to the south. As a beginning, the snow-bank around the ship was cleared away, and a ditch of a couple of feet cut around her, so that she was free from the floe on all sides. At her bows the canal was then begun. The floe was sawed into strips with a long jagged ice-saw worked by four or six men; the resultant pieces were then broken with ice-drills and hauled on to the floe with ropes and grapnels. Several blasts of gunpowder were inserted under the ice on the end of a long pole and fired with a fuse, but they, none of them, effected as much damage to the floe as we looked for. For two weeks the work slowly and intermittently proceeded, for the ice proved much thicker—15 to 25 feet—and our tools less effective than had been supposed. But the greatest obstacle was perhaps the temperature. After a relatively mild August we looked for spring in September, but looked in vain, for on the very first day of the month the thermometer fell to -20° F.; on the second day it dropped five degrees lower; on the third it was down to -26° F. in the early morning, and after a few hours rising to 8° with a westerly wind, it fell again to -20° at nightfall, with a ground minimum of −33°: then with an occasional drop to the vicinity of zero the temperature remained more seasonable, but it had been low long enough to undo much of our work, and, what was more, to firmly congeal once more the shifting floe towards the mouth of Scotia Bay.

It would have been folly to continue to waste labour on this almost futile task, so we turned, though not without reluctance, to other occupations, and waited for natural forces to do their work, and release the *Scotia* in due time.

While this work had been in progress, the engine fires were again lighted, and steam was never far off. The Captain was at first very sanguine that the canal would be cut, and hence Gravill had orders to have all ready in a few days; but after a fortnight's warmth and cheeriness in the engine-room and stock-hole— particularly acceptable in the evenings of the severe cold snap—those regions reverted to their former dismal and frigid state, and ceased again to be the evening rendezvous. However, the labour of cutting out was not by any means wasted. The anchor chain had been cut out of the ice, and the anchor heaved up and cat-headed ready for use, should the floe go out; and equally important was it that the *Scotia* was all round clear of the floe, in a little dock of her own, as it were, which would quite effectively prevent the otherwise conceivable possibility of her floating out firmly adhering to the floe.

But as September and October ran their courses and still no release came to us, the crew waxed impatient, and being nearly all whaling men, and so with the beliefs common to that service, decided there must be a "jinker" on board, whose sacrifice was essential to ensure a change in weather. For a day or two preparations had been going on in the fo'c'sle, when one evening the crew announced that the South Orkney jinker, accused of adversely affecting the weather, would be tried. A life-size effigy, whose fate was covered in the meantime, was paraded round the deck, and then carried aft to the cabin door, and the face revealed to view. Then for the first time I found that it was myself who was the jinker, and who was to be tried. The likeness was excellent, the shaggy red beard and moustaches unmistakable, and what made the semblance stronger was that the effigy was clothed in an old suit of mine, which I had unwittingly given away to help in the manufacture of the victim. My offences were read out solemnly, the Captain was duly asked, as always on these occasions, if I was guilty, and, as always, his silence was taken as an affirmative, and I was sentenced to be burnt. Out on the floe, a hundred yards to leeward, I had the unique experience of setting fire to myself after pouring half a gallon of spirit over myself to aid the conflagration. It was a very enjoyable evening; but despite the sacrifice of the jinker, the weather refused to change, and the floe held firm.

But we had still plenty to do in collecting and photographing every aspect of the newly awakened bird-life; coal and stores were landed, to last a year or more if necessary, and then the ship was got ready for sea, and in one way or another the days were filled until November was not far from its close. One Sunday evening (November 22) the wind blew from a rather unusual quarter (N.E. by N.), and the Captain's hope began to swiftly rise, for he had always, from a study of the ice conditions obtaining at Laurie Island, looked for such a wind to play havoc with the floe.

The rest of us were, I confess, a little sceptical after so many false alarms, and much, therefore, was the surprise and delight on board when early next morning the water was nearer, and from the mast-head great strips of floe could be seen floating away to sea. It was a day of great excitement and, at last, fulfilled hope. The wind, clearing away some loose pack to the south, allowed the ocean swell to reach Scotia Bay, and no floe can resist the action of waves of swell; so that all day long the break-up continued, getting more rapid as the head of the bay was reached. At 4 P.M. a crack ran right across the ice about the ship, and Mossman, with a sledge party taking a few final things ashore, had a run for it over the now drifting ice. By 7 P.M. the bay was clear, and the *Scotia* lay at anchor.

Glad as all were to be set at liberty, there was an undeniable touch of sadness in seeing old familiar hunting-grounds and well-known bergs and hummocks swept ruthlessly out to sea, and one felt at once the narrow confines of the ship in contrast to the wider freedom the frozen bay afforded.

The chief and his boat-party of five were still away, but the same day Pirie and Cuthbertson arrived overland to bring us word that the whole party were encamped at Point Thomson in Brown's Bay. On Tuesday morning Pirie left early to give Mr Bruce the welcome news of the ship's release, and at noon that day the *Scotia* got under way to steam round to the camp at Point Thomson to pick up the party. We encountered no pack to speak of, but heavy swell was running, and the ship, being light, knocked about considerably. We rounded Capes Burn Murdoch and M'Vitie, went up Washington Strait, and, passing between Nigg Rock and Eillium Isle, crossed Jessie Bay, then rounding Pirie Peninsula, were soon in sight of the camp. Brown's Bay was surging with a confused swell, and a broad strip of heavy pack and slush cut us off from Point Thomson. We saw them try to launch the gig to reach us, but the attempt had to be abandoned, as progress through such ice was next to impossible. There was nothing for it then but to return to Scotia Bay, which we did, arriving there at 10 P.M., to await the return overland of the sledge-party next day.

On Wednesday evening all returned on board, having left their boats at Point Thomson, to be picked up when the sea moderated. The following day, when the *Scotia* again went round to Brown's Bay, this was successfully accomplished, and we lay that night at anchor in Uruguay Cove. The shore-party, consisting of Mossman, Pirie, Cuthbertson, Ross, and Martin, with Bill Smith as cook, finally took up their abode in Omond House that afternoon, and at daybreak on November 27 the *Scotia* put to sea, bound once more for civilisation, and to announce to such of the world as cared at all about it, what discoveries we had made.

CHAPTER VIII

SLEDGE AND BOAT JOURNEYS

PREPARATIONS FOR SLEDGING—EXPERIMENTAL TRIP—LIFE IN CAMP—DEATH OF RAMSAY—A STIFF CLIMB—NEARLY ADRIFT ON PACK—HEAVY HAULING—ORCADIAN GEOLOGY—MISTY WEATHER—SNOW-BLIND—RETURN OF PENGUINS—A FORCED MARCH—BOAT-TRIP—GIANT PETRELS—SHAGS—NERVES— CAPE PIGEONS—RINGED PENGUINS—A BLOODY FIGHT— RELEASE OF THE SCOTIA.

EVER since our arrival at the Orkneys it had the chief's intention to map out as much of islands as possible, for our experience in hunting for a harbour to winter in had showed us that existing charts were woefully deficient, and subsequent events proved that they presented nothing like the real shape of the land. But it is not to be wondered at, considering that the whole group was surveyed (*sic*) in four days by men who were really on the look-out for seals, especially when it is remembered that the light-and-shade effects of the dead black and white are such that a deeply indented coast-line, seen from sea-level a mile or two off shore, often looks perfectly straight and flat.

We had hoped to have some trips in the autumn, before the days became so short as to make it unprofitable to undertake such work, but it was not to be. A few short excursions from the ship—afternoon strolls, in fact—made it clear that the extremely steep nature of the hills would make it wellnigh impossible to go any distance by land over the glaciers. The sea-ice conditions were most unsatisfactory. On the north and west side of the island the land-floe never held more than about a couple of miles from The Beach. As late as July 17, after a north-west wind and swell which broke up the ice, a south-west wind carried out the pack, and there was nothing but open water in sight; then the pack-ice

75

would drift back, become frozen together, but sooner or later undergo again the same breaking-up and drifting-out process. On the south side the congealed pack-ice remained in the greater part of Scotia Bay the whole winter, and sometimes held as far out as Ailsa Craig in the mouth of the bay, and round Cape Burn Murdoch. Outside of the Craig was almost always a strip of open water, beyond which the steady easterly drift of the bergs and pack-ice could be noted from the ship.

But hoping for better conditions in the spring, we had everything prepared during the winter months,—tents made, and the dogs accustomed to harness and sledge-hauling. As our work was intended to be mainly at sea, extensive sledge-trips were not anticipated, and our supply of dogs was correspondingly small—two Samoyede dogs brought from home and six sheep collies obtained at the Falklands. Of the eight, one of the Siberian dogs and two of the collies were killed through accidents, and a third, an old dog, died, so that our total was reduced to four. Our experience of the collies was very satisfactory: they stood the cold well and pulled well in harness, their only weak point being the paws, which are not so hard as those of the Samoyedes, and were apt to be cut when on rough ice.

The first trip was partly an experimental one to find out how our apparatus and provision scale worked. Our venue was Delta Island, at the eastern extremity of Scotia Bay; and the object of the trip, in addition to that already mentioned, was to survey the neighbourhood and to take some series of soundings. The party consisted of Wilton, myself, and William Martin, one of the A.B's., an extremely able and intelligent companion. The outfit was as follows: One sledge carrying three one-man reindeer sleeping-bags, one small aluminium cooking-stove of Nansen's pattern and suppy of methylated spirits, biscuits, tinned or "bully" beef, bacon, oatmeal, tea, cocoa, sugar and butter, chocolate and cheese. The sleeping-bags went on the front of the sledge, and the provisions in a box behind. In the latter was also a gun and some cartridges. The sledge-covers being fastened over these, the tent was lashed on the top, also some long bamboo poles and flags to serve as survey-poles. A small sledge was towed behind carrying a hand sounding-reel, with a couple of hundred fathoms of wire, an ice-drill and shovel, and a measuring line a hundred feet long.

We ourselves were clad in thick grey woollen Norwegian sledging-suits (knickers and jumpers), with leggings of the same material, and wore ski boots over two pairs of socks. In windy weather we put on over all a wind-suit made of closely-woven gabardine, which served excellently to keep out wind and snow-drift.

We set out on July 8, a bright calm day, with the thermometer just about zero. The surface of the ice was excellent, and the dogs took the sledge out to the camp in style. Cuthbertson accompanied us and took the dogs back to the ship, save Russ, who preferred to remain. The first business was to pitch camp. The tent was of the pattern invented by Dr Koettlitz when with the Jackson-Harmsworth

Expedition to Franz-Joseph Land,—a four-sided pyramid with a bamboo pole running up in each corner, the lower end being firmly planted in the snow. All round the base projected a snow-cloth, twelve or eighteen inches wide, and on this snow was piled to keep the tent in place. In one side was a circular hole, about two feet in diameter, with a short canvas tunnel, or bag without a bottom, sewn on round it. To get in or out it was necessary to creep through this, and then the bag was tied up, purse-string-wise, inside or outside the tent as the case might be. This method of ingress and egress was a little awkward at first, but snow-drift was effectually precluded from getting into the tent,—a great consideration.

A survey of our quarters yielded some interesting geological facts. The island was found to be almost cut in two by a gap with sharply perpendicular faces, which appeared to run along a line of fault. The top, which reached an elevation of ninety feet, was covered with loose boulders, and some of these were found to consist of a variety of greywacke-conglomerate, not occurring *in situ* on the island, but found on some islets to the north-west, between Delta Island and Point Davis. The probability is that these boulders have been carried hither by the action of land-ice, and the rounded outline of the island, sloping gradually up from the north-west and presenting a steep face to the south-east, is in favour of the view that it has at one time been over-ridden by an ice-sheet coming down Scotia Bay. As there is now a depth of ten fathoms between the island and the mainland, the general elevation of the land must at that time have been considerably greater, as the ice-sheets seem to have attained their maximum possible development with the present gathering-ground.

Eight days were spent working in this neighbourhood, and I shall describe a typical day's work. About seven o'clock the cook for the day crept shivering out of his warm sack, lit the cooking-stove, and put on to melt the ice which had been brought in the last thing at night: in three-quarters of an hour the cry of "Burgoo ahoy!" roused out the other two, and a large plate of porridge was served round, and swallowed as hot as it could be borne. Meanwhile, some slices of bacon were frizzling nicely in the frying-pan,—these and biscuits formed the second course. At first we tried to be very economical of spirit, and ate the bacon raw, but this was soon voted not good enough. Some more ice was then put on to melt, sufficient for a large mug of cocoa each; during the interval we dressed— i.e., took off the extra dry socks which were worn at night, pulled out the mitts which had been placed next our chests to dry, and worked our way into our boots: these, though put under our heads to keep soft, were more like cast-iron than leather. Soon after nine we sallied forth with the sounding apparatus, measuring-line, and prismatic compass for surveying.

About thirty soundings we found as much as could be done in a day: each involved cutting a hole through ice at least thirty inches thick, often rather more. Frequently several bores had to be made till a place was found clear of the old hummocky ice.

Lunch was taken out on the floe: this consisted of biscuit, butter (which was quite hard and crumbly), cheese, a stick of chocolate, *and* a pipe. It did not delay long, as we were usually glad to get to work again to keep warm.

Dusk at six found us once more back in camp. The two lucky ones snugged down in their sacks, while the third cooked dinner. This meal consisted of more biscuit, thawed meat, and a large mug of tea. How the thoughts of that hot tea kept us going all day! The recollection of it is the strongest I have of our camping-out experiences,—how both hands having clasped the cup so as not to lose any heat, the warm glow gradually spread and spread, till at last even the toes felt warm ere the cup was drained. Truly it was a cup that cheered.

The day's work was then plotted out by the light of a guttering candle, and a pipe and chat passed away an hour ere we wooed the drowsy god. The moisture from our breaths and from the cooking-stove of course condensed as snow on the walls of the tent, and a considerable amount found its way into our sacks. This, together with some snow which one could not help carrying in about one's clothes, and the frozen socks and mitts, gave us a good deal of thawing to do in bed; but, notwithstanding that and the howling wind which sometimes threat-ened to carry the whole tent away, we slept the sleep of the just, with never an ache or pain such as would almost certainly be the result of sleeping out in more temperate but less healthy climes in similar wet conditions. And the secret of it all is—No microbes there!

Animal life was very scarce at this time of year. A few seals and some shags, gulls, giant and snowy petrels, were all that we saw.

A very fine geological section of bedded greywacke was exposed on the east side of Mill Cove: the strata could be seen running right up from sea-level to the top of the cliff, some 600 or 800 feet high. This cove was closed at its head by the terminal ice-cliff of a glacier occupying a narrow col, and which, we found later, was continuous with the ice-sheet at the head of Brown's Bay, on the north side of Laurie Island.

We returned to the ship for the week-end, but went out again on Monday, August 3, Brown taking the place of Wilton, who had had three fingers rather badly frost-bitten. Our work was practically finished as far as was possible with the state of the ice, when the camp was brought to a sudden termination on August 6.

Ross and Cuthbertson came out early in the morning with the news that Ramsay was much worse. He had been going gradually downhill ever since March, and the last two months had been spent almost entirely lying in a deck-chair in front of the cabin stove. Three days before, when I saw him last, he was not noticeably worse, but the end came suddenly. Hurrying back that morning, I found him suffering great agony, which I was able to relieve, but could do no more. He passed away peaceably in the afternoon. Poor Ramsay! he died a mar-tyr to a mistaken sense of duty. Of a quiet retiring disposition, he kept his troubles very much to himself, for he had felt it even before we reached Port Stanley, but said nothing then, in case he should be sent home, and land us in difficulties without an engineer. It was not until considerably later—too late—that I found out he was suffering from heart disease. Even then, when he was knocked off all work, I thought he would pull through the winter, but the cold was too trying, and rest and all remedies proved unavailing.

Two days later he was buried on the north side of The Beach—"the side nearest home." That scene we can never forget: one of those perfect days we sometimes had—crisp, clear, and cold, but absolutely calm; the melancholy little procession to the shore, headed by the piper playing "The Flowers of the Forest" and "The Old Hundredth."

He gave his life for others, and gave it uncomplainingly. What greater praise can be given to any man? There are those, I know, who envy him his last resting-place beneath the shadow of the ice-capped hill that is named after him, where throughout the ages the sea-birds wheel in their restless flight, and the waves crash on the shore save when frost holds them in its mighty grip, and there is stillness deep as death.

Although a gloom was cast over us by the loss of our comrade, work of course had to go on, and there was plenty of it to keep us from brooding. Five days later the same party of three set off on another trip. This time the scene of operation lay to the west—in Wilton Bay. To get there it was necessary to cross the steep ridge lying between that bay and Scotia Bay. The height was nothing great, only some 500 feet, but the descent on the far side was very steep. To negotiate this safely, almost the whole crew turned out and dragged up our outfit, which was practically the same as on the previous trip, and also another sledge carrying two whale-lines—*i.e*, some 200 fathoms of stout manilla rope. The lines were spliced, our sledge was made fast and lowered gradually down the steep ice-slope, over the more gently sloping part of the glacier, and finally down a small terminal snout on to the floe. The rope was then made fast to a rock on the summit of the ridge, and left in position for hauling up again. Helping to pull the sledge up I lost my mascot—a lucky horse-shoe; and to this, of course, was attributable all the misfortunes which occurred on this trip. Our camp was pitched on a small islet a little way off the shore, but not far distant from the spit by which we got off the glacier on to the bay ice.

The following morning our cooking-stove burst up, and breakfast had to be made off half-cooked oatmeal and raw bacon. This we discovered was due to our leaving the frying-pan in the stove underneath the porridge-pot. Wilton returned to the ship for a new spirit-lamp, while Martin and I took angles from our camp as one end of a base line, sank a trap near the island, and then set out for the south end of the bay to finish the survey. This, however, proved impossible, as drift and mist came on so thick that all landmarks were completely blotted out. There was nothing for it but to crawl inside the tent and indulge in the sailor's privilege of grumbling. The following day was not much better,—a strong north-erly wind with mist and driving sleet, and a temperature about 34° F.; but it was sufficiently clear at times to enable us to fix the main points of the coastline, and run a line of soundings across the mouth of the bay. The last part was risky work, the ice being much broken up, and in the dusk it was difficult to distinguish between solid ice and lanes of water covered over with slush. By this time we were more like walking icicles than human beings, so, being Saturday night, we "guessed" it would be decidedly more comfortable at home in Scotia Bay. It was a weary pull up the whale-line, and at the top I managed to let one ski disappear down the glacier before me. It was hopeless looking for it in the dark, so I had to hobble down on one as best I could. Next morning we returned, and had a most exciting day. Mr Bruce came with us, and later on some of the crew came over, fossicking for curiosity,—Sunday, of course, being a holiday. We wished to make our way as far west as possible, but found the road barred at Cape Davidson. The strong north wind had cleared the pack-ice off the coast and a heavy swell was coming in, lifting the ice some five or six feet. The floe was much cracked, but as yet holding. In my ignorance I was for pushing on,—wanting to know what was round the corner. It was lucky for me that Mr Bruce was with us: but for his seeing the danger (knowing ice of old), I had soon been off to sea on a on a trip of my own on an ice-floe,—a trip that had surely ended in Davy Jones's big locker.

Baffled in this direction, we cut across the bay to the south side to explore it a little more thoroughly, and were rewarded by finding a fine geological section showing alternating beds of shale and greywacke, and by seeing a sort of pocket-edition glacier nestling in a little hollow of the cliffs. This baby glacier ended in an ice-face, where the cliff again became too steep, and the face showed the strati-fication due to successive years' snowfall, only they were not horizontal as in the larger ice-sheets, but sinuous, following exactly every rise and fall of the under-lying rock. It could not be examined in detail, however; the ice was beginning to move out of the bay, great strips were breaking off like slices of a gigantic melon, and drifting lazily out to sea, while flocks of snowy petrels were diving in and out of the cracks, evidently finding a rich store of nutriment in the shape of *Euphausiæ* and other animals that had collected on the under surface of the floe. At first we struck homewards leisurely, but had gradually to go quicker and quicker, till finally it was a race between us and the ice, such was the rate at which it was breaking off. Jumping the ever-widening cracks, we got back to the islet the camp was on, tore down the tent, bundled the things on to the sledge anyhow, and dashed for the spit of the glacier. We had won! The trap was the only bit of gear lost. Mr Bruce and Johnny Smith actually had it pulled up to the surface, but had not time to slew it square to come through the hole in the ice: they had to drop it and jump for dear life. Packing the sledge properly, we made it fast to the end of the whale-line and climbed up the hill. That trip was over. By the time we were at the top the ice was almost wholly out of the bay, and in our own winter quarters there was open water a good mile inside Ailsa Craig. We began to have visions of the ship being free very soon: little did we think there was more than three months to go, and that our coldest spell of weather had yet to come. In the next two days the floe did indeed break off to within a mile of the ship, and the boats, traps, &c., were lifted on board in case of accidents; but the accident did not come off. For a month the ordinary routine work of the winter went on: the house ashore was getting ready for habitation, the young Weddell seals claimed attention, and an abortive attempt was made to cut the ship out. On September 21 a day's excursion was made to Cape Whitson, farther east than we had ever reached before; and as the ice appeared to be holding as far as Cape Dundas, the chief decided that now or never was the time to complete the survey of the eastern part of the island, and the following day we set off. This time the party consisted of Mr Bruce, Wilton, Cuthbertson, and myself. Instead of single sleeping-bags we took two two-men sacks, and had provisions sufficient to last us three weeks. In the event of the ice breaking we trusted to being able to make our way back somehow overland, or else being rescued by boat. We took no sounding machine, but had a trap, a sextant, and artificial horizon for check observations on our position: these, and the extra provisions needed for a fourth man, made a very good load on the sledge. The chief and I set off early, *viâ* Ailsa Craig and Murray Islands, to link up these with our survey. Near Ailsa Craig there were numerous pressure ridges in the ice, huge hummocks being squeezed up ten and twenty feet above the general level of the floe. It was generally easy, however, to pick a road between them, and travelling was not very heavy, as drift-snow had filled up many of the inequalities of the surface. But between the Craig and Murray Islands it was much harder work. The ice was not actually so heavy, being chiefly small, rounded, water-worn pieces of ice with occasional level floes, but there was very little snow on the surface, and ski would not "bite," but slipped in every direction. One mile per hour was about the utmost we could do.

The Murray Islands are a small group of rocks about half a mile in circumference. They were named by Weddell in 1823. The largest has a very distinctive tower, which formed a conspicuous object on the eastern horizon of Scotia Bay. We did not succeed in quite reaching the top of this, but from a point near it had a magnificent view of the whole southern coast-line of Laurie Island, with its black frowning bluffs alternating with bluish-white ice-cliffs, the whole being backed by a complex maze of serrated peaks, all of the purest white. To the northeast the land gradually sloped down into a low plateau, rising again in the terminal hill of Cape Dundas—our goal.

On the islands were a fair number of shags, all paired, also snowy petrels, paddies, and a few seals with their young. The land-floe was not holding beyond—in fact, it was impossible to get quite round the south side owing to the presence of a lane of open water, which we could trace running towards Cape

Dundas. Dusk coming down, we made our way across to Cape Whitson, where it had been arranged the two parties were to meet. We found camp just set up: the others had had the same experience as us—a rough road from Delta Island onwards.

The following day we had typical South Orkney weather—mist and heavy snowdrift. There was no call for a forced march, and no useful work could be done with the landmarks all invisible; so we sat tight for the day, smoking and sleeping in the intervals between meals. The double sacks proved more comfortable in every way than the single ones, being both roomier and warmer. The succeeding day was the very antithesis of this one—bright clear sunshine, with just a breath of northerly wind and a comfortable temperature about zero. We had breakfast under way at half-past five, made a local survey of the neighbourhood, discovered a large sea-cave whose floor was raised some ten feet above the present sea-level, and then headed off north-east across the ice. The order of march was as follows: At the head of the main drag-rope on which the dog; were pulling, two on each side, was Cuthbertson, picking out a road amongst the hummocks; Mr Bruce and I hitched on to two shorter ropes like the two outer horses on a Russian troika; and Wilton, with his ski off for convenience in quick shifting from side to side, kept by the sledge, steering it clear of hummocks, and doing his best to keep it on an even keel. His was the hardest task, for he was often floundering along in soft snow-drift almost up to the waist, and had to balance a sledge which had sometimes one runner on a hard high hummock and the other down in soft drift; or again, getting some unexpected way on before he could stop it, the sledge would dive nose first into a hole between two hummocks, bringing the team up with a jerk. It was then a case for all hands setting the apple-cart up again with many a "Heave-ho!" and sometimes even stronger expressions. To reach our destination we had only about three miles to go, but it took full six hours to get over that ice,—six hours of the hardest pulling I ever want to have to do. How the tea went down after it! "If this is Science," said Willie, "she's a hard mistress; give me Art." But the reward came soon. Layers of shale, which cropped up every here and there amidst the greywacke, were more abundant near the camping-ground than in any other part of the group visited. Hunting over these, I was fortunate enough to find three fossil remains. Much splitting up of shale yielded no further treasures. They were not good specimens, but still sufficient to identify pretty closely the age of the rocks.

One specimen consisted of some stipes of graptolite belonging to the genus *Pleurograptus.* The other two were fragments of a crustacean carapace, probably closely allied to the form *Discinocaris.* These two forms indicate that the rocks correspond in age to the uppermost beds of the Lower Silurian or basal rocks of the Upper Silurian. It is further interesting to note that the greywacke and shale of the South Orkneys are practically identical in character with the rocks of the same age in North Wales and in the southern uplands of Scotland.

The presence of isolated islands such as the South Orkneys, and, still more so, South Georgia, composed entirely of sedimentary rocks and surrounded by deep waters, proves a former much greater extension of land in this area of the earth's surface. These rocks were originally laid down under water; subsequently earth-movements on a large scale must have raised up a great part of the South Atlantic into dry land,—quite possibly continuous with what is now South America and South Africa,—the same movements bending, folding, and fracturing the rocks into much their present condition. Still later changes have again depressed most of the area under the ocean (a lot of good farm-land wasted!), leaving these tiny islands as sole remains of a lost continent. This story, of course, holds good of the rocks whatever their age; but the finding of these fossils enables us to take another step in tracing back the history of this corner of the globe. Rocks of similar age occur on both sides of the Andean Chain in Bolivia and Northern Argentina, and also in the province of Buenos Aires in the Sierra Tandil and Sierra de la Ventana. The ridging up of the Andean Chain—a long wrinkle on the earth's surface formed as it grew old and cooled—brought these beds to light from the bottom of the sea; the probability is that the same ridge which we see bending eastwards in Southern Patagonia and Tierra del Fuego once continued still farther south-east, and the rocks of the South Orkneys, which are folded along a north-west and south-east axis, lay on one flank of this sub-Andean chain. How it became cut across by what is now called Drake Strait is for future exploration to decide, but probably much of the story is for ever hidden from us—lost beneath the waves of the stormy Cape Horn seas.

We had camped at first on an island,—Graptolite Island, as it has been named—but on September 27 moved over on to the mainland just opposite. There was often a little movement of the ice, more than the mere rise and fall of the tide: it was greatly cracked, and looked as if very little would drive it out, in which case we had no desire to be marooned even in the company of the graptolite.

The same day some half-dozen gentoo penguins arrived—the harbingers of spring. I grieve to say they were promptly sacrificed; but my grief is only for the individuals, not for the species in general, for they made a most welcome addition to our *menu*. The day following hundreds appeared. It was a great sight to see them come;' marching across the narrow neck of land from the open water on the north side, like a regiment of soldiers, walking upright on the level where rock and glacier met, tobogganing down the ice-spit on their breasts, then up again on their feet across the strait to the island, where they squatted. Many stopped to examine us and the tent on their way past, but with a stare and a shake of their stupid old heads they soon passed on.

I shall now give some extracts from my diary as written at the time. They give a graphic enough account of the unsatisfactory weather conditions we had to do survey work under.

September 29.—"S.W. wind, thick snow-drift; can't see quarter of a mile.

Cleared up in the afternoon; went back to the cove lying just east of Cape Whitson and finished the mapping of it,—a low glacier, similar to that at the head of Mill Cove, seems to lead over by a col to the north side. (This we found later was the case, both of them opening on to Brown's Bay.) To the west it is shut in by a steep saw-like ridge. Willie stayed behind and hung up our sacks to dry a little; they are quite soppy and pulpy."

September 30.—"Another bad day. Wind N., but it does not seem to matter what direction it has or what the barometer is doing—the mist and snow-drift come all the same. Tried to do some charting, but it is not easy sitting in a sack with the consistency of a peat-bog and a steady drip coming from the top of the tent on to the paper. Cleared about 3 P.M. Mapped the north side of Ferrier Peninsula; found it is joined on by a neck of land only about a hundred yards wide. Saw numerous gulls, nellies, snowies, and shags, also a few gentoos and Cape pigeons."

October 1.—"Another beast of a day the whole round of the clock. Wilton returned from the ship."

He had gone to get some more biscuits sent out, for it was evident that we had put ourselves on rather short allowance, and that our stay was to be prolonged. With clear weather we could have done in one week easily what it took us full three to do, and that not quite completely with regard to the position of the hill-tops, though the coast-line was thoroughly surveyed.

"All well at the ship. His arrival was quite an event,—like a long letter. What will it be when real letters from home come!"

October 2.—"Temperature dropped during the night. Door not properly closed; woke to find a good half inch of snow all over us, and a good deal actually inside the sleeping-bags. We had still enough heat left in our bodies to melt this, and make the bags even pulpier than before. Heavy wind and drift all day— mapping impossible, but had a good ski-run to warm us up."

October 3.—"A lovely day at last—bright sun, almost no wind, temperature a little under zero. Put all the contents of the tent out on the rocks, and by night we had once more beds which were almost dry—only a little ice in them. The chief took observations for latitude and longitude. I mapped the south coast of Ferrier Peninsula, and the others went to Cape Whitson for the extra biscuits which had been cached there."

October 4.—"Only a thin mist to-day. Mapped the west side of Fitchie Bay. Being Sunday, indulged in a pair of dry socks and had a wash—*i.e.,* we rubbed our faces with snow."

October 5.—"Clouded over again. Can't get hill-tops which we want badly to carry our triangulation over on to the north side. Found a seal near a small seal-hole in the floe outside Graptolite Island. Killed the seal for dog-food and sunk our trap through the hole. Wilton's eyes beginning to be painful."

October 6.—"Another soft day, no wind, but thick mist and snow. This is sickening. Adelia penguins have arrived now, and seem to have all paired already. Their courtship must be shorter than that of the gentoos, which still wander about in single blessedness. Numerous gulls, snowy petrels, and Cape pigeons, shags, paddies, and nellies, but no skuas or ringed penguins to be seen so far. Rounded Cape Dundas: numerous lichens there, but no sign of the grass that Weddell speaks of. Can he have mistaken the green lichen for a grass, or has it died out? Sleeping-sacks are soaking again: make excellent wet packs, but we have not high temperatures that require bringing down."

And so on *ad nauseam* till—

October 11.—"Best day we have had for some time—low ground all clear. Worked our way north-westwards past a cape which seems to correspond with d'Urville's Cape Vallavielle. A wild sheer coast it is. The ground rises towards the coast, and much morainic stuff has been deposited west of Cape Vallavielle. The ice-sheet we travelled over must be the largest on the island, being continuous from Ferrier Peninsula to Ferguslie Peninsula. It terminates in Fitchie Bay in one continuous ice-cliff while on the north side it reaches the sea in four separate places—it cannot be said by distinct tongues or glaciers. Rather stuck for bearings, as hills never clear. Mist came down very heavy about 4 P.M.: how very lost one feels on the inland ice with nothing whatever to indicate direction, and not a sound to break the stillness! I never heard (!) a silence so intense. Wilton's and Willie's eyes rather bad: curious this snow-blindness coming on in thick misty weather, because it is generally supposed to be due to the glare of the sun off the snow. Five days' grub left."

October 12.—"Climax. A clear day; the chief out before breakfast taking angles for the hill-tops. On coming in he announced we would start on our homeward journey. I went off to fetch in the trap, while the others were to pack up at the tent. Came back to find them all with their heads buried like the proverbial ostrich—crocked with snow-blindness: their eyes felt as if hot sand were in them, and the tears simply streamed over. Darkness and cocaine indicated. Travelling out of the question. As the opportunity was too good to be lost, I went up to the 800-foot flag-staff we had raised on a *nunatak,* and took a splendid round of angles—embracing the coast-line from Murray Islands round by Cape Dundas to Cape Buchanan, and including Saddle Island away to the north-west, then made my way over the ice-sheet almost to MacDougall Bay. It and Brown's Bay beyond both open: no road to the ship that way. (Later we discovered it was possible to get round the head of MacDougall Bay but not round the other, the hill-ridges coming sheer down to the water, in several places forming an *impasse* to a sledge.)

"Found Wilton's eyes so bad on my return that I asked the chief to let me take him back to the ship. This was agreed to, so we set off in the dark a little after 8 P.M., and, arm-in-arm, we stumbled along through the hummocks, had exciting times with tide-cracks round the various capes, relieved the monotony of the way with snatches of song, and finally arrived "home" about 2 A.M., finishing up by tumbling into the trap-hole underneath the bows of the ship. My right eye—the compass-eye—had collapsed by now, but in the kingdom of the blind the one-eyed are kings."

As Mossman was expecting a N.W. gale, I requested Brown and Walker to go off to the camp next morning. This they did. Walker turned up again two days later wanting some biscuits to be sent out and a pair of ski to replace breakages. His eyes showed signs of giving way, and as mine had now recovered, I returned on October 16, accompanied by Martin and Johnnie Smith. The day was bright and calm—rather too hot for comfortable travelling. They accompanied me the whole way, carrying a load of about 15 lb. of biscuits each. Did the journey in four hours. Found Mr Bruce and Cuthbertson quite recovered after a couple of days' darkness in the tent. Graptolite Island was now one huge penguin rookery, mainly of adelia penguins, and on the mainland they were also very numerous. There must have been literally millions of them.

October 17.—"Final break-up of camp. In the forenoon went over to the north coast to clear up some survey points. Strong northerly wind with a heavy swell coming in, and we could see the ice breaking off the edge of the land-floe to the south: there was open water well inside the Murray Islands. It looked as if it was high time for us to bundle and go, so returned to camp at three, had tea, cached our remaining food, and set off homewards at 5 P.M. Reached Cape Whitson in an hour and three quarters: the surface was infinitely better than when we took six hours to come out. It was very dark before we reached Delta Island, and we were decidedly fagged. Had a small 'nip,' the only time we have used alcohol out of doors. It certainly had a temporary stimulating effect, but we would not have taken it even then had we not been sure of a warm cabin awaiting us at the journey's end. Reached the ship at 10.15, not quite played out, but very ready for bed."

It was just as well we returned, for a couple of days later the ice was found to be entirely broken up a little beyond Delta Island.

After our return the shore-party flitted from the ship to their quarters on The Beach, and the meteorological observations were transferred thence; but we had only been a bare week ashore, and beginning to feel at home in the house, when, early on the morning of November 2, word came from Mr Bruce to be ready to set off on the out-trail once again. This time the trip was to be by boat along the north side of the island, picking up the coast-line at the point we had reached from the Cape Dundas camp, and thus completing the map of the island.

It was the anniversary of our departure from Troon. The gig and dinghy were dragged across to the north side of the beach, launched and loaded up. The equipment on this occasion was a larger one, as the party consisted of six persons,—Mr Bruce, Wilton, Cuthbertson, and myself, and in addition MacDougall, our third officer, and Walker, commonly known as "Tanks," from his duties in charge of all lamps and store tanks on board. Both men had ample experience of boats "up North" when engaged in the pursuit of the wily leviathan, and knew what they were about among ice. Rowing out to the mouth of what we then called the North Bay, but which has since been termed Uruguay Cove in honour of the Argentine war-sloop *Uruguay,* which rescued Nordenskjöld and his party and took our successors away from the Orkneys, we were then able to set sail on the gig, in which a mast had been stepped, and take the dinghy in tow. With a strong westerly wind we fairly flew along. There were a few "bergy bits" of ice about, but they were easily dodged; it *was* good to have "left once more the solid motionless land, and, entering a ship, to sail, and sail, and sail." But the sail did not last long: in some three and a half hours we had found a suitable camping-ground on the west side of MacDougall Bay, where there was a little bit of level ground and a low ice-foot on to which we could pull the boats. The impedimenta were soon landed and tents pitched; Mr Bruce, Willie, and Mac occupying one, Wilton, Tanks, and myself the other. For beds we had this time three-man sacks, and found them even better than the two-man ones, though when any one wanted to turn, it was almost a case of "When Pa says turn, we all turn." Walker made an excellent middle-man: he had a way of disappearing to the lower half of the sack, and made a first-class foot-warmer; but how he breathed is still a mystery to me.

The day following was one such as occurs seldom in a lifetime, so full of interest was it: of wind and cloud there was none, and we were bathed in sunshine whose heat was tropical rather than polar. It began with a climb up the rocks behind the camp, hunting for snowy petrels' nests. There were no eggs as yet, but I was rewarded by an unexpected tumble down a steep slope, which resulted in nothing worse than a few scratches. We then crossed over "Mac's" bay, and, proceeding farther over the eastern ice-sheet, were able to link up our position with landmarks already fixed by our Cape Dundas survey. From a convenient ice-covered *nunatak* on the far side of the cove to the east of Watson Peninsula, there was a magnificent panorama embracing the whole north-east coast of the island with its long narrow peninsulas and intervening bays, at the heads of which were high ice-cliffs from which bits of ice, tiny bergs, were every now and again breaking off with a noise like a cannon-shot. On this side the glaciers were big enough to force their way so far that the terminal cliff was constantly washed by the waves. On the south side their rate of motion was so slow that the sea kept them truncated at high-water mark, leaving a strip of beach exposed at low-tide.

The only thing lacking in the day was colour: the sunshine was too intense to have the many delicate shades that frequently relieved the monotony. To-day there was only black, white, and blue,—greeny-blue ice, light-blue sky, and dark-blue sea flecked by the white of some pack-ice away towards Saddle Island. But what a delightful sensation it was to breast such a hill with the feeling that you were the first human being whose foot had ever trodden its summit, and whose vision had drunk in the beauty of the scene that lay spread out below you!

On a moraine to the north of this hill I found a large rookery of giant petrels, and a little later in the day we came across another one out on Watson Peninsula. At each locality there must have been about two hundred nests, placed fairly close together, though not crowded in the same way as the penguins. The nests are great affairs, composed entirely of small pebbles—about half a bushel to each nest. They run from two to three feet in diameter, and have a shallow depression in the centre, in which the bird sits. The birds were then sitting very close, but as yet there were no eggs. To get photographs we at first began stalking them yards away, but there was no need for such caution; they sat quite unconcernedly till we were within a few feet, then, with a reproachful look, shuffled off and waddled away a few yards in their ungainly manner and sat down to watch us. They seldom took flight right away unless literally rushed at. Farther out on the same peninsula was a mixed rookery of adelia and gentoo penguins.

On getting back to camp the tents had to be shifted; there was a little glacier at the back, and the strong sun had melted so much of the surface-snow that our site was being flooded. We found a drier one, and the water came in most useful for culinary operations, and by filling up the boat's breakers we had a store which saved much time in cooking. That night we had neighbours, some ringed penguins appearing on the scene. The first fellow to arrive popped up on the ice-foot, gave himself (or herself?) a shake, walked up to the small moraine here, picked up a stone and staked his claim for a nesting-site. The *quagh* of the ringed penguin is harsher than that of either of the other two species; and when two are love-making they stand facing each other, and, stretching out their necks, stick their heads straight upwards, uttering their notes,—which are more like a donkey's bray than anything else,—swing their heads backwards and forwards and in and out, then relapse once more into solemn contemplation.

November 8.—"Paid a visit to the Rudmose Rocks, where we found numerous nests of the blue-eyed shag or cormorant (*Phalacrocorax atriceps*).

"These birds resemble closely in size and shape the common shag of this country (*P. carbo*), but the plumage is very different. Instead of the uniform sooty black they have their under parts white, while the plumage of the back is brownish black with a greenish metallic lustre. Their big splay webbed feet are crimson, round the eye is a very prominent ring of a bright metallic blue, and at the base of the bill is an orange-coloured wattle,—altogether a variety of colour unrivalled in the Antarctic avifauna. Their nests are crowded together almost as closely as the penguins', and are quite elegant structures, formed of seaweeds, lichens, moss, and feathers. They evidently build on the same site year after year, for some of the nests were balanced on the top of a little pinnacle of old ones. Most were secure on the rock, but we saw a few on ice pinnacles. These must have been built on the snow, which, being protected from the sun's rays by the nest, had not melted away so quickly as the surrounding snow had done. They sat very close on the nest, even allowing themselves to be stroked. If one, more timid than its neighbours, flew off, the chances were that ere its return there was no nest to come to,—for they are arrant thieves, and those whose nests were still unfinished let slip no opportunity of getting building material thus easily. And yet we are told that only man is vile!—Perhaps.

"Laying had just begun. We obtained a dozen eggs in all, some in couples, but mostly single. The eggs are small, sharply pointed, and of a chalky light-green colour.

"At Cape Geddes, just opposite, the high cliffs showed very finely the marked dislocation and crushing the rocks have undergone in their long history, and the reefs just off-shore bore the marks of another of the many agents which modify the earth's surface—viz., floating ice. Stranded floes surging backward and forward under the influence of wind and tide have given those rocks a rounded, polished outline, different in character, however, from the polish of land-ice, and lacking the directional strife which result from the boulders carried along in the lower part of a glacier. Here we found another rookery of giant petrels, but no eggs as yet.

"In the evening we crossed over to the penguin colony near Cape Buchanan for a supply of fresh eggs for the larder—real fresh eggs, none of your Baltic and Siberian sort. A penguin's egg, tasty as a plover's, made a most appetising addition to our bill of fare. Coming back, we had a stiff time making our way through some pack-ice which was tightening under the influence of a faint north-west wind. We were more often on the ice pushing and lifting the boat than in the latter rowing: sometimes it was necessary to lift her right up on to a floe to avoid being crushed between two pieces of ice."

November 9.—"Shifted camp over to Point Thompson, on the west side of Brown's Bay. Had a similar experience to yesterday getting through the ice—only rather worse, as there were two boats to manoeuvre instead of one. Fair site for tents up on the glacier, but rather a rocky landing-slip for the boats. Visited an island near by on which was another colony of shags: many had three eggs in a clutch. With them was the usual complement of paddies (*Chionis alba*). The thieving parasites!—I saw one actually boring under the wing of a sitting shag to suck the eggs!

Being the King's birthday, as loyal subjects we celebrated the occasion by an extra feed of penguins' eggs and drinking the King's health in our medical supply of whisky: there was about a teaspoonful to each of us."

At this camp a stay of about a fortnight was made. The coast-line was soon mapped, but there was the same difficulty as at Cape Dundas in fixing the position of the hills, and the number of peaks visible from here was very great. Time hung rather heavy on our hands before the end, and one or two of the party were frequently off at the ship on holiday, for we had found quite a good road across: it was passable even for sledges, though it involved two rather steep hauls through passes in the hills. Familiarity with the road ultimately bred contempt, till one day, crossing in the mist, Walker and I, scoffing at the idea of needing a compass, lost our way on the mile and a half between the two passes. On the level ice-sheet our sense of direction was absolutely lost. We described almost a complete circle, wandered into a badly crevassed region, and finally climbed round on a spur above the pass, not knowing we were over on to the Scotia Bay ice-sheet until, descending in sheer desperation to see whether anything was visible nearer sea-level, to our great astonishment we found ourselves within about a mile of the ship. On another occasion, when out with Wilton and MacDougall, I experienced the worst fright I have ever had. Going across a steep glacier parallel to the terminal ice-cliff below, we came on a part where the surface-snow had all melted, leaving the hard blue ice exposed. Wilton and Mac, who were on ahead, pegged steadily across. I began to ruminate on what would be the result of a slip, and there is little doubt it would have meant a slip over sixty feet of ice-cliff into the sea below, without time to shake hands with myself and say good-bye. In the middle of the blue ice I stopped, paralysed with fear, afraid to move on or go back. I was just able to shout for Wilton and hang on with my ski-stick, till his jaunty unconcerned way of recrossing the patch gave me back my confidence, and I proceeded in safety. But the acute mental pain and sense of impending sudden death I had in those few seconds is a feeling I have no wish to experience again, nor yet the feeling of disgust afterwards at having allowed one's "nerves" to get the upper hand when in a little bit of a tight corner.

We were anxious to run a line of soundings along the length of one of the bays on the north coast to find out whether they were of the nature of rock-basins scooped out by the land-ice, but the constant northerly wind kept some ice always jammed up in the bays, and we never managed it. But a line we ran across the mouth of Brown's Bay, giving depths of up to eighty fathoms, is rather against their being basin-shaped like the Scottish and Norwegian fjords, shallower at the mouth than farther up.

One day we went back to Cape Geddes to collect giant petrels' eggs: as is the case with the majority of petrels, the egg is pure white, and usually there is only one, but in two instances we found two eggs in a nest. To get the eggs the birds, had to be literally kicked off: they would then sit down a yard or two off and eject the contents of their stomachs at the intruder. There was no doubt then why they received the epithet of "stinkers," commonly applied to them by the old sealers in the southern seas. They never actually attacked us, though there are instances recorded of men fallen overboard who have been attacked by them.

The Cape pigeons were nesting in thousands about the shore-cliffs, their nests being formed of a few small pebbles on a rock-ledge, or a slight hollow in the earth and stones of the scree slopes. They sat for almost six weeks clucking and cooing like doves, though it must be remembered they are not really pigeons but petrels; but laying did not actually commence till December 2, and, curiously enough, for three or four days before that date they seemed to vanish from the islands entirely, for not a bird was to be seen, although just at that time we were keeping a very close watch on birds.

Ringed penguins we studied closely in a small colony located just in front of our tenth. We could see all the routine of their daily life,—how one fetched pebbles for the nest while the partner guarded it; how, when apparently sleeping, they were very much awake and on the look-out for an opportunity to steal stones from their neighbours; how the neighbour objected forcibly with beak and flipper, while the others looked on amused or watched their chance to steal unobserved. It was as good as a sociological study of human beings. If their bad habits seemed to bulk more prominently just now (and they certainly were the more amusing to us), later on their good qualities were more in evidence when the young had to be protected, though each parent, however tender to her own offspring, was merciless to any neighbours' who might wander within reach of her beak.

A terrible example of "Nature, red in tooth and claw," was seen one day. Two skuas (*Megalestris antarctica*) fought to the death while a third, perched on a hummock near by, looked on—probably they were two males fighting for the female. Despite our abstract recognition of the doctrine of survival of the fittest and the weak to the wall, our sympathies were with the loser, especially at his terrible end, for before he was quite dead a giant petrel came up—like all carrion birds they can see their prey from afar—and literally tore him to bits. We tried a charge of No 4 shot, but they were on a floe out of range.

On Monday morning, November 23, Wilton, Mac, and Walker, who had been over at the ship for the week-end, returned with the welcome news that the open water was inside Point Davis, and if the wind lasted the ship should be free in one or two days. This was not quite unexpected, as a heavy swell had been running for some days.

Having nothing particular to do, Cuthbertson and I set off. Reaching the pass on to the Scotia Bay ice-sheet, we saw the open water only about a mile from the head of the bay, with fresh cracks opening and great pieces of floe drifting off merrily. On arrival at the ship we found every one in great spirits,—the bored expression and melancholy of the past two months had vanished; from skipper down to ordinary seaman they were one and all like schoolboys on break-up day. This time it was not a case of hope deferred. At 5 P.M. the good ship was once more afloat on the ocean wave and tugging at her cables, impatient, like all on board her, to be off.

But the final departure was delayed till the morning of the 27th, for two days passed ere it was possible to steam into Brown's Bay to lift camp, and then the dinghy and tents had to be brought back to The Beach for the use of the shore party.

CHAPTER IX

TO BUENOS AIRES AND BACK

FAIR WINDS—SOUNDING—THE BURDWOOD BANK—A DANGEROUS MISHAP—A RICH HAUL—THE FALKLANDS AGAIN—UNWELCOME NEWS—H.M.S. BEAGLE—A GOOD START—A CHAPTER OF ACCIDENTS—AGROUND—CHRISTMAS PROSPECTS—BUENOS AIRES—AN ENLIGHTENED GOVERNMENT—THE FRITHJOF—SOUTHWARD—THE HOME-LIKE FALKLANDS—PORT STANLEY—"LAME DUCKS"—SEA-LIONS—MANY BIRDS—CAPE PEMBROKE—A PLEASANT LAND—A DISCOURTEOUS SHIP—A NOVELTY IN SEA-SICKNESS—SCOTIA BAY AGAIN.

FROM the South Orkneys to the Falkland Islands, though a short journey in point of mileage, is one which is very liable to be protracted for a sailing-ship. The prevalent winds to be encountered in the Cape Horn seas are from the north of west, which is almost a direct head-wind on the course the *Scotia* had to make, and blowing, as they often do, with the force of gale, there was no question of our steaming against them. If we experienced such winds we would be driven away eastward of our course at once.

However, contrary to the accepted belief at sea, sailing on a Friday seemed to favour us. We started from the coast of Coronation Island, sounding as we went, amidst uncertain squally winds off the land; but once clear of the islands and heading N.W. by W., the weather became calm and the sea quite smooth but for a big head swell.

The water rapidly deepened as the land was left behind: that evening we had 1746 fathoms fifteen miles off the land at Penguin Point, deepening the following day to over 2000 (2180 in 59° 23′ S., 49° 8′ W.), about which depth it remained until the bottom rose up again toward the South American continental shelf.

The weather held fair and calm for another day, and we took advantage of it to make as much "westing" as possible, for then, in the event of a westerly gale, we would have less ground to lose. No ice was seen after we once were clear of Jessie Bay, and the softer air began to foretell more temperate lands than we had known for a twelvemonth. Birds were very plentiful: albatroses (*Diomedea exulans*) and sooty albatroses (*Phœbetria fuliginosa*) continually swooped in their long curve of motionless flight about the ship, and whenever we stopped for sounding the mottled brown-and-white Cape pigeons settled in the water to be fed with scraps. We often caught these birds by simply scooping them out of the water, when the ship was lying, with a large landing-net. It was curious to note their inability to escape when once liberated on the deck, for all these petrels (it was the same with the giant petrel) require a long run before they can rise on their wings, and the size of the *Scotia* would not permit this. They have the same offensive but effective habit of repelling intruders that the giant petrel has.

On Sunday evening a fair breeze from the S.S.E. filled the square sails, and the *Scotia* did over seven knots all night until we lay to again next day for sounding in thick driving snow. Practically all day was spent in this operation; and though we lost in the forenoon a deep-sea water-bottle and thermometer, with over 2000 fathoms of sounding-wire, we were more successful in the afternoon, and found the sea shoaling to 1943 fathoms. But the breeze held fair, and that night we did eight knots, and the following afternoon found ourselves on the Burdwood Bank, a day earlier than we had expected.

This is a long bank 200 miles east and west and about 60 north and south, covered with a depth of from 25 to 100 fathoms of water, and lying some 90 miles south of the Falkland Islands. We were very anxious to take a haul of the dredge on this shoal, since it promised a very rich fauna, little or nothing of which was then known. Preparations were at once made, and the trawl was put over in ninety fathoms at eight o'clock. On this occasion we experienced one of the few serious accidents that fell to our lot throughout the voyage. The winch had just made a start of hauling in the cable, when suddenly there was a terrific crash, and down came the trawling derrick on deck, smashing at a blow the port pin-rail amidships, and deeply scoring the deck before impact with the covering board brought it to rest. The pin (technically the "goose-neck") of stout 2-inch iron, by which the derrick was hinged to the main-mast, had broken right across and so released that end. It was fortunate that in its career the heavy beam met no one, for it was always one man's duty to stand below and read the meter placed there to record how many fathoms of cable had passed. Luckily for him, he had at that moment moved aside, and so without a doubt saved his life.

However, we contrived to get the trawl on board with some difficulty, and truly we had a rich reward. It was full of beasts—many fish of all sorts, tunicates and sea-urchins by the hundred, crustaceans of every kind, but particularly a wealth of bryozoa, and hosts of sponges from a few inches across to a perfect giant over two feet in height: in all, there must have been a ton of specimens in that one haul, which was far the richest of the whole voyage. Before long the laboratory was knee-deep in animals, and still the sailors brought them in by the bucketful, till Wilton and I were in despair what to do with everything. The ship was rolling heavily, and the sky had a dirty look away in the west; and as bad weather in those seas gives little warning, we deemed it inexpedient to leave any valuable specimen unpreserved, for, since all we knew, the morrow might be a day on which work of this kind would be impossible. It was long after midnight when Wilton and I had stowed away the biggest and most perishable animals, and we only turned in when Bruce came on duty for the morning watch.

Luckily that evil sky brought nothing with it, and Wednesday dawned as fair a summer day as one could wish to see. Again we worked at the catch, and many a beast was found on deck or in the interstices of the trawl that had escaped us in the darkness.

The last bottles were being stowed away shortly before noon when a report of "Land ahead" brought every one on deck. There, far off on the port bow, shimmering in the heat-rippled air, was a long purple streak on the horizon. It was like being home again to see that; we felt again linked to the world, and already the Antarctic seemed far behind.

Soon after land had been sighted Fitchie developed a bad cold: of course he blamed the land and civilisation, and he might have had cause if there had been an off-shore wind, but there was exactly the opposite. We had fain to believe that he was such a hardened sailor that the very sight of land upset him. The night of December 2 had fallen as we passed Cape Pembroke Lighthouse, dipped our ensign in salute to its astonished occupants, and entered Port William. There we stopped to drop our big trap among the kelp, and in a blaze of moonlight passed through the Narrows into Stanley Harbour. The little town seemed asleep: a few lights were blinking, but no one was about to notice our arrival despite Kerr bravely piping as we steamed up to our anchorage off the dockyard. Hardly was the anchor down than from a little British sloop-of-war a boat was to be seen approaching us. In a few moments Lieutenant Marriott, of H.M.S. *Beagle,* was on board to welcome us back, and ask us who we were and whence we came from, while we as eagerly bombarded him with a thousand questions. Then we first heard that the Swedish South Polar Expedition, under Otto Nordenskjöld in the *Antarctic,* had not been heard of since their ship left Ushuaia for the south, thirteen months ago, and that now two relief expeditions were at work searching for her. The wardroom officers of the *Beagle* most considerately sent us a heap of newspapers and periodicals, and were not a little surprised to hear we had plenty of food, and were not in the least starving. It was a strange picture that evening in the *Scotia's* cabin, and one that neither we nor Lieutenant Marriott will soon forget,—the neat uniformed officer sitting at the table, and, crowding round him, the weather-beaten explorers, clad in their well-worn and grotesquely patched clothes and rough jerseys, and with their shaggy untrimmed beards. It was a contrast between civilised and uncivilised, and only then did I realise what seeming savages we had become. Next morning we went ashore to fetch our letters—a boat-load full,—and spent a bewildering and happy morning in trying to read them all. As to the year's newspapers, we gradually read some in succeeding weeks, but soon discovered how much of the contents of a newspaper is but of ephemeral interest, and how little is vital: still to this day I am always finding gaps in my knowledge of the history of 1908, and amaze my friends with my ignorance of some of its events. We spent a week at Stanley getting stores and coal on board, and effecting a few urgent repairs. The Governor, His Excellency Mr (now Sir William) Grey-Wilson, again showed us every courtesy; and Captain Elliott and the officers of H.M.S. *Beagle* made us so free of their ship that we almost lived on board her. The first day after our arrival the Captain, Mr Bruce, Wilton, and I lunched in the wardroom, and greatly amused her officers, when they asked us what we particularly wished for, by expressing a desire to lunch on fresh potatoes and beer, two luxuries we had long been strangers to. All on board the *Beagle* were interested in natural history. Captain Elliott's favourite study was botany, and some pleasant walks in search of plants he and I had together; Surgeon Bowen spent his spare time in zoology, and Lieutenants Marriott, Cameron, and Isaacson were all keen naturalists, and many hours they one and all spent on board the *Scotia* among our collections. It was singularly appropriate that the namesake of the vessel in which Darwin made his famous cruise should be captained and officered by such men.

On December 8 the Pacific Steam Navigation Company's s.s. *Orissa* arrived on her way from Valparaiso to England, and brought with her the welcome tidings that Nordenskjöld and his fellow explorers had been rescued and brought to Buenos Aires in safety. It was good news; for to search for men in the Antarctic is much like the proverbial hunt for a needle in a haystack, and at the time we did not learn the succession of fortunate happenings that had greatly aided the search-party in finding the shipwrecked men.

The same day Mr Bruce left us on board the *Orissa* for Monte Video and Buenos Aires to cable home—for there is no cable from the Falkland Islands—and to arrange several things for us in Buenos Aires and so save time, for the *Scotia* could not expect to be there for eight or nine days at best.

Early the next morning, amid cheers from the *Beagle*, we stood out of Stanley Harbour at the height of a sou'westerly gale. Clear of Volunteer Point, out of the shelter of the land, a heavy sea was running, and the light *Scotia* rolled and pitched madly, yet made splendid progress northward at over eight knots; but unfortunately the gale did not last, and for the next four or five days we had varying fortunes of light winds and head winds, until on the morning of December 15 land loomed up ahead.

It was a stretch of low-lying sandy hills and dunes that lay before us,—evidently the coast some seventy miles west of Cape Corrientes, a headland which we had to weather. But the wind was north-east—dead against us, and our coal supply very low; so—for anchorage on the coast was unsafe—the *Scotia* was put about to S.E. by S., and crept out to sea again. Three times we tacked that day and night, but morning found us off the same coast only about five miles to windward of yesterday's position. Two more days we beat aimlessly to and fro in this manner, hoping always that the persistent north-east wind would veer a little. On the 17th Mogotes Point light was sighted ahead, which meant we were slowly creeping round Cape Corrientes; but for another three days that lighthouse was visible off and on, and we unavailingly battled with the head-wind. The little town of Mar del Plata was in sight these days; but its anchorage is quite open, and was then exposed to a heavy swell; so any hope we had of anchoring there and sending ashore a message to Mr Bruce in Buenos Aires had to be abandoned, though we knew by this time he would be getting anxious over our non-arrival. This part of the Argentine coast is a very dangerous one, for shoal-water runs far out to sea,—many days we were never in more than forty fathoms,—and from La Plata right round to Bahia Blanca is not a single safe anchorage for a ship of any size. We therefore always kept the coast at a respectful distance, especially at night, and our Thomson sounding-machine had little rest. Insects began to be very numerous on board, particularly house-flies, which rapidly became a pest, and we would willingly have dispensed with the mosquitoes, which were increasingly numerous as we reached warmer weather. This was again the sea for sun-fishes, near where we had captured one on the voyage out; and at times the dorsal fin of one showed above the surface, but we were in no mood to hunt them now.

The morning of the 20th found us off Medano Point Lighthouse, and instead of being wind-bound, for a change we lay becalmed amid a glassy sea, when suddenly, a few minutes after noon, a spanking breeze came away from the south-west, and, under full sail, we at last moved northwards. The sea being calm, there was nothing to impede the ship's progress, and it seemed that at last our old luck for good passages had returned. At 11 P.M. we passed Punta Piedras lightship at the mouth of the Rio de la Plata, and at dawn in mirage saw the Uruguayan coast; then we turned westward and headed direct for what we took to be Punta Indio light-vessel, past which the tortuous river channel lay.

Navigation in the Rio de la Plata is at all times a matter demanding care and a more than usually close look-out for dangers of many kinds. We were well prepared in having the charts of the estuary on board, and these, needless to say, had received much careful study on the captain's part. But matters are not facilitated by the no doubt necessary but exasperating warnings sprinkled through the charts and sailing-directions to tell the mariner that this lightship is reported irregular, that that one is not to be entirely depended on, that all are very liable to drift and be moored anew in slightly different positions, that other vessels are occasionally substituted without notice, that the buoys cannot be relied on, that the contour of several of the banks is imperfectly known, and that the depths vary considerably with the wind prevailing at any time.

However, we seemed to be on our right road, when suddenly, about 8 A.M., there was a heavy bump, and then another, and the *Scotia* stopped dead. The engines were rung to "Full speed astern," but to no avail—the *Scotia* was aground. A sounding showed only 13 feet of water, and the ship was drawing 14 feet 1 inch. But how it came that here, apparently full in the navigation channel, we should come on such shoal-water was beyond our comprehension. Speculation, however, was futile—we must try and get off. The water-ballast tanks were emptied into the bilge by knocking a few rivets out of each, and then the water was pumped overboard; the boats were lowered into the sea, but still, try as hard as the engines could, we made no movement. Several steamers passed us about a mile off, but we were not yet reduced to signalling for help. Towards evening a little pilot cutter was sighted bearing down on us, and soon her master was on board. Then the mystery of our whereabouts was cleared up. The lightships had been shifted; the one on the horizon was not Indio, but a new one between Indio and Chico, and we were aground in a nasty part of the Ortiz Bank. Our charts were naturally a year old, so the Captain, who had faithfully followed them, was in no way responsible for the mishap. The cutter took a letter to Buenos Aires, seventy-five miles off, informing Mr Bruce of our plight, and the pilot stayed on board. It could hardly be expected to cheer us much to hear that we had run aground in exceptionally high water, and that, there being no tides in the Plate, the rise and fall depends entirely on the way the wind is blowing. Certainly the water was steadily falling, and, as it fell, the *Scotia* bumped ominously, and lay over to starboard till her deck was a hillside; but we all had faith in her strength, and as yet there was not the least danger, though the pilot, who seemed to think her as frail as an iron ship, was not so much at ease. "If it come away to blow like hell from nor'-east ve clear out to lightship," he warned us; but I think that even in the event of that occurring he would have had to go alone. The full ignominy of our position, however, came home to us when the two red wreck-lights were hoisted on the foremast at night. Next day the pilot was out in a boat sounding in all directions for the nearest deep channel. The water rose a little and the *Scotia's* bows were free, but the deeper after-part remained fast. To ease her we tried to weight down the bows with two tanks of water and a whale-boat full of water hanging from the jib-boom, but to no avail. Equally futile was the attempt to haul her off by dropping a kedge firmly in the bank and hauling away with the winch at a steel cable attached. It was a poor prospect for Christmas, now only three days off. Our fresh meat and eggs and vegetables were done; our fresh water was more or less sour, and the temperature was 82° F. On all sides the broad sluggish river met the horizon, only broken in one spot by a lightship and in another by a half-submerged wreck, unless at the intervals in which a steamer passed. But the water continued to rise, and I awoke next morning to bear the pilot shout, "Ah, Capitano, she valks avay like hell," and, rushing on deck, I found that in truth the *Scotia* was afloat. At noon we reached the outer roads, and there had to anchor, for our coal-supply was utterly exhausted; and though the docks and town lay only fifteen miles farther on, we could not raise the steam necessary to take us there. So we lay that night among the multifarious shipping in the roads and watched pass us—though we little knew then who it was—the *Français*, with Dr Charcot's French Antarctic Expedition on board, southward bound. On Christmas Eve, with the help of a tug, we entered the docks, and so at least gained our Christmas ashore.

.   .   .   .

The month we spent in Buenos Aires was fully occupied in dry-docking the *Scotia*, repairing her broken derrick, and adding much-needed stronger brakes and supports to the drums of trawling-cable, and effecting sundry other small repairs, besides coaling and provisioning,—all of which were hampered, beyond what we had anticipated from the dilatory character of the inhabitants, by a great dock strike. However, we were helped in every way by the Naval Department, largely through the kind instrumentality of Dr Francisco Moreno, who from the day of our arrival to that of our departure was absolutely untiring in his efforts in all directions on our behalf: without his help we might have been twice as long. Mr Carnegie Ross, C.B., the British Consul, busy man though he was, always found time to assist us in a hundred different ways.

The welcome news was cabled us that funds were available—again through the generosity of Mr James Coats, jun.—for a further six months, and we could therefore make plans for another voyage toward the South, and hoped thus to be able to complete much of the projected work that time and ice had prevented us from doing the previous summer.

The plans Mr Bruce had cherished of making at Omond House, South Orkneys, a permanent meteorological station were now happily fulfilled. The Argentine Government, through its Meteorological Office, agreed to undertake the upkeep of the station for the following year if we would give a passage to the men and stores. The readiness with which the Argentine Government consented to this agreement was very largely due to the energetic enthusiasm of the head of the Meteorological Office, Mr Walter G. Davis, who, with far-seeing thoughtfulness, realised at once the importance of this observatory in relation not only to the weather knowledge of the Argentine, but to meteorological science in general. Mr W. H. Haggard, C.B., the British Minister, also gave all his weighty influence to the furtherance of the project. It is significant to note how the Argentine Government willingly spent money on a scientific object such as this, while nearer home we have had the deplorable occurrence of an ignorant Government closing one of the most important meteorological observatories in its country. It has remained for one of those oft-abused South American republics to give Britain the lead in this respect.

In Buenos Aires we had the pleasure of meeting two other Antarctic ships—the Argentine sloop-of-war *Uruguay*, which had lately returned from the rescue of the wrecked Swedish Antarctic Expedition, and also the Swedish relief ship *Frithjof*, who, under the command of Captain Gylden, had been despatched on a similar mission, but had just been forestalled by Captain Irizar on the *Uruguay*. The *Frithjof* was now on her return journey to Europe, and the freemasonry of Antarctic exploration joined her officers with us in many a happy evening before she left. In fact Buenos Aires, and particularly the British residents, treated us well, and our stay there was one round of festivities and entertainments, until we began to long to get to sea for a little respite. After many delays, we at length were ready to sail, and on the afternoon of January 21 bade good-bye to our many friends in Buenos Aires, and cast off our moorings and steamed into the river. As we left the docks, we exchanged salutes with the Italian cruiser *Liguria*, with H.R.H. the Duke of Abruzzi on board—himself a polar explorer.

There were now on board the *Scotia* three Argentines for Omond House: L. H. Valette, already a far travelled man, went as naturalist, while H. Acuña and E. Szmula went as assistant meteorologists, Mossman having consented to remain in charge, and Bill Smith having agreed to stay as cook.

The voyage back to the Falkland Islands was uneventful, and, if the winds were sometimes not all we wished, we at least had none of the exasperating experiences of the month before on our northward journey. The weather became rapidly cooler and more bracing, a not unpleasant change after the tropical heat of Buenos Aires. Several sperm whales (*Physeter macrocephalus*) were sighted, with at one moment their tails and another their truncated heads clearly in view above water. Occasionally a *Velella* floated past, but the water was getting too cold for jelly-fish of that sort.

Penguins were soon met with again (in 45° 30′ S.), and the many masses of floating kelp showed us that we were entering southern waters.

Nine days after leaving Buenos Aires, land was sighted, and at daybreak following we found ourselves once more in Stanley Harbour.

This was our third and last visit to the Falkland Islands: the first time, in January 1903, we had three weeks here; on our return from the South, in December 1903, six days; and now we spent another ten days here. On each occasion we made several excursions, both by land and water, but, unfortunately, the duty of packing and sending home collections largely curtailed our opportunities to get far afield. The first impression that the Falkland Islands gave me, and it is one that grew rather than lessened as I knew them better, is the remarkable similarity they bear in scenery to the wilder and more barren parts of western and northern Scotland. The coast-line is similarly indented by landward running lochs, and outlying rocks and islets gird the iron-bound shore. Vast stretches of undulating moorland, interspersed with peat-bogs and swamps, constitute the general type of country, unless where the land rises into rocky ridges or higher into jagged hills. In place of heather, the "diddle-dee" (*Empetrum rubrum*), a close ally of our blaeberry, grows in prolific abundance, clothing the moorlands for miles upon miles, and each in its own particular haunt various kinds of sedges flourish. The absence of trees on the islands is very noticeable. Beyond a struggling Scots fir or two and a not very thriving monkey-puzzle in the town, all of them growing in shelter, not a single tree is to be seen, for none could face the frequent strong winds that, summer and winter, sweep over the land. Possibly, however, a different state of matters once obtained, for at Hope Island, in the north of West Falkland, Mr A. H. Felton had, just before our arrival, made the discovery of several large tree-trunks and roots embedded in a clayey stratum below peat. It is, of course, not unlikely that these may be stems that have drifted across from Tierra del Fuego, but Mr Felton assured me that several of them were so placed that they gave him strongly the impression of having grown on the spot. But, speaking generally, the flora of the Falklands, though it contains very few species identical to our Scottish ones, is strangely akin, especially to a non-critical eye. No doubt similar surroundings working upon different plants have brought about this kindred facies. There is, however, one plant whose strange appearance at once struck me—that is, the bog balsam (*Bolax glebaria*), which grows in curious more or less hard cushions over rocks and stony ground, each cushion covering an extent of from a square foot to some three square yards, and being composed of hundreds of closely-set plants. It is noteworthy that in the island of Kerguelen, where much the same physical conditions obtain, though the climate is more severe, another allied plant shows the same habit.

But the most characteristic feature of the Falkland Island flora is the huge kelp (*Macrocystis pyrifera*)—a sea-weed whose long leathery fronds grow to a length of twenty to thirty and even fifty feet. A fringe of this kelp encircles all the shores and outlying rocks of the Falkland Islands, as well as the other lands in these latitudes. Its long strands are a welcome warning to sailors when they are nearing the many dangerous rocks that stud the coast, but the kelp is a less desired companion when one is trying to row a boat through its tenacious clutches. The oars stick at every stroke, and little progress can be made until one catches the trick the islanders have learnt of drawing the oars inwards over the gunwale at every pull.

The Falklands are bountifully supplied with harbours on every side, especially for smaller vessels, and there are few finer natural harbours in the world than that of Stanley—a noble stretch of three miles in length and half a mile across,—entered through the Narrows from Port William, itself a long inlet of the sea which effectually protects the harbour in all winds. Dredging would vastly improve this harbour, but with the little shipping that now enters there is ample anchorage where the depths are from twenty-five to thirty feet.

Straggling along the southern side of Stanley Harbour, in the shelter of the Murray Heights, is the little town of Port Stanley, the capital of the Falkland Islands, where about 900 of the 2000 inhabitants of this isolated colony live. Composed chiefly of wooden houses, with a few older stone crofts and a few newer and more pretentious brick houses,—some the exact counterpart of London suburban villas,—the town is not imposing; and the spireless Gothic cathedral, planned on an ambitious scale, looks strangely out of place among its dwarfed and primitive surroundings. But most visitors to Stanley do not see it with such critical eyes. Its harbour is the hard-gained refuge of many a sailing-ship, battered and smashed by the savage winds and seas off Cape Horn, and there is seldom a week when one of these "lame ducks" is not to be seen lying off the town. During our short stay there were, I think, five ships refitting broken masts and smashed bulwarks, or otherwise preparing anew for sea. The dozen or so of old hulks moored in the harbour each told its tale of some fine ship which had met its fate at the hands of storm or fire, and had struggled in here never to sail the seas again. Among these hulks lies one of historic interest—namely, the *Great Britain,* which, built in 1845, was the first iron screw-steamer and the precursor of all the modern liners. Later she was cut down to a three-masted sailing-ship, and came into Stanley with her cargo on fire some fifteen years ago. Condemned as unseaworthy, she has remained there ever since. The town of Stanley, beyond its export trade of wool, hides, and tallow, derives a lucrative income from the refitting and repairing of these victims of the sea. The inhabitants, too, have many among them who have originally come as shipwrecked sailors and elected to settle there. Half a score of little Nova Scotian and British Columbian sealing schooners make Stanley their winter quarters, whence they send home their summer's catch. They are naturally unwilling to divulge the exact whereabouts of their sealing-grounds; but doubtlessly many sub-Antarctic islands are well known to them,—better known, perhaps, than scientific geographers would believe. The few fur-seals which remain in some of the islands of the Falkland group are a Government monopoly, and, though the governor very kindly gave us permission to take a couple for specimens, we failed to find any. On Seal Rocks there were none, and time would not permit a visit to the farther-off Jason Islands. On the tussock-covered islands in Port William we heard that sea-lions (*Otaria jubata*) were to be found in large numbers; so one day half a dozen of us set sail to see them, in a crazy little 20-ton schooner yacht, the *Zillah.* With a pleasant breeze we soon covered the distance, and lay to off Tussock Island. On the rocks ashore and among the edge of the dense tussock thicket several large sea-lions could be seen. Their fine massive heads are crowned with a very creditable mane, and when they rear up on their fore-flippers to emit a long deep roar, they seem well to deserve their name of lion. They have, among the islanders, the reputation of being somewhat savage animals, and awkward customers to meet with among the tall grass; but, as I have said, there were several on the rocks, where Wilton shot a fine specimen, which with great difficulty we towed off to the *Zillah*, where our united efforts were only just sufficient to haul it on board. It was 10 feet 8 inches in length, and scaled 1200 lb. With our prize safe on board we now set out on the return journey, when, true to its wonted habit, the wind failed entirely at sunset, and we were becalmed six miles from the *Scotia*. There was no likelihood of a breeze springing up until morning, so we had to make shift to row the *Zillah* home. Only then did we quite realise what remarkably bluff bows she had; and if we had failed before to notice it, the long matted growth of seaweeds and tunicates upon her hull became at once most obvious. At barely a knot an hour we crept onwards, working like galley-slaves, and it was after midnight when the *Zillah* reached her anchorage, and we, her tired crew, put off to the *Scotia*.

On our way out we had visited the haunts of the jackass penguin (*Spheniscus magellanicus*) on William Island. This penguin lives in burrows varying from a foot to a couple of yards in length among the roots of the tussock-grass, and, with caution, one can see him sitting at the mouth taking the air, but at the least alarm away he rushes into the safety of this underground dwelling. It has a curious habit of sitting far back in its burrow eyeing the intruder, with its head turned sideways, now on one side, now on another. This penguin derives its popular name from the very close similarity between its cry and an ass's bray. Other species of penguin, notably the gentoo, breed on the northern shores of Port William, and the king penguin (*Aptendlytes patagonica*) is a not unfrequent visitor to the islands.

At the mouth of these burrows and in the nests of the gentoo are often to be found a few pebbles. The impulse of the penguin to collect these is no doubt derived from the habit either in itself or its ancestors which necessity demands in the Antarctic, where no other nest-material is available. The suggestion that these stones are used as ballast inside the penguin to enable it to dive for food is one that is hard to countenance, and it reminds me strongly of one of Bill Smith's yarns. He insisted that cranes always carried ballast in the shape of pebbles, which they "threw overboard" when they wished to rise. This he told with all gravity, and any suggestion of a smile on his listeners' faces was met with "Sure as I'm standing here, it's a God Almighty's truth," an assertion of veracity which he felt put an end to all doubt. On this island were also to be seen many pink-breasted gulls (*Larus glaucoides*), a species which, as its name indicates, has a beautiful rosy blush on its breast. Shags (*Phalacrocorax imperialis*) were also numerous; and I noticed one or two of our old friends, the giant petrels of the Antarctic (*Ossifraga gigantea*). The Falkland tussock-grass (*Dactylis cæspitosa*), though of a different species to that of Tristan da Cunha and Gough Island, is very similar in general habits. It grows in clumps to a height of six or eight feet on small elevated "bogs," as they are locally called. These "bogs" are formed no doubt by the rain washing away all the earth not bound together by roots: it is under them that the penguins burrow. The grass is largely used for feeding horses, and several boats are constantly employed in conveying it to Stanley: that, indeed, was the *Zillah's* usual work.

An excursion along the shores of Port Stanley and onwards to Cape Pembroke Lighthouse was full of interest, particularly in the many kinds of birds met with. Steamer ducks (*Tachyeres cinereus*) were very common in the placid waters of the harbour, many of them with a brood of young. This duck apparently has earned its name from its mode of flight, which is to scud along the surface of the water, sending a series of ripples behind it. They fly badly, and cannot remain long on the wing. On the shore many sparrows (*Chlorospiza melanoderma*)—a bird very like our native yellow-hammer—flitted about; and farther inland I saw one or two specimens of the brilliant crimson-breasted starling (*Sturnella militaris*). Our way led over grassy slopes and rough moorland, and the track which did apology for a road soon vanished altogether. There are indeed no roads whatever in the islands outside of Stanley, and hardly any tracks. But beyond the end of the harbour the character of the ground changed to a plain of drifting sand with a few half consolidated dunes, and which continued about three miles to the lighthouse. A few pairs of the kelp goose (*Chloëphaga hybrida*) were here met with wading about among the kelp at low-water, the male pure white, the female brown. These birds are said to pair for life; and at any rate they appear content with their one companion, for they are seldom, if ever, seen in flocks. They are extremely difficult birds to approach, not only by reason of their haunts among the kelp, but because of their extraordinarily keen senses, which warn them when the hunter is still quite out of range. A rare species which we managed to include among our collections was the king quawk (*Nycticorax obscurus*), allied to the herons. This bird is black in colour, merging through grey into white on the throat, but is at once conspicuous by the waving white plumes tinged with yellow upon its head. It would seem by the accounts of the islanders to be comparatively rare, and certainly we saw very few. At Cape Pembroke the light-keeper, Mr Pearce, met us with a hearty welcome, and had the many jars we left him the previous year well filled with specimens of all kinds. It was of interest to hear from him that one of the almost extinct sea-elephants (*Macrorhinus leoninus*) had come ashore near the lighthouse a few months past. Mr Pearce, knowing how anxious we were to secure a skeleton of this animal, had tried to kill it, but he had no rifle, and a shot-gun made not the least impression on its leathery hide. During the year another had come ashore in Port William, seemingly to die, but the skin had been taken by some sailors, and the skeleton was so buried in sand that it would have required several days' work to excavate it, not to speak of the difficulty in locating it: and so we had to rest content without this rare specimen to enrich our collections.

There could be many less congenial places to live in than Stanley, despite the bleakness of the surrounding country. The climate is very pleasant, never much above 60° F., and seldom cold enough to allow snow to lie on the ground, and rain is not excessive. The great drawback must be the scarcity of supplies and the expensiveness of every commodity except mutton and whisky. Mutton of the very finest quality ranges from 2d. to 4d. per lb., and is always plentiful; but beef is scarce, and want of enterprise makes fish somewhat hard to procure. Milk and other dairy produce is difficult to obtain, and vegetables—even potatoes and cabbages—are largely a luxury. On our third visit the little town was in a state verging on excitement over an extraordinary shoal of small herrings that had entered the harbour. It was quite an event for Stanley, and fish was for days the staple diet of the inhabitants. Probably it was the Pacific herring (*Clupea sagax*), a species well known off the coasts of Chili, which had migrated round the Horn in search of new feeding-grounds.

But generally excitement is not one of the drawbacks of Stanley, for it is one of the most isolated places in the world, with communication but once a-month from Britain and once a-month from Chili, unless an occasional cargo-boat happens to call or a warship pays a flying visit,—a delightfully uneventful place for one who loves peaceful quiet.

On February 9 the *Scotia* once more turned southward to the unknown regions. This time fortune favoured us, and we made a splendid passage across the Cape Horn seas. The *Scotia* bowled along under full sail at seven knots; a heavy swell ran after the ship and caught her on the starboard quarter, making her roll a bit, but she was deep with stores and coal and so felt it relatively little. The second day out we sighted a large three-masted ship under full sail homeward bound from the Horn. As a matter of course we flew our blue ensign, and expected her to at least show her colours; but that she refused to do—and so, out of pure laziness no doubt, committed what is considered an act of unpardonable discourtesy at sea.

Poor Acuña had been far from well on the voyage to the Falklands, and now he again took to his bunk. Home-sickness was responsible for much of his depression, though he insisted that he was sea-sick; but, if he really was, I never before saw a sea-sick man who got through three large meals a-day, beside an extra lunch at 11 A.M. of a few cold chops.

The hourly meteorological observations had again been resumed as soon as we left the Falklands. Wilton took his regular water samples every four hours for density determinations, and I continued my collecting of *plankton* samples, occasionally, however, at such high speeds suffering the loss or bursting of a net. But otherwise little scientific work was done, for we were pushing on to more southern and less known waters. Had the wind allowed it, Mr Bruce hoped to steer for midway between the South Orkneys and Clarence Island to determine by a sounding if a submarine ridge joined Orkneys and Shetlands; but the wind hauling into S.S.W. this proved impracticable, and we headed for Laurie Island. On February 14, at 3 A.M.,—that is, four and a half days after leaving Stanley,—

land was sighted. We steamed along the northern coast in blustery and snowy weather, sighting ice again for the first time this voyage. As we turned into Jessie Bay we saw again The Beach and settlement; and when the Scottish Lion ran up at the cairn we knew we were seen by the inhabitants of Omond House. Soon after the anchor was let go in Uruguay Cove, and Mr Bruce went ashore to greet the party and bring them all on board to enjoy a dinner of fresh mutton and fresh vegetables. The story of how the summer had been spent will be told by Pirie's pen.

Summer was now fast going, and time was consequently very precious if we wished to get far into the Weddell Sea before winter forced a retreat. But the Argentine stores had to be landed, and a busy week was spent at Scotia Bay in doing this and in getting our men's goods and chattels aboard and fixing a new wooden roof on the house over the old canvas one. But all hands worked well, and with favourable weather to aid us we were ready to say good-bye to Mossman and his party on February 21, and set out on our second voyage of discovery.

CHAPTER X

THE SUMMER PARTY ON THE SOUTH ORKNEYS

MAROONED—LIFE IN OMOND HOUSE—THE OLD MAN OF THE SEA—SUMMER THAWING—INSECTS—A VISIT TO A RINGED PENGUIN ROOKERY—CAPE PIGEONS—SNOWY PETRELS— STORMY PETRELS—MIDSUMMER WEATHER—GLACIER MOVEMENT—HOURLY OBSERVATIONS—CHICKENS—MASSACRE OF THE INNOCENTS—SKUAS—SHEATHBILLS—HIGH-DAYS AND HOLIDAYS—ANXIETY FOR SCOTIA—*PREPARING TO TIGHTEN OUR BELTS—A THIRTEEN-MONTHS' MAIL.*

THE party of six left on The Beach in "Omond House" during the absence of the *Scotia* was made up as follows: Mossman, in command; Cuthbertson, Ross, and myself; William Martin, who had left the ship's company and signed on to the scientific staff at the time of the transference of the meteorological observations from the ship to the shore in the end of October, and was by this time an experienced observer; and last, but not least, William Smith, commonly known as Bill, second steward on the ship, cook and handy-man ashore, and a thoroughly handy-man he proved to be. But "Russ," our Samoyede sledge-dog, must not be forgotten; he remained behind while the others were taken back to Port Stanley. Our instructions were to carry on the hourly meteorological observations, and to do as much other scientific work—physical, geological, zoological, and botanical—as possible.

Who took the observations during the day was usually a matter for daily arrangement, and depended on the other work that was going on. The night-watch began at 10 P.M., and was taken every second week by Mossman,—Ross and Cuthbertson coming on alternately the other week. The duties included keeping the stove alight, and after taking the 3 A.M. observation, the preparation of a cup of coffee or cocoa for the morning-watchman, who was wakened at 3.30. The morning-watch ran from 4 A.M. to 8 A.M., and was taken alternately by Martin and myself. Bill had to be awakened at six o'clock to prepare breakfast, and the remaining sleepers roused up at intervals between seven and eight o'clock. We had only one washstand, hence the necessity of coming *seriatim*. A morning cold tub was a luxury not indulged in, as we were none of us enthusiasts enough to take a dip in a sea whose temperature never rose above 33° F., and was more commonly about 30° F.—*i.e.*, under the freezing-point of fresh water. But do not suppose we never had a bath; the porch made an excellent bath-room, even if a little snow-drift did blow in on one; and a good tubful of hot water could be had in the evening merely for the trouble of bringing in a few extra lumps of ice to melt in the big pot on the top of the stove.

A short description of the internal arrangements of the house may not be out of place here: the building thereof has been dealt with by Brown in a previous chapter.

The internal dimensions were about 14½ feet square. To the left of the doorway on entrance stood the stove or "bogie," bagged from the ship's fo'c'sle; behind it was a set of rough shelves for pots and pans, and alongside stood a large copper for holding water. From the funnel to the wall behind were stretched wires, over which wet clothes or washing could be hung to dry. Along the west side were slung four hammocks, two tiers of two abreast; underneath the guys and along the walls were ranged our kit-bags.

The two beds were formed by spring-mattresses from cabin berths resting on boxes of baking-powder, pickles, and such other provisions as could not be risked in the outside store for fear of damp or frost. In the corner nearest the door was the "pantry press," built of packing-case wood, and between it and the east window the washstand. That and the chest of drawers in the far corner were taken from one of the ship's cabins, and were the only things in the house out of keeping with their surroundings. They offended one's sense of the fitness of things. What right had machine-cut boards, bevelled glass, and glaring varnish where everything else bore the stamp of individual workmanship, and was in perfect artistic sympathy with its environment? To be consistent, I suppose we should have followed the law, "To cast out that which offendeth." In that case, perhaps the spring-mattresses should also have gone, but being hidden beneath homely blankets, they did not offend the eye; and in extenuation of our inconsistency, let it be said of all the articles which offended our artistic sensibilities, that they ministered very materially to our creature comforts, and might hence plead justification for their continued existence. Over the chest of drawers were a couple of bookshelves, and between it and the north window hung the station barometer. The sill of the window projected inwards as a small table, and this formed the meteorological office. In the centre stood the dining-table, about four feet square, and formed of boards fastened on to two large cases of cocoa. At meals one of the party sat on the edge of a bed, which came close up to the table, the remainder gathered round on camp-stools.

We had a stock of coals and provisions left sufficient to last a full year, in case of any unforeseen event preventing the return of the *Scotia*; but we were by this time so fond of penguin that, in one form or another, it appeared at every meal of the day. Breakfast usually consisted of porridge and penguin eggs, with bacon on Wednesdays and Saturdays, and coffee or cocoa week about. For mid-day lunch there were eggs again, with bully beef, or bread-and-cheese and tea. Dinner at five consisted most days of the week of penguin "hare-soup," stewed penguin, with some farinaceous pudding or preserved fruit to follow.

When the day's work was done we would gather round the stove for a quiet smoke and yarn, varied occasionally by lively, if somewhat diffuse, arguments on such subjects as Evolution, The Irish Question, Idealism in Art, Socialism, &c. At yarning it was a case of one man first and the rest nowhere—for Bill, when wound up, would relate his salted-down experiences and adventures in every corner of the globe. How they all came to be crowded into one life is still somewhat of a mystery, for on adding up the number of years we ascertained he had spent on different ships and ashore, we found he had lived, at the most moderate computation, a hundred and forty-three years! Good old Bill! But the yarns were excellent and inimitably told, for he was a born raconteur. So much for our life indoors. The first piece of work to be done outside was to put up the two tents, one to be used for bird-skinning and the other for general zoological work; and after that two boat-slips had to be dug through the ice-foot, one on either side of The Beach. On the Scotia Bay side the ice-foot where the floe had broken off was from twelve to fifteen feet thick, but consisted largely of compact drift-snow, and was fairly easily shovelled.

On November 29 the summer warmth was already making itself felt, and in the middle of The Beach, which was lower than either of the two sea-fronts, was a small pool of water partly formed from snow melting *in situ*, and partly from water running down from the cliffs on one side and the glacier on the other. As the summer wore on this pool gradually enlarged until nearly half The Beach was free of snow, and it formed a very convenient water-supply, although it became necessary to dig through some part where it was still snow-covered, as the open pool was a favourite bathing-place for skuas. On this date I found some insects amongst the stones at the bottom of the pool: they belonged to the *Collembola*, and were quite lively although under a foot and a half of water at a temperature of 32° F. Only two other species of insects were found in the islands,—one a small black *Acarinid*, on stones about the beach and penguin rookeries, the other a tiny red mite, living amongst patches of moss.

During the first fortnight of December our excursions were mainly to the north; after that we were restricted to Scotia Bay, partly on account of the difficulty in hauling the dinghy across The Beach when the surface was clear of snow, and partly because of the heavy surf and rough bouldery beach on the north side.

In that time we did a little sounding and dredging from the boat in Uruguay Cove, but went mainly after birds. Out at Route Point there was a large rookery entirely composed of ringed penguins. The rookery extended along the low rocky coast at least half a mile. It was so crowded that many of the birds were forced to climb to a height of two or three hundred feet up the rising ground at the back in order to find room for a nesting-site; the highest must have had nearly a couple of hundred yards' journey to and from the shore,—quite a long walk when much of it consisted of jumps and hops from rock to rock. There was on an average one nest per square yard, and I reckoned there were about 200,000 birds in this one rookery.

The nests were very rough affairs—only a few pebbles scraped together; probably the supply was too small to go round. Each contained two, or very rarely three, eggs, similar in size and colour to those of the other two species. Of these we gathered a large number, both for culinary purposes and for collections. The habits of the ringed penguin are very like those of the black-throated species, but the former is even more pugnacious and more game than the plucky little adelia penguin.

On approaching the confines of a rookery a very babel of harsh, shrill, angry cries commences,—not that it was quiet before, far from it, but now the noise is deafening. You can see their "back hair" standing up straight, a trait which they share with the black-throats, and one which gives them a very fierce expression. Their fighting qualities become more apparent when one is in their midst: they believe in doing as they expect to be done by,—only doing it first, and often attack the intruder unprovoked. Even high sea-boots are not always an adequate protection, for I have seen them take a running jump and fasten on behind, inflicting a hard bite with their beak and at the same time striking vigorously with their flippers. Even Russ, who could out-manoeuvre most penguins, was fain sometimes to retreat, tail between his legs, before a properly enraged ringed penguin,—and that a single bird—not one in a rookery, into which he would never venture.

In the steep cliffs under Mount Ramsay, and on the somewhat less precipitous shores on the opposite side of the cove, were numerous nesting-places of the snowy petrel (*Pagodroma nivea*) and Cape pigeon (*Daption capensis*). The former made its nest—or, rather, laid its single egg—usually in deep cracks or crevices of the rocks. A large cave under Mount Ramsay was evidently a favourite nesting-place, for the floor was deeply carpeted with guano, in hollows of which about a dozen eggs were found. This cave, about twenty feet above the present sea-level, is beautifully polished by the action of the waves, and, along with the various raised beaches around the island, shows there has been a fairly recent slight elevation of the land,—although previous to this there are, as I have already mentioned, evidences of depression.

The Cape pigeon, on the other hand, made its nest of a few small angular fragments of stone on the open ledges of the cliffs, or scraped a hollow in the earth of the scree slopes. Although known to breed on South Georgia and Kerguelen, the eggs had hitherto never been obtained, so that on December 2 we made a good find in getting several specimens, and on succeeding days were able to add considerably to our stock. Like most petrels, they have a single, pure-white egg, large in size proportionately to the bird. Collecting the eggs of these two species was not altogether pleasant: they have developed to the full the petrel habit of ejecting the contents of their stomachs at intruders, and the oily red semi-digested *Euphausiæ* on which they feed had an evil smell which clung very persistently about one's clothes.

The downy slate-coloured young were not hatched till January 13, giving the long incubation period of six weeks.

One day, while after Cape pigeons, I heard a curious whistling coming from a cleft rock close to the shore, and, on investigating, found a nest and what I took to be a pair of Wilson's stormy petrels, but on capturing one found it to be a slightly larger bird, all black except the white under surface and white-tinged rump feathers. It turned out to be the species known as *Fregetta melanogaster*, previously known in South Georgia.

The dainty little stormy petrel of Wilson (*Oceanites oceanicus*) was common in the cliffs above the house, and doubtless all round the coasts. The nests, under boulders in the screes and in deep narrow cracks of the cliffs, would seldom have been found if we had not had Russ to smell them out. Their eggs were not laid till the middle of January, and no young had hatched when we left the Orkneys on February 21. They seem habitually to lay too late, or else there had been a succession of cold summers previous to this one, for, along with the single fresh egg, two or even three unhatched eggs of previous seasons and occasional dead nestlings were almost always to be found. This little wanderer seems to nest only in the various sub-Antarctic islands, but at other seasons ranges far and wide across the oceans, being found even as far north as Labrador.

The weather of December was not of the character one usually associates with midsummer. The mean amount of cloud (overcast sky = 100) was 93, greater than that of any month except March; snow-fall was recorded at 212 of the hourly observations, a record only just exceeded during the month of August; but the total quantity that fell was small, and accumulation on the glaciers is certainly not at a maximum in summer here as it appears to be in Graham Land, according to the observations of Nordenskjöld. The mean shade temperature for the month was actually under freezing-point, being 31°.5 F., but the range was small, only from 40°.8 F. to 25°.4 F. Notwithstanding this apparently low temperature it felt much warmer, and we frequently went about quite comfortably in shirt-sleeves and bare-headed, or else wearing broad sun-hats for protection from the sun and the reflected glare off the snow. There was not much bright sunshine,—

only seventy-three hours for the month,—but what there was, was very warm, the black bulb *in vacuo* registering once 165° F., which was more than it ever recorded in the tropics.

These relatively warm temperatures had a great effect on the scenery: much more naked rock was exposed, and some plateau-like places were found thickly carpeted with moss, some patches of it being nearly an acre in extent, and several boat-loads of this moss were brought up to cover over Ramsay's grave.

The ice-foot, between the action of sun and sea, gradually diminished in size, so that about the beginning of February, instead of having to haul the boat up fifteen feet of a slip by means of a "handy billy" rope and tackle, it had to be pulled over the shingle on oars as improvised rollers.

At the house the melting had rather disastrous effects, for it was discovered that the ground sloped very rapidly away from the wall nearest the sea, and the foundations had not been quite sunk to the solid beach. Sand is notoriously bad to build on, but snow in summer is worse, as we found when the wall began to collapse. Some underpinning and rebuilding of the walls had to be done, and ultimately a buttress terrace built right along the east side and in front of the door, till it looked like the stoep of a South African house, only lacking the verandah. Luckily the building material was easily obtained from the adjoining screes,—there was no quarrying to be done, as in the winter building.

The effect wrought by summer on the ice-sheets was not less striking. On the terminal snouts most of the surface-snow melted, exposing the hard blue ice underneath. Ribs of water traversed the surface, and sometimes plunged into the depths through crevasses or moulins, to emerge again as small cascades on the terminal ice-cliffs, or underneath the sole of the glacier. Travelling over the surface became less pleasant: it gave one a nasty jar when a snow-bridge gave way alongside one's ski, exposing a yawning crevasse extending deep into the ice. I was keen to be lowered down a crevasse to examine the structure of the ice, and take its temperature at various levels. Observations in the winter showed that with a range of 56° F. in the air temperature, a thermometer sunk six feet into the glacier only showed a range of 9° F., and waves of heat or cold took five days to reach that depth. It would have been very interesting to have found out where a constant temperature was maintained, and what that temperature was, but want of tackle prevented my going down. A thermograph lowered to a depth of about sixty feet in a crevasse for some hours kept steadily at 32° F., but whether that was actually the same as the ice temperature is uncertain.

That these glaciers or ice-sheets moved very slowly was shown by the long persistence of the snow-talus in front of the ice-cliffs, and the infrequency of ice-falls. Direct measurement from a line of pegs sunk in the ice gave a rate of under three feet for the nine months, April 1903 to February 1904. That is even slower than Mark Twain's famous glacier journey in the Alps.

Throughout the summer, trapping, dredging, and tow-netting were systematically carried on, but nothing very strikingly different from the winter catches was obtained, unless, perhaps, some large brachiopods, and a new species of heart-shaped sea-urchin. In addition to this, various lines of sounding were run over parts of the bay untouched during the winter months.

Mossman and Martin took several sets of hourly magnetic observations over five-day periods to ascertain the daily variations: these were in addition to the ordinary observations for dip, variation, and intensity. Somehow they generally managed to light on a period of snow and drift, when the interior of the observatory hut was not improved by the frequent opening of the door to let in the observer, who had first to carefully empty his pockets of any iron articles, and at night took the readings with a copper lantern. Even such small details as an absence of metal buttons on one's clothes had to be attended to when taking these delicate observations.

Such was the enthusiasm aroused for hourly observations, that one member of the staff actually kept some penguins tethered near the house for the purpose of taking their temperature every hour, and pressed other members into the service so as to have a complete record for the twenty-four hours. I must state that at the end of its spell each bird received its well-earned liberty, and thus escaped the fate of so many—the frying-pan.

There are two ways of preventing the cold from lowering the body temperature to an undue degree—by producing more heat, or by preventing its escape. The flying-birds of these regions seem to follow the first plan mainly, for a temperature similar to that of most birds (108°-110° F.) is maintained with little more subcutaneous fat than is found on sea-birds in more temperate climates. The penguins and seals have adopted the other plan, and the escape of heat is prevented by the thick layer of blubber underneath the skin. In the winter this layer is about four inches thick in the seal, and from half to one inch in the penguin. The temperature of the seals is about 96°-98° F., and of the penguins 103°-105° F.

Man follows both principles—he wears more clothes and eats more food, especially such heat-forming substances as fats and cereals; but we never suffered from that "fat hunger" so eloquently described by Nansen in his 'First Crossing of Greenland,' finding that a liberal diet of carbohydrate food (bread, biscuits, oatmeal, &c.) served amply for the supply of the necessary caloric.

The most interesting part of the summer work was the study of the young birds in their rookeries. The adelia and gentoo penguin chicks were hatched about the middle of December, those of the ringed penguin some three weeks later, and for the first month the parent birds had a busy and anxious time feeding and protecting the youngsters. The young adelias are covered with a dark, almost black, down. The ringed species is of a pale grey tinge, but becoming darker before the down is cast, while the colour of the gentoo chicks is of an intermediate hue, only darker on the back than in front.

12. *The piper and the penguin*

13. *The crew of the* Scotia *on the ice off Coats Land, 12th March 1904*

14. *The* Scotia *icebound off Coats Land*

15. *The ship's engineer, Allan George Ramsay*

16. *Allan Ramsay's grave on Laurie Island*

17. *The expedition shore house on Laurie Island, Omond House, named after Robert T. Omond who had advised Bruce on the design of an Antarctic observatory*

18. *The cook, William Smith, inside Omond House*

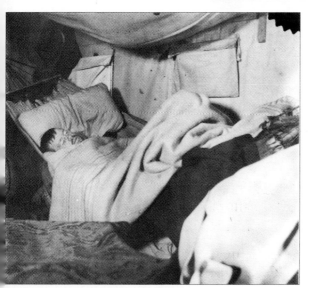

19. *A well-earned rest in the comfort of Omond House*

20. *Scottish and Argentine scientific staff at Omond House*

21. *The* Uruguay

22. *The Scotia returns to the Clyde after a 20-month voyage of discovery*

The young have voracious appetites and grow rapidly. It is a funny sight to see a poor emaciated parent being chased by two fat chicks as big as herself, demanding loudly to be fed, with cries of Maa, Maa, like a young lamb.

By the time they are three weeks old they carry quite a little geological museum of pebbles in their stomachs; but whether they pick these up on their own account, or receive them with their food from the parent bird, I never found out. When about a month old they begin to lose their down, and at this time present a very dirty bedraggled appearance, for the rookeries by then are like quagmires, and the birds are daubed and caked all over with the mud and dirt. At the same time the stench is abominable: when the wind was in the proper direction we used to be able to smell it strong at the house, a mile and a half away.

After a month the young are left more to their own resources, clumps of ten or twenty of them standing about the rookeries with only a few old birds on the outskirts for protection. When about six weeks old they are able to take to the water and forage for themselves. The old birds quickly fatten up, for in the beginning of February we found them of sixteen and seventeen pounds weight, and they had almost disappeared from the islands by the middle of that month, apparently leaving the young to follow them out to the open sea The adelia penguins have at first white throats, but after moulting the adult black-throated stage is reached.

In the water the penguins have only one enemy, the sea-leopard, which has been seen to come up alongside a floe on which the penguins were resting, seize one in its huge jaws, and sweep down again with its prey.

But on shore during the nesting-season they have several natural enemies to contend with,—paddies, skuas, and nellies,—and the death -rate among the young birds must be high. The giant petrels or nellies are probably the worst offenders: if not so numerous they are larger, and certainly more rapacious, than the others. Abundant remains of recently-killed chicks may be found all over the rookeries, while nellies, filled to repletion, waddle round the outskirts or sleep on the neighbouring snow-slopes. Nemesis, in the person of Russ, sometimes overtook an unwary sleeping murderer and sent him to join his victims in the happy hunting-grounds; and at almost any time, when pursued, they had first to disgorge some of their ill-gotten meal before being able to take the wing, even with the necessary preliminary run.

The skuas (*Megalestris antarctica*) took their toll of the penguins chiefly in eggs, to a lesser extent in young chicks. Their nests were made in the patches of moss which covered some of the rock plateaus at heights of from one to four hundred feet near the penguin rookeries. One or two were also found on the moraines,—hollows excavated in the earthy *débris* and lined with moss and lichens. Two eggs were laid, very similar in colour to those of the common gull. An amusing trick was played on one skua by substituting a penguin egg for its own. The deception was not at first discovered, for the bird was seen sitting happily on the egg afterwards; but in the course of a few days the change was found out, and doubtless the egg was eaten: at all events, no trace of it could be seen on our return visit.

Soon after the young skuas were hatched they would run from the nests on our approach and hide in holes in the moss. It was then almost impossible to find them, so like were they in colour to the light-brown of the dead moss. Meanwhile the parent birds would be shrieking defiance and flying around, making great swoops within a yard or two of our heads, but never actually attacking.

The skuas were frequent visitors to The Beach, on fine days to bathe in the large fresh-water pool,—a pastime of which they were very fond,—and at all times in search of scraps of food. It was no uncommon sight, when seated at meals, to see through the doorway three or four skuas fighting over the remains of a penguin from which our dinner had just been cut off, and to judge by their attitudes and loud screams, the language they used must have been very bad indeed,—worse even than that with which penguins greeted visitors to their homes, and hurled after them as they sped the parting guest.

The last enemy of the penguins is the sheathbill or paddy (*Chionis alba*). This bird is unique in the Antarctic avifauna in being non-web-footed, and since the land produces nothing in the way of nourishment, it lives in a state of practical parasitism on the other birds, dependent on their leavings and refuse. Every rookery had its complement of paddies, and their nests were built in rock-clefts or in holes under boulders, in close proximity to the nests of the penguins. They were not content, like Lazarus, to wait for the crumbs to fall from the rich man's table, but believed in helping themselves, as their nests testified, being built of egg-shells, and bones and feathers of penguins. I must confess to a dislike to this bird,—illogical, of course, for it was simply obeying the first law of nature— self-preservation; but its thieving ways seemed so mean and despicable compared with, say, the straightforward, bold depredations of the skua. They laid three deeply-blotched eggs, and brought forth young with bare patches at the base of the bill, more repulsive-looking than their parents.

Having now described the bird-life at some length, I may return for a little to our own doings. Most days passed off very quietly in the routine of work, but it happened that three of the party had birthdays to celebrate during the absence of the ship. These and Christmas and New Year's Days were observed more or less as holidays, and honoured with special banquets. The *menu* of Christmas Day was Bill's *chef-cl'œuvre*. Here it is in full:—

Tomato Soup.
Roast Pheasant.
Penguin à la Scotia.
Potatoes.   Brussels Sprouts.

Plum-Duff à la Drift.
Preserved Fruit.
Coffee.   Cigars.

The wine-cellar was ransacked, and a single bottle of champagne was discovered to have somehow found its way ashore. With this we drank the toast of "Absent Friends," and then proceeded to have a lively argument on the subject of Home Rule, coming to the conclusion that it would be far simpler to do without any government at all. Were we not getting on very well without one in our No-man's Land?

We were, in fact, advocates for, and practical exponents of, the Simple Life; for such a feast as that just given was a rare exception. Tobacco was almost our only indulgence. A single glass of grog was allowed to those who wished it on Saturday nights; more was not usually desired, for after one celebration at which this moderate limit was exceeded, even the old shellback Bill had to admit to a headache next morning.

In January the weather conditions were very similar to those of December, but with even more cloud (93 per cent) and less sunshine (49 hours). The mean temperature, however, rose to 32°.3 F., actually over freezing-point; snow and drift were almost absent, and very light winds prevailed. This last feature was perhaps the most marked difference between the summer and the other seasons, in which wind was the *motif* of the weather-song, with gales, blizzards, and hurricanes for variations of the theme.

We tried on various occasions to have kite-flights for the purpose of investigating the meteorology of the higher strata of the atmosphere, but always unsuccessfully. Most days the wind was too light to raise the kite, and the others were too squally. The situation was largely responsible for the squalls,—The Beach being like the constriction of an hour-glass between the two wide bays, and with high cliffs on a third side,—but no other was available. The kite three times carried away and had to be rescued by boat from the water.

All summer seals were frequent visitors, especially our winter companion the Weddell seal (*Leptonychotes weddelli*). Often a hundred could be counted lying on a small raised beach on the west side of Scotia Bay, asleep on the pebbles. Their custom seems to be to have a square meal consisting largely of cuttle-fish, but also fish, small crustacea, and mollusca, which they must grub off the bottom, then to come ashore and sleep for a week while digesting. They sleep turned over almost on their backs, every now and again giving a scratch with the uppermost short fore-flipper. When approached they look up with a sleepy stare and then go asleep again, and will not move off unless vigorously roused. Most of them were changing their coats in January, and many had scars about their bodies. These have been attributed to grampus, but from their situation I think they are more probably inflicted by each other, though a few may be the results of cuts by rough ice. The spotted sea-leopard (*Stenorhynchus leptonyx*) was the next most common. This seal often attains a length of eleven or twelve feet; it has a long slim body, and a big ugly head armed with a vicious mouthful of teeth. It cannot be played with in the same way as the Weddell seals, on whose backs we used sometimes to ride, as a certain individual is said to have done on turtles, but is best approached behind a loaded rifle. Its teeth show that it is a true carnivore, but when penguins and fish are not available it is not above eating shrimps and other crustacea such as the *Euphausiæ*, which form the staple diet of so many Antarctic birds and beasts.

A few specimens of the crab-eating seal (*Lobodon carcinophaga*) were seen. This seal is more typically found on the pack-ice of the open. Why it is called crab-eating is rather a puzzle, as Antarctic crabs are almost as rare as Iceland snakes. Its diet is chiefly the small crustacea which swarm about the ice-floes, and its teeth seem to serve the same purpose as the baleen of the right whale— viz., that of a strainer to separate out its food from the water.

Only a single Ross seal was observed.

We were fortunate enough to get some more bird novelties before the *Scotia's* return. Two fine albino penguins were captured—one of the adelia species, which had a slight mousey tinge where the normal black feathers are; one of the ringed species, pure snow-white, with just a suspicion of the bridle round the neck, sufficient to recognise the species. This bird was also remarkable in having a few insect parasites,—a very rare thing here, in marked contrast to the infested birds of the Arctic.

Several specimens of the "Macaroni penguin" (*Catarrhactes chrysolophus*) were captured. This fellow has a fine yellow crest over each eye, and as the crest is known sometimes to be of a deep orange, it may have been this bird that Larsen reported, ten years previously, from the islands. Two of the birds were quite young, and must have been reared in the group. The nearest previously known habitat was South Georgia, 500 miles away, so that this find made a great extension southwards of its range from the sub-Antarctic region into the home of the more truly Antarctic birds.

Towards the end of January we could talk of nothing but the probable date of the ship's arrival. We were longing for news from home, and at the same time it was very tantalising to see the fine open summer slipping away, and with it our chances of pushing far south into pastures new.

A grand sweepstake was opened, but no one drew the prize, as all the dates were short of that of the actual arrival.

When February dawned we began seriously to wonder whether some accident or misfortune had not befallen her, and to discuss schemes for our own future. One winter we could face easily enough, and two at a pinch, but afterwards . . .? If the ship had by any possibility been lost, we had to depend on ourselves for relief, and our chances of making Cape Horn or the Falklands, 800 miles away and against contrary winds, were small enough. The dinghy was impossible; the old whale-boat was our forlorn hope, but it would have needed a lot of patching up.

Such a possibility was never really anticipated, but in case of eventualities, the second week of February was devoted to putting the walls of the house and store in thorough repair. Clothes were patched up, and some experiments in preparing seal's skins for boots were commenced. We took stock of our provisions, and were to go on strict rations on Monday the 15th. On the Sunday forenoon I was engaged in making a set of chess-men with which to help pass the winter, the others were darning and mending, when Martin went out to take the mid-day observation. He seemed a long time over it. Then we heard a shout, and saw him cutting capers and gesticulating wildly. Surmising at once what was up, we ran up our flag on the cairn to show all was well, and went over to the north beach to see the ship, which was by this time well into the bay. Seeing a strange flag on the fore-peak, we guessed it was an Argentine one, and that the chief had succeeded in bringing down a party to carry on the Station. Not to seem too anxious, we returned to lunch and allowed the visitors to seek us out, but all the same were very glad to go on board to greet the old friends and welcome the new arrivals. It was a treat to see some new faces, a pleasure to once again taste fresh food; but best of all was the news from home. Just think of it,—thirteen months without a letter or a paper! It was well into the night before the letters were all devoured, and luckily none of us received bad news. After letters, pictures interested us most; newspapers could wait.

CHAPTER XI

SECOND CRUISE IN THE WEDDELL SEA

ALBATROS—SOUNDING ON A WHALE—ROSS SEAL—A GREAT ICE-BARRIER—COATS' LAND—PART OF THE ANTARCTIC CONTINENT—NIPPED BY THE ICE—ANXIOUS DAYS—PREPARING FOR ANOTHER WINTER—EMPEROR PENGUINS—FREE ONCE AGAIN—DIFFICULT TRAWLING—ABYSMAL FAUNA—"CHANTEYS"—THE END OF ROSS' DEEP—TEMPESTUOUS SEAS—"ANOTHER BERG ON THE LEE BOW, SIR"—LOSS OF A BOAT—DIATOM OOZE—FAREWELL TO THE ANTARCTIC—SHALLOWING WATER—GOUGH ISLAND IN SIGHT.

ON February 22 we bade our final good-bye to the South Orkneys, Mossman remaining behind in charge of the Argentine party,—also Smith, who had volunteered to stay on as cook. We skirted the north coast of Laurie Island to fix the position of two outlying rocks (too far out to be marked on the accompanying map), then the survey, so far as we were concerned, was finished.

We were once more southward bound—following the traditional policy of the inhabitants of Scotland, laid down at least as far back as the Old Red Sandstone days, and faithfully adhered to during successive æons. Even in those early days of the world's history, if the geological record is to be believed, the fishes meditated invasions of England, for their fossil remains are found *all* with their heads turned southwards towards the border!

We did not, however, go due south, but south-east, with the object of cutting between our two tracks of the previous year. Within fifty miles of the land, in addition to Cape pigeons, Wilson's stormy petrels, and snowy petrels, we met in with sooty albatroses (*Phœbetria fuliginosa*), blue petrels (*Halobena cerulea*), and silver petrels (*Thalassæca glacialoides*); the two former of these were never seen at the Orkneys, and the latter only very rarely.

On the 25th, when stopped for sounding, we obtained a specimen of Hutton's albatros (*Phœbetria cornicoides*). This species differs from the sooty albatros only slightly, in having the plumage of the back and breast greyer, and the stripe on the mandible is pale-blue, and not yellow as in the better known sooty albatros. Both these species range farther south than the great white or wandering albatros (*Diomedea exulans*), which always keeps some distance north of the ice-pack. It was the shooting of a sooty albatros, as narrated in Shelvocke's 'Voyage Round the World' (1726), that supplied Coleridge with the idea elaborated in 'The Ancient Mariner.' The bird hovering about them for days while they had tempestuous contrary winds was imagined from his colour to be of ill omen, and shot.

They often followed us and were occasionally shot, not as ill omens, but for museum specimens: their flight is not quite so graceful as that of the wandering albatros, as they not unfrequently flap their wings, which the wandering albatros never seems to do.

The weather was quiet, very few bergs were encountered, and no pack-ice seen until we came to the Antarctic circle in about 32° W. long. Here we met in with some loose streams of pack which appeared closer to the south, so that we were compelled to make a slight detour eastwards to round them. Sounding there on February 27, a curious incident occurred. When about 1000 fathoms of wire were out, the machine stopped dead as if the bottom had been reached, but then ran on again, touching bottom in 2630 fathoms. The probability is the sounder landed on some large fish or on a whale—there were some playing around the ship at the time, but it seems an impossible depth for them to descend to: whatever it was, I expect it had rather a surprise when sixty pounds of iron dropped whack on its back—a novel form of bolt from the empyrean.

On the 28th we captured a youngish specimen of the Ross seal (*Ommatophoca rossi*). This seal, perhaps the rarest of all seals, only occurs singly in the open pack. On the *Scotia* only two were seen altogether, one on each trip, and one was observed in the summer at the Orkneys, but not captured. It has a somewhat striped hide, and is described by M. Racovitza of the Belgian Expedition as "le plus phoque des phoques, car chez lui toute forme de quadrupede a disparu. Son corps n'est plus qu'un sac fusiform pourvu de membres trés reduites." Its most remarkable feature is the thick neck, giving it an appearance not unlike a pouter pigeon. This swelling is caused by a great development of the larynx, which, acting like a resonator, gives the animal a very curious voice.

On March 1 we crossed our track of the previous year, getting a clear run to the south under canvas only, where a year before there was impenetrable pack, and a sea freezing up for the winter. There is little doubt the summer 1903-04 was a very open one all over the Antarctic, and had circumstances been such that we could have struck south a month earlier, a much larger part of new coast-line might have been traced. But regrets were vain; there was nothing for it but to make the most of the time still remaining.

March 2 was a "Stratus 10" day—i.e., completely overcast: with a strong northerly wind and considerable sea we still boomed merrily south-east, encountering a few bergs, but no pack until the following morning, when we were brought up short in 72° 18′ S. lat., 17° 59′ W. long. Taking a sounding, we found the depth to be only 1131 fathoms,—up till now it had seldom been under 2500. This sent the skipper up to the crow's nest with a run, and the excitement was great when he reported "Land ahead." Steaming towards this, we found it to be a lofty ice-barrier similar to that first discovered by Ross on the other side of the Pole: it stretched in a north-easterly and south-westerly direction, but heavy pack-ice prevented a nearer approach than two miles. This ice was much heavier than any we had hitherto seen, rivalling in thickness, if not in extent, the great ice-fields of the Arctic. Birds, which during the last day or two had been very scarce in the open, were now found in numbers, including antarctic and snowy petrels, giant petrels, terns, and emperor penguins; of the latter three were captured after an exciting chase on an ice-floe.

The wind coming away strong from the north with thick snow, we were compelled to retreat a little to avoid being nipped in the ice. This weather continued most of the next day while we dodged along to the westwards about one knot per hour, the coal-bunkers being refilled from the hold,—a proceeding which, though very necessary, made the usual lovely mess of dust on board, and rendered all other operations impossible.

The mist lifted a little in the evening, and we had a good distant view of the Barrier with a magnificent ice-blink over it—the bright reflection in the sky of the white surface of the great ice-sheet. The 5th of March was also overcast, and the Barrier still remained more or less of a mystery. Two hauls were taken with an eight-foot net within 100 fathoms of the surface: the catch included numerous pteropods (a form of soft-shelled mollusc with an expanded wing-like foot), some small crustaceans, brilliantly coloured bristly chætopod worms, and fathoms of what we thought was a nemertine worm, but has turned out to be the tentacles of some unknown siphonophore jelly-fish, probably of great dimensions. Birds were abundant, and some grampus were seen playing in the open water. Large bergs were numerous, and one small piece of banded berg-ice was noted studded with rock fragments, but it proved impossible to geologise on account of the brash-ice surrounding it.

The 6th, being a Sunday, proved rather a better day, and we were enabled to trace the Barrier to a point about 150 miles south-west of where we had first encountered it. It was in sight practically all day, save once when we passed the mouth of a bight, the head of which was not visible. The surface of this great Inland Ice, of which the Barrier was the terminal face or sea-front, seemed to rise up very gradually in undulating slopes, and faded away in height and distance into the sky, though in one place there appeared to be the outline of distant hills: if so, they were entirely ice-covered, no naked rock being visible. Pack-ice kept us always some distance off, but a sounding, two and a half miles from the Barrier by range-finder, gave a depth of only 159 fathoms. This made it certain that we were really off a new Antarctic land, which has been named "Coats' Land" in honour of Mr James Coats, jun., and Major Andrew Coats, the two chief sub-scribers to the Expedition. Whether this land is a large island or a part of the Antarctic continent remains for future explorers to finally decide, but the latter hypothesis seems the more probable one. Mr Bruce is of the opinion that the coast-line of "Antarctica" runs more or less continuously eastward from Coats' Land to Enderby Land, as there appears to be no other way of accounting for the obstructions which Cook, Bellingshausen, Biscoe, Ross, and Moore all met with in attempting to penetrate south in that region. Weddell, in 1823, was probably also not far from discovering the edge of the Antarctic continent when he turned homeward in 74° 15′ S., for the large number of birds he observed there accords with the distribution we found in relation to the discovery of Coats' Land.

The skuas, terns, giant petrels, antarctic and snowy petrels, and the black-throated penguins which we had found retreating northward the previous summer, all go to show that not far distant were the beaches and rocky cliffs of some actual land where they could nest. The ice-barrier, a vertical cliff from 100 to 150 feet in height, stretching in unbroken majesty for at least 150 miles and probably for many more, is the seaward edge of part of the great Inland Ice of Antarctica, which covers an area probably larger than that of Australia. The ac-cumulated snowfall of ages, altered into solid though plastic glacier ice, creeps slowly but steadily down off the land, pushing its way some distance over the sea-bottom until it reaches water deep enough to float in; then part breaks off and becomes one of the large tabular icebergs so typical of the Antarctic seas.

That the land is of a continental character is shown by the boulders brought up in the dredgings taken in the vicinity,—boulders which have been picked up by the ice-sheet from the underlying rock and deposited on the floor of the ocean by the melting of the bergs. Amongst others, granites, schist, gneiss, quartzite, sandstone, slate, and limestone were found, all rocks characteristic of an old con-tinental land-surface.

Its discovery in this latitude was very unexpected. Sir John Murray, basing his calculations on Ross's sounding of 4000 fathoms no bottom (which we had still to prove fallacious), put the outline of Antarctica about 400 miles farther south in this longitude.

The Weddell sea has turned out to be considerably less in extent than was previously supposed, and our soundings also show that its depth is very much less.

Early on the morning of the 7th the *Scotia* was caught in a north-east blizzard,

121

and despite all efforts to get free, was beset in slush and heavy pack-ice. During this and the following day the pressure from the driving pack became great, the ice piling up against the ship's sides almost level with the top of the bulwarks.

It happened to be my week as night meteorological observer, and it proved "dreich" and eerie sitting there alone in the watches of the night. Silent watches they were not, for the crushing of the ice made the good ship's timbers creak and groan, and every minute I was wondering whether the ice would not rise still farther and overwhelm us altogether—a fate which has overtaken many a ship ere now. Although not specially built with a rounded hull like the *Fram*, we found afterwards that the ice had gone right under the ship, lifting her bodily out of the water some four feet, and it was doubtless in consequence of this that the *Scotia* suffered no injury from the tremendous pressure.

At the end of two days the gale abated, and we then found we had been driven into a bight of the ice-barrier. To the westward was a low part of the great ice-sheet, probably soon to break off as a berg, and over it could be seen the tops of distant bergs where the line of the Barrier turned more sharply to the south just beyond our position. We were in lat. 74° 1′ S., long. 22° 0′ W., the farthest south point we attained.

The immediate danger was past, but there lay before us the prospect of having possibly to spend the winter there, frozen up in the pack. This was not altogether enticing: of the necessities, food and coal, we had sufficient to get along on, but our supply of light was limited, and the prospect of nearly three months' total darkness was not inviting. Also we thought, what would be the feelings of those at home: it was known we had no intention of spending another winter in the south, and if we did not turn up at Cape Town in May or June they would. naturally imagine the worst. Three days later our chance of escape looked even gloomier. There was no open water in sight to the north, and the temperature having dropped to near zero, the pack was freezing up hard.

Hope was not altogether given up, but the question of having to winter was seriously entertained. The topgallant yards were sent down from aloft so as to offer less resistance to the wind, light was at once cut down to a minimum, and a tally of stores taken preparatory to going on to strict rations.

Had the mental horizon not been somewhat cloudy, nothing could have been finer than our situation. The air was calm, crisp, and beautifully clear; from the crow's nest one could see to the north only huge bergs—"ice mast high going floating by"—and pack-ice, with every here and there a black dot where a seal or a penguin lay. To the south lay the Great Barrier, sublime and mysterious, inclining one to be in pensive mood brooding over its awful silent loneliness; but the hum of voices from the deck below, or the shouts ascending from the large floe nearby, which served for the nonce as a football field, soon brought the wandering thoughts back to the worries of our microcosmos, stranded on the edge of the chaos of ice.

A large trap was sunk in a depth of 161 fathoms—two miles off the Barrier—and collections of the marine fauna made, including a fine specimen of feather-star (*Antedon*) and abundant small amphipod crustaceans, which soon cleared the flesh off the penguins used to bait the trap. A number of emperor penguins, which were here very numerous, were captured: in the event of wintering they would have served as food, but as it turned out it was only their skins that had to do duty. To test the effect of music on them, Piper Kerr played to one on his pipes,—we had no Orpheus to warble sweetly on a lute,—but neither rousing marches, lively reels, nor melancholy laments seemed to have any effect on these lethargic, phlegmatic birds; there was no excitement, no sign of appreciation or disapproval, only sleepy indifference. Some of them when weighed turned the scale at close on eighty pounds, and it was just all that one man could do to lead one up to the ship: with their beaks they bit fairly hard, and with their long flipper-like wings could hit out decidedly hard.

March 12.—"An exciting but tantalising day; the wind came away faintly from the south-west, and our hopes ran high. Under its influence, the ice being no longer pent up against the Barrier, the floe spilt into great fields separated by long leads of open water, the whole mass drifting westwards in front of the Barrier. The fields gradually cracked up into smaller pieces: about 4 P.M. a wide lead ran far to the north-east from the stern of the *Scotia*, but midships and at the bows she was still fast, and remained so despite futile efforts to blast the ice with tonite and gunpowder, and to break it by poling and by the whole ship's company jumping on it, Newfoundland sealer fashion. It was not till 8.30 P.M. that the ice spilt, and the *Scotia* slid down from her icy cradle and was once more afloat; but, alas! the lead had closed, and we could make nothing of our partial freedom, but wait in patience to see what the future had in store."

March 13.—"All morning we lay jammed in the ice, powerless to move or help ourselves, but in the afternoon the pack loosened a little, and after five hours' dodging, ramming, and butting our way 'twixt the floes, we were some two or three miles nearer the open water. It was risky work for the propeller, which frequently brought up sharp against projecting tongues of ice, but it was neck or nothing, and something had to be risked. A small piece was, indeed, snapped out of one blade, but luckily not enough to seriously interfere with its action.

"The uncertainty was very trying to our equanimity, every one being in a state of nervous tension, obvious or suppressed as the case might be."

On the 14th, with the first dawn the engines were again under way, and by breakfast-time our freedom was assured: we were out of the heavy pack into young pancake-ice, where the sea was just beginning to freeze over. It was none too soon, for the wind was again round to the north. How we blessed our engines! —without them we might have tacked till doomsday and not succeeded in forcing a passage through the maze of leads between the floes and hummocks.

Our course was now clear. The Antarctic summer was over, and we had had sufficient warning not to force the *Scotia* again into the pack, so we turned north-eastward towards the "Ross Deep," an examination of which was part of the programme of the expedition.

The water rapidly deepened to over 2000 fathoms until after a day or two, when, as the sea seemed open in that direction, we set an easterly course, which brought us into rapidly shoaling water, until in 71° 32′ S., 17° 15′ W. it was 1221 fathoms, showing we were getting near the continental shelf.

On March 16 and three subsequent days the trawl was down each day under somewhat extraordinary circumstances. The first day the trawl came up without having reached the bottom, fouled, turn after turn of the cable being twisted round the net, but as none of it kinked it was possible to unravel the cable without cutting.

On the second occasion, in a depth of 2370 fathoms, we had 3000 fathoms of cable out, but again it came up without having reached the bottom, although not fouled: previously in depths of 2500 fathoms we had had no difficulty in touching ground with 3000 fathoms of cable, using the same tactics with regard to rate of lowering and steaming.

The depth was only 1410 fathoms on the third day, and we allowed 1000 fathoms extra cable. This time we were successful, and had the richest deep-water haul of the whole cruise. Over sixty species of animals were brought up, mostly in excellent condition, and some in considerable numbers. There were curiously-shaped deep-sea fish and numerous crustacea, especially of a large, bright-red, spiny species. Red and purple, by the way, are the two most common colours in deep-sea animals, and it is an interesting though unsolved problem what purpose such vivid colours can serve in a world where all is darkness, save perhaps, for the few fitful gleams of some phosphorescent animals. Correlated with this darkness is the fact that most of the animals are either blind or have developed eyes of extraordinary size to make the most of the little light there is. There were also mollusca and lamp-shells or brachiopods, and, as is usual, a big selection of echinodermata, including many brittle-stars; some crinoids or sea-lilies,—a stalked form much more abundant in previous ages, but now dwindled to a small family only found in fairly deep water; numerous holothurians or sea-slugs, some of a deep purple colour, a foot in length, and with a circlet of tentacles around the mouth, others like transparent celluloid, and in shape and size resembling the handle of a bicycle. There were stout siliceous sponges, more like strong walking-sticks than the ordinary bath sponge, and a considerable quantity of large tough sea-anemones. One of the latter was growing on the ear-bone of a whale. This is noteworthy as being the only ear-bone we dredged. In some parts of the ocean, notably in the Pacific, far from land, where the deposits accumulate with extreme slowness, the floor of the ocean is thickly strewn with sharks' teeth and whales' ear-bones. These are hard, dense structures, resisting the solvent action of sea-water, and are the remains of whales and sharks that have lived and died in these waters for thousands of years back. In the Antarctic, on the other hand, although whales are probably quite as numerous, their bones are soon covered up by the blue mud which must accumulate rapidly from the great amount of *débris* brought down by the ice-sheets of Antarctica and dropped far and wide over the floor of the southern ocean by the dispersion and gradual dissolution of the icebergs.

The fourth day the depth was only 1221 fathoms, and, though we allowed 2000 fathoms of cable, the trawl again came up without showing any sign of having been on the bottom. The only feasible explanation of these repeated failures seems to be in the existence of a strong undercurrent which swept along the trawl bag, instead of allowing it to sink down quietly on to the bottom. Such a current, if it were a north flowing one, might account for another puzzling circumstance connected with the deposits on the floor of the ocean. All over the Weddell Sea diatoms are extremely abundant in the surface waters, but none are to be found in the blue mud from the bottom. Where do they go to when they die? North of 60° S. lat. the diatoms, though still abundant, are not quite so marked a feature of the plankton, but on the ocean bed the ooze—diatom ooze it is called—is composed of the skeletons of diatoms to the extent of from 30-70 per cent. May they not have been carried off by this undercurrent, only gradually subsiding as they went northward?

Trawling days were fairly heavy ones, especially so when they came four on end. The usual mode of procedure was as follows: Before breakfast a sounding was taken while the officer on duty was preparing the trawling apparatus—i.e., raising the derrick, leading the cable round the winch ends and over the dynamometer which hung from the end of the derrick and registered the strain on the trawling cable, and lastly, coupling on the large otter trawl. After breakfast we proceeded to lower away, by far the most ticklish part of the whole business: it had not to be done too quickly, else the cable was apt to sag underneath the trawl-bag, which offered more resistance to the water and sank more slowly, and then there would be a glorious tangle. If lowered too slowly, it would stream out as the ship steamed ahead, and possibly not reach the bottom. The ship had to be manœuvred at the proper speed, and at the same time kept clear of the ice. When the trawl was judged to be on the bottom and a sufficiency of cable let out to allow of its being dragged without lifting up the mouth clear of the ground, the engines went full speed ahead for about half an hour, or until the dynamometer showed a strain of five or six tons. Then the winding in began. The heavy part of the lifting was done by the deck winch, with much rattle and vibration, at the rate of from 1000 to 1200 fathoms per hour, but the slack of the cable had to be wound by hand on to the store-drums in the 'tween decks. Staff and crew assisted at this, working five men at a time in half-hour spells. To keep revolving a drum which weighed six tons when full was splendid exercise in cold weather, though the work was easier this trip than the previous summer on account of the alterations which had been made at Buenos Aires on the brakes. The work was often enlivened by songs—regular old sea-chanteys. The fashion was thus: Some one with a bit of a voice and a capacity for "making up" as he went along sang a line, usually in a high minor key, and then the others joined in with the refrain. Our best leader or chantey-man was Cornelius Schneider, "Dutch Harry," one of the new hands shipped at Buenos Aires, and the favourite songs were "Heave away Rio," "Homeward Bound," "Sally Brown," and "Rolling Home." When the trawl came up to the surface there was always great excitement to see what was in it, and it was very amusing to hear the names given by the crew to the various animals. A sailorman is never at a loss for a name, and it is a curious "fact" that he has always "seen that beast before, or one exactly like it, up the Gulf, or out in the Colonies, or in some other blanked place." At this time we had two live emperor penguins on board which we were attempting to take home, or at least, as far as Cape Town for the Zoo. Their diet was the difficulty, as nothing would persuade them to take fish or crustacea even out of a bucket of water placed beside them. When fish was forced into their bills they swallowed it, and for a few days we hoped to keep them going on preserved fish, but it did not agree with them, and though continuing to take it they gradually became thinner and soon died. We were unlucky in our attempt to bring back live specimens. Two paddies which had been brought from the Orkneys, and which, with their peculiar scrap- and refuse-eating habits ought to be able to live anywhere and anyhow, both met with accidental deaths, one being drowned in a barrel of tar and the other in a tin of methylated spirit.

On March 23 a sounding was taken in 68° 32′ S., 12° 49′ W., where Sir James Ross had reported a depth of 4000 fathoms, *no bottom*. We obtained an excellent sample of blue mud—depth 2660 fathoms. So after sixty years the "Ross Deep," and with it the hypothetical contours of the South Atlantic based thereon, have been obliterated from the map. This, however, implies no disparagement of the splendid work of Ross in his exploration of the Antarctic. Probably his error was due to the defective sounding-apparatus which was then at the disposal of oceanographers. A woodcut in his "Voyages" shows how his tall-hatted and peruked sailors sounded from open boats with hemp-lines wound on enormous wooden drums turned by hand. We think it likely that there were really 4000 fathoms of line out, but that it was swept along by the undercurrent already referred to, and never actually reached bottom.

A series of water-samples brought up from different depths and compared, as regards their temperature and salinity, with similar observations which we took in other localities will, when fully worked out, doubtless shed more light on this problem.

From this point our course—when we could keep it—lay about due north along the meridian of 10° W. long. It was not a path strewn with roses, but a rough road with wondrous ups and downs, and the way was long, and the wind was cold. Most of the time it blew half a gale, and if not half a gale, then a whole one. They were chiefly from the N.W. and N.N.W. those "brave west winds," so that our progress along a line due north was slow and particularly uncomfortable The seas ran high, and as our coal-supply was running low, the ship was very light and "tender," rolling and pitching like a thing possessed. Scientific work, other than the meteorological observations, could only be carried out intermittently, and seldom was a sounding taken without loss of gear, wire, water-bottles, or thermometers, as the case might be.

I shall give a few extracts from my log to illustrate what we had to put up with.

March 26—"Still choppy seas, tried sounding in the evening, but owing to the jabble the weights would not stay on, so had to give it up."

March 27—"66° 57′ S., 11° 13′ W.—Being a Sunday, had better luck. After two failures, had a successful sounding in 2715 fathoms. It is not pleasant work standing up on the sounding-bridge for an hour or two in a biting wind. The man who has to grease the wire is particularly unlucky; a perfect stream of ice-cold water comes off the wire, soaks through his mittens, and freezes hard. Then, being out on the weather side, he gets well douched with spray, and by the end of the time is thoroughly chilled, and more like an icicle than a sentient human being.

"Had a bit of a wash-out in the cabin at night when Brown opened the door to go out and take one of the observations."

March 29—"63° 54′ S., 10° 42′ W.—Booming northward with the wind dead on the port beam. The most uncomfortable day we have had. Sea 6-7 (the amount of sea running is estimated according to a scale which runs from 0 to 9,—0 being dead calm, and 9 so bad that there is just time to record the observation before the ship goes down). Ship rolling as much as 47° from the vertical.

"Everybody growling. The only consolation is, the rust in the water-tanks is so shaken up that drinking the water is as good as a visit to Spa, but there is only about three weeks' supply left. Tea made with it, however—ugh!"

March 30—"Sea gone down very quickly; comparatively quiet to-day. Sounded in the afternoon in 2764 fathoms, the deepest we have yet found. Afterwards took a series of water-samples from different depths in the big Pettersen-Nansen water-bottle. Caught several chains of a compound ascidian (*Doliolum*) floating on the surface. Several silver petrels (*Thalassoeca glacialoides*) shot and albatros seen, the first since leaving the ice."

March 31—"Blowing again from the north. Ship put off on the starboard tack, rolling and pitching so badly at night that no one aft got any sleep."

April 1—"60° 33′ S., 12° 0′ W.—Good Friday. Drifting sideways out of the Weddell Sea. Wind dying away during the day, but the barometer falling steadily —over an inch in the twenty-four hours. In the evening the wind came away from the south west and was soon a living gale. Another sleepless night. Ship did one record roll of 56° to starboard and 43° to port: taking meteorological observations under these conditions is a treat—especially for the night-watchman who has to carry a lantern as well as the observation-slate, and at the same time open the thermometer boxes and hang on the mizzen rigging to keep himself from careering over the poop, and it might be over the rails into the seething sea below.

"At 11 P.M. the spar from which the gig was slung broke, and as it was being lashed up it was cheering for us miserable wretches down below trying to wedge ourselves into our bunks to hear Mac shouting to the skipper (who was on the bridge all this and the preceding night), 'There's another berg on the lee-bow, sir!' I must confess to being glad I have not the responsibility of keeping a look-out for bergs on these wild dark nights, but it is good to feel we are being well looked after, as we are.

"Running under lower topsails till midnight, when they were taken in, as it was too risky with so many bergs about. That is another business which is no joke, clinging to yards often nearer the vertical than the horizontal, clawing up a hard frozen sail with benumbed fingers, and fumbling in the dark at the gaskets to make it fast."

Saturday—"To cap the excitement of last night a heavy sea struck us on the port side just at breakfast-time. The ship lay over to starboard, and the fore-lashings of the gig carried away. As she slowly righted again the gig hung battering against the side, and had to be cut adrift. Shipping it solid green several times to-day; the engineer's, mates', and boys' berths all afloat; one sea lifted the laboratory skylights and thoroughly dowsed the place, but did not do very much damage; the cook's galley was swept several times, with only the loss of one pot, however."

Easter Sunday—"56° 55′ S., 10° 0′ W.—Even the elements are at peace to-day, the wind having entirely died away, and the swell is rapidly going down.

"Followed Captain Dougal Dalgetty's plan of provisioning for three days when the opportunity offered.

"Seized the chance of sounding, and brought up a fine sample of diatom ooze—no more monotonous blue muds, hurrah!"

[This sample, on further examination, turned out to be 55 per cent composed of diatoms—a very sudden change from the previous bottom sample, in which there was not a trace of diatoms: the remainder was almost entirely volcanic mineral particles, probably derived from the South Sandwich group of volcanic islands, which lay due west.]

"Numerous albatros about—the sooty species and the yellow-billed albatros (*Diomedea melanophrys*), also many hump-backed whales, but never any of the bowhead or right whale, which carries the gold-mine in its mouth.

"Proposing to trawl to-morrow."

Monday, April 4.—Man proposes, but——.

"Sounded in the morning in shallower water, 2270 fathoms only; but the barometer was falling and the wind and sea rising, Trawling postponed; strong gale by night time, backing from N.W. to N.E., driving us away to the westward."

During the next three days we were only able to make about seventy miles of northing. If this wild waste of waters had lain on the regular track of any ships, it would have been named the "Furious Fifties," I should say. Compared with these latitudes the "roaring" of the "Forties" is as the bleat of a lamb to the melancholy howl of a hyæna or the dismal wail of a lost soul.

A cluster of about a dozen bergs was passed on the night of the 5th, almost the last ice we saw, an outpost of the Antarctic army. We were bidding farewell to the land of mist and snow,—for most of us probably a farewell for ever. Ah, well! it had been a good time. Monotonous, dreary, and uncomfortable days there had been, but where do these not exist? In the future we knew there would often come a longing to be back again, however much we might rail against the present. The ice had cast its indescribable mysterious glamour over our souls, and oft in our day-dreams would we remember how,

> "When a scarlet sun doth rise
> Like a scarlet fleece the snow-field spreads,
> And the icy founts run free,
> And the bergs begin to bow their heads,
> And plunge, and sail in the sea."

Ay, and many another scene too of wondrous beauty and grandeur.

April 8—"52° 33′ S., 9° 47′ W.—Although there was still a considerable swell running we were able to sound, but at some cost in instruments. At the first attempt a Buchanan sounding-tube and 1300 fathoms of wire went; the second time bottom was reached, but the Admiralty pattern tube snapped off. The third attempt, using our last Buchanan sounder, was successful, although no deposit was brought up: it had been on 'hard ground.' The depth was now under 2000 fathoms." This was a discovery of the highest importance, as it showed a continuation of the mid-Atlantic rise nearly a thousand miles farther south than it was previously known to exist. Very probably this comparatively shallow water extends to the Sandwich group and to Bouvet Island, and another link has been added thereby to the strong chain of evidence accumulating in favour of a former land connection between South America and South Africa, but which I need not enter into more fully here.

On the 9th, 12th, and 13th we had, marvellous to say, three days fit to trawl on. The first catch was a poor one, owing to the trawl fouling on the bottom; on the second occasion, although in quite shallow water—only 1322 fathoms (about a mile and a half)—there was doubt whether the trawl ever reached the bottom, —at all events it came up empty; the third time we had a good haul—not a great variety, but all in very fine condition. Curious how our luck always held the third time!

April 14—"46° 35′ S., 10° 10′ W.—Our Indian summer, a calm warm day with a slight haze like the smoke of distant camp-fires. Fell in with a school of porpoises, sporting like merry boys in the ripple of the sunlit sea.

"The day spoilt only by the operation of coaling,—a necessary evil, with its dust and grime."

April 15—"45° 54′ S., 10° 10′ W.—Sounded before breakfast and brought up a typical globigerina ooze."

[This is a deposit formed largely of the limy shells of foraminifera, single-celled protozoa, one of the simplest forms of animal life, though their shells are often of extreme beauty and complexity. It is the ooze over which "the shell-burred cables creep," when linking Europe and America across the North Atlantic.]

The wind rose steadily all day, and at 4 P.M. we passed right through the centre of a cyclonic disturbance, the barograph curve showing a sharp V where the pressure, which was falling rapidly, began suddenly to rise again just as quickly. The gale—a contrary one, of course—lasted nearly four days, just to show us that the "Forties" could roar a little when they tried. At the end of it we had dodged up to within about 180 miles of Gough Island, and late on the night of the 20th April the island was sighted. Another stage of our long voyage was completed.

CHAPTER XII

GOUGH ISLAND AND SOUTH AFRICA

A FORGOTTEN ISLAND—ANTICIPATIONS—A BEAUTEOUS LAND—DIFFICULT LANDING—PLANTS AND BIRDS—RUINED HUTS—GEOLOGY—BETTER WEATHER—TRAWLING—SOUNDING MISHAPS—NEARING CIVILISATION—PHOSPHORESCENCE—A BREAK-DOWN—TABLE BAY—A DISAPPOINTING TOWN—A HAPLESS COLONY—ALONG THE COAST—SALDANHA BAY—BOER VILLAGES—THE VELDT.

LYING about 1500 miles from the Cape of Good Hope, and 2000 from Cape Horn, Gough Island (or as it should be more correctly called Diego Alvarez Island) may certainly be regarded as one of the most isolated islands on the face of our globe. The only land near it is the tiny island of Tristan da Cunha and its two adjacent isles some 280 miles to the N. by W. And yet, despite its isolation, it is strange that Gough Island should have been so wholly forgotten, as is the case. The *Challenger* on her world-circling cruise missed it, and the *Valdivia* did not go so far west; and our previous very meagre knowledge about the island consisted of a few casual notes in the voyages of sealers, and a few remarks as to its configuration by one or two men-of-war, enterprising enough to have wandered off their routine tracks. Discovered in the sixteenth century by the Portuguese, and named by them Diego Alvarez, it seems for long to have been lost sight of until, in 1731, Captain Gough, homeward bound in his ship *Richmond* round the Cape of Good Hope, sighted an island in the South Atlantic, which henceforth went by his name; and it was only slowly that geographers came to the conclusion that Diego Alvarez and Gough Island were one and the same island, and then the former name gradually disappeared from charts. In size the island is about eight miles east and west, but, small though it is in area, it can be seen from afar with its peak of 4380 feet.

Strange to say, Gough Island is claimed as British territory, and apparently has been since Captain Gough reported it, but on what grounds this claim was made, and is still retained, no one, not even the Colonial Office, can say. To all intents and purposes the island must be considered outside any sphere of influence.

This tiny island offered us particular attractions, for we knew we would be the first scientific explorers ever to set foot upon its shores, and it promised, by reason of its extreme isolation away in mid-ocean, to reveal many treasures in the way of plants and animals, no less than rocks.

But there was perhaps an even greater fascination, almost a glamour, about the thought of Gough Island. We knew well it would be a land free from the embrace of snow and ice, a land where we might again tread on soil and grass, and again see green leaves and perhaps enjoy the scent of flowers once more. To those of us who had not known for fifteen long months what all these simple pleasures were, there was certainly an alluring prospect about Gough Island, and the long delays and four weeks' incessant battling against contrary winds had only increased our expectations and strengthened our desire to get there. The adjacent island of Tristan da Cunha is relatively well known, and from various accounts of it, which we had carefully read, we knew in a general way what we might expect in Gough Island. Let it not be supposed that we dreamt of tropical luxuriance and fragrance; far from it, we pictured an island somewhat bare, perhaps even desolate in appearance, but with a certain amount of green vegetation; not perhaps a very tempting prospect to one coming from a happier clime, but to eyes long accustomed to look over snow and ice, and from sea to sky, this was something keenly to look forward to. All night the *Scotia* lay off the island to leeward, and I, happening to be on watch that night, enjoyed to the full the glorious fresh scent of grass and soil wafted off the land on the breeze.

Early next morning we steamed round the weather side of the island. Great as had been our hopes, they were more than surpassed when we found the whole island, from the water's edge to almost its summit, beautifully clothed in green, and saw the numerous cascades of water pouring out of their lofty hanging valleys, and leaping over the sheer precipices some hundreds of feet clear into the sea. The whole island is very precipitous, cut with narrow glens into steep ridges, and everywhere facing the sea in towering cliffs. Inland it rises into a lofty peak of over 4000 feet which is lost among the clouds. Valleys and ridges also, to a height of almost 2000 feet, are densely covered with a small stunted buckthorn tree (*Phylica nitida*) and thick impenetrable masses of tussock grass (*Spartina arundinacea*) both growing vigorously, and seeming to enjoy the wildest winds: the cliffs, too, are green with their covering of moss and ferns, while even the highest crags appear to have a coat of green, probably some sort of lichen.

We cruised up and down the eastern sides of the island, but nowhere was there any possibility of effecting a landing in face of the furious swell that dashed in angry breakers on all the shores. In fact, we saw only one place where, if we did land, access could be gained to the interior: that was on the eastern side, where a rocky glen, ending in a little beach, partially sheltered by a projecting headland, seemed to run towards the heart of the island. At other places were beaches, but there was no appearance from the sea of there being any likelihood of gaining the higher ground from any of them. However, the following day, Friday, brought some abatement in the sea, rendering an attempt at landing possible. So, soon after nine o'clock, the whale-boat put off from the ship with a picked crew, and the whole scientific staff, armed with cameras, collecting apparatus, and, not least important, in case of accidents, several days' food. We chose the place that I have spoken of above, but on approaching within about a couple of cables' length, we found far more surf than a view from the ship had revealed. Under the circumstances it would be quite impossible to attempt to beach the boat. But as there was no great probability of our getting a day with a calmer sea, we determined to try and get ashore then and there. Fortunately we had an admirable boat and a skilled crew, both of which greatly facilitated matters. We lay off on our oars and waited for a lull in the waves, which occurred every few minutes: when it came the boat was quickly backed in, and just before the wave returned seaward one man jumped from either side into the sea, and scrambled up the steeply sloping beach as best he could. In this way, with a little trouble, Mr Bruce, Wilton, Pirie, Cuthbertson, Ross, and myself got ashore, and by wading out again waist-deep, we safely transferred everything from the boat to the shore, though the cameras had a perilous passage. We, of course, were wet through with sea-water from the waist downwards, but as it happened to be raining in torrents at the time, that made little difference: moreover, the water felt comparatively warm, and the air temperature was nearly 60° F. Down the glen, at whose mouth we then found ourselves, a rushing mountain torrent flows over its stony bed, between thickly grown banks, until it merges into the sea in the shelter of the small projecting headland. Through this headland runs a curious tunnel, along which the waves, forbidden free play in so confined a space, boil and fume in a fury of seething waters. Just above the beach on either side of the stream is a small level stretch of ground, perhaps nearly an acre in extent. On the south it is covered with grass, but on the less sunny and damper north it is thickly overgrown with small tree-ferns (*Lomaria boryana*), wild celery (*Apium australe*), and several kinds of docks (*Rumex frutescens* and *R. obtusifolius*). Pushing our way through this tangled mass of vegetation, we suddenly came on the ruins of two huts. The uprights were still standing, and various timbers and pieces of corrugated iron lay around; and half overgrown, among docks and celery, we found a broken stove, a tub, a pail, and the remains of several barrels. The timbers had all a charred appearance, which indicated that whoever had once inhabited these huts had for some reason or other burnt them down.

Gough Island, like all these southern sub-Antarctic islands, used to be the haunt of fur-seals (*Arctocephalus australis*) and sea-elephants (*Macrorhinus leoninus*), and on that account was occasionally visited by American and British sealers. These were doubtlessly the ruins of their encampments, for the sealing-schooners used to leave men on various of these southern islands during the season, and return to take them away with their catch in some months' time. The seals and elephants are now practically exterminated, and Gough Island has, in consequence, long ceased to be visited. A little way along the beach to the north we came on another sign of man. In a rude natural cave, just above high-water mark, were to be seen traces of a shelter in the shape of iron staples, bits of canvas, a piece of board, and a short length of very corroded chain fixed to the rock, while near by was painted the inscription, "Fred. Andrews, 1892." Here we felt we had surely come on the track of some shipwrecked sailor who had been cast ashore on this lonely island, and constructed this rough shelter to live in. But on second thoughts that appeared less likely. The huts or their ruins must have been there long before 1892, and why then should a shipwrecked man have chosen to live in a cave exposed to sea-spray when he could have rigged up, if he did not actually find ready, a more comfortable shelter?—and, moreover, would a shipwrecked man have had paint to record his name on the rock with? It seemed more probable that Fred. Andrews had been one of the sealers, and yet I confess I was not convinced, and half expected to find among the neighbouring vegetation the bleached skeleton of a man.[1]

We spent the whole day ashore rambling about and collecting birds, plants, and rocks. Lively little green and orange finches (*Nesospiza goughensis* and *N. jessiæ*) flitted to .and fro under the trees feeding on the berries, or hopped about on the beach wonderfully unconscious of our desire to harm them; gorgeous black and scarlet water-hens (*Porphyriornis comeri*) darted about among the undergrowth by the banks of the stream, and skuas (*Megalestris antarctica*) and several kinds of albatros were always to be seen. In the adjoining cove, which, unfortunately, we could not land in, were a few belated penguins (*Eudyptes chrysocome*) who had not yet left for their winter holidays at sea. The stream, at the mouth of which is the ruined settlement, forks some way inland, and from the ridge between the two tributaries, but some distance below the summit of the island, there rises up a large rounded column known as the Apostle. This has a darker colour than the surrounding rocks, and appears to be quite bare of vegetation. We were unable to get close enough to be sure of its nature: it may be either the stump of an old volcanic neck or of a "Tower of Pelée." On the other hand, it may be of the nature of one of the phonolite bosses which are so common

---

[1] At Cape Town this little mystery was solved. I found Fred. Andrews, and he told me he had been one of a party of sealers of the schooner *Wild Rose*, who had lived on Gough Island from January 1891 to February 1892; and he further told me that on leaving the island the crew had, in a drunken frolic, fired all the huts.

in South Atlantic islands—e.g., "Lot" and "Lot's Wife" at St Helena, the peak at Fernando Noronha, and the Ninepin Rock on South Trinidad. For the rest, as far as Pirie had opportunities of ascertaining, the rocks are entirely of volcanic origin, except for one solitary piece of coral limestone with quartz pebbles which was picked up on the beach. Little importance, however, can be attached to this, as it may have been brought there by human agency. Had it been found *in situ* in the agglomerate it would have told a different story.

The captain had warned us not to go far afield, for he might have to hurriedly recall us if the wind increased, since the *Scotia* had a very insecure anchorage, and would only be safe in a gale if she put to sea. In consequence our wanderings were limited to a mile or so up the glen, but there was plenty to see and enjoy even in so short a distance. Trees and shady nooks,—for the sun shone strong between the showers,—grassy banks and mossy grottoes, the pleasure of wading knee-deep through the burn, of walking on springy turf; and of bathing in delightful rock-pools, of lunching amidst ferns and leaves once more, but, above all, the joy of mingling again with the abundance of nature, of treading on land, and of drinking in the smell of earth,—all contributed to make this one of the most delightful days of the whole voyage. At evenfall we again put off with another soaking in the surf though the sea had subsided a little, and all that evening, and well into the night, we laboured at preserving and storing away our scientific treasures.

The following day landing was again out of the question, for a high sea was running, and fierce squalls rushed down from the high land. We therefore spent it in trawling off the island, and wild work that was with the *Scotia* rolling madly in a big beam sea. The sea proved as abundant in its wealth of life as the land, and after two hauls in 100 fathoms we had enough fishes, corals, and zoophytes, not to mention other animals, to fully occupy our attention for the rest of the day.

Our plan of visiting Tristan da Cunha had, I regret to say, to be abandoned, for the coal resources of the *Scotia* would not at the time admit of her steaming about 250 miles into a strong head-wind. Two hundred tons, our utmost coal capacity, even at the low demand of three to four tons daily which our engines made, would not last for ever; and so we were compelled to square away under full sail for the Cape.

On our easterly course there was every prospect of fair winds in this longitude, and sure enough our expectations were fulfilled. We suffered occasionally from too little wind, but never from a head-wind, and our only difficulty was to carefully harvest our rapidly diminishing coal-supply. It was required as much for ballast as for coal, for the *Scotia* was getting very light, and heeled over uncomfortably in a fresh breeze. The temperature was now appreciably milder, and with 55° F. we felt that the regions of ice were indeed behind us, though there was still a remote possibility of meeting with a far-straying iceberg. Our course lay across the track of outward-bound sailing-ships to the east, but yet we sighted none, and the ocean remained as lonely as the Weddell Sea. This part of the South Atlantic was so far uncharted,—that is to say, no knowledge was extant as to its depths, and no animal had ever been brought from its bottom; in consequence we proceeded as near as possible along the 40° parallel, keeping the track of the *Challenger* several degrees to the north. In 39° 58′ S., 8° 36′ W., in a sea ideally calm for the purpose, we sounded in 1807 fathoms. The stillness of the ocean and the calm on that occasion may be imagined from the fact that all sails were set, but still no steam was required to keep the *Scotia* steady. The canvas hung idly from the yards with hardly a perceptible quiver, and the ship lay quietly as in harbour. Perhaps an exploring party is singularly hard to please, for we desired strong breezes no more than calms; for while a calm used too much coal, a strong breeze meant we covered too much unexplored ground, and that the sea was too disturbed to admit of sounding and trawling. But wish and grumble as much as we liked, at sea, even more than ashore, one must accept one's allotted fate; and so, before the weather admitted another sounding to be made, we were over the meridian of Greenwich. The water was much deeper, and the 2500 fathoms of wire on the machine proved insufficient to reach bottom with. However, the day following we were more successful, and lowered away the trawl with 4000 fathoms of cable in 2645 fathoms. The weather was getting too warm for such work as winding in the slack cable, and this, added to the fact that the trawling-drums were slowly working slack, and in consequence becoming more liable to jam at every roll of the ship, made it an unusually hard day's work. Excitement was therefore all the keener when the last 100 fathoms of cable were running over the winch, and up came the trawl without a hitch. Half a dozen of us stood ready on deck with buckets, basins, and trays to carry away the catch, but, alas! when the trawl was swung on deck it was absolutely empty: the cod-end was open, and all the catch had escaped. Such eventualities are never totally unexpected in deep-sea trawling, but one is always sanguine enough to believe that *this* time, at least, all will go well, and a failure after so much time and labour is always disappointing. There was nothing for it but to wait till daybreak and try again, and on the morrow things went better. We ran in the 4000 fathoms of cable in under three hours, and when the trawl was emptied on deck, a large catch kept us busy long into the night. The usual dark purple jelly-like sea-cucumbers (*Benthodytes sp.*) were there in numbers, as well as others of the same family, with curious projecting processes scattered sparsely on their bodies; brittle-stars (*Ophiuroids*), as usual in deep trawls, were in profusion; but best of all were three small fish. These particularly delighted the chief; as he claimed them as a record for fish in depth. The Captain lost no time when once the trawl was up: he gave a glance, saw it was successful, and in a moment the foresail was set, the topsail yards were going up, and hands were aloft loosing the top-gallants. Sailors ran to and fro, ropes dragged in all directions over the deck, and eager scientists wallowing among mud and water excitedly found another and still another specimen. It was a scene of wild animation but not of confusion, for by this time we had learnt to each and all pursue our business on the restricted space of the deck, without, to any great extent, preventing others doing the same. The unsteadiness of a ship and its cramped and confined space teach sailors nimbleness of limb and neatness of finger. As we drew nearer to Africa the chart evoked even greater interest than it used to do when the Captain spread it each day on the cabin-table, but he himself was certainly as excited as any one: he measured and re-measured the distance to Cape Town, as Wilton said, to see if he could possibly convince himself that the *Scotia* was a mile nearer home than she really was.

Next day the water was 2900 fathoms, and the loss of a sounding-tube still further reduced our stock of sounding apparatus, which was fast reaching a minimum. The day following we repeated the process, both the sounding and the loss of a water-bottle, but now our deep-sea work was over, for we had entered the fairly well charted seas lying around the Cape of Good Hope. The current in these days was playing fine tricks, and upsetting the Captain's most careful calculations. One day it took the ship eastward, so that her course was altered a point to the north, and then, as if to mock us, next day's observation showed that the *Scotia* had come exactly true to her course, and was too far to the north. These seas are noted for their treachery to mariners. My diary reminds me that May-day was celebrated by my producing a genuine Christmas pudding for dinner, much to the delight of the cabin, who welcomed the change from the usual Sunday duff—not that the latter was not excellent, but the resources of the cook were naturally limited.

I had received that pudding the February before at the Falkland Islands, too late for Christmas, but had carefully stored it away in the event of the ice compelling us to spend another winter in its clutches, as it so nearly did. Then a real Christmas pudding would have been to us nothing short of the food of the gods. As we neared the Cape preparations for civilisation went on apace, and wet paint was on every side. Even Pirie and I caught the painting mania, and, challenged by the Captain, undertook to paint all the brown wood-work on the deck-house in three hours. It was a tremendous race, and when completed no doubt left some room for criticism; but we won, and our painting enthusiasm was, for the time being, satisfied.

As land was approached I noticed a very marked increase in the phosphorescence of the waters. A haul with the tow-net showed this, as usual, to be largely due to myriads of small crustacea, whose eyes were aglow with purple fire. A curious phenomenon was one night visible alongside the ship. Streaks of phosphorescence could be seen winding to and fro about the stern, sometimes even appearing to emerge from the water, or dive deep down about the propeller. It was no doubt due to some inquisitive fish following the ship, and either the fish was luminous, or, as is more likely, it stimulated to phosphorescence the crustacea it came in contact with, just as the disturbed waters in a ship's wake are always more aglow than on either side.

Fate was to treat us no better in our approach to South Africa than she did last year when we sought to reach South America. Early in the morning of the day we sighted land, Haynes reported that the boiler was leaking, and that he had had to draw the fires without delay. The leak seemed serious; in fact, he suspected a crack, and that could certainly not be repaired at sea, so the *Scotia* was once again a "wind-jammer." Then our troubles really began. We were becalmed for several hours until a nice breeze came from W.N.W., very favourable to us, only to almost at once go into the N.N.E. straight out of Table Bay, and for hours we tacked to and fro, trying to beat up against it towards the land.

All day the splendid panorama of high land and mountain peaks comprising the Cape peninsula was in view, fading away towards the east in the headland of the Cape of Good Hope. Table Mountain was covered with its cloth, and the sunlight only filtered through in long lifeless streamers between the heavy clouds. This first glimpse of the continent was in strange contrast to one's boyish dreams of Africa—of rich sunlit plains and dense forests; of scorching coasts and broad sluggish rivers. Here before me was a scene as wild and bleak as any in the wildest west of Scotland, and but for the lighthouse on the Cape of Good Hope, the only sign of human life, I could readily have imagined myself gazing on an unknown land in mid-southern ocean. The hope of lying peacefully at anchor that night seemed very small, when the engineers gave the welcome tidings that the boiler was sufficiently repaired for use: at once all available hands cheerfully undertook the task of pumping water into the boilers. By evening we were under way, skirting the outlying seaward suburbs of Cape Town, and, picking up light after light, passed the lepers' prison on Robben Island and entered Table Bay, anchoring safely in shelter of the breakwater at 11 P.M. It was on May 5 we thus returned for the second time from the perils of the Antarctic seas, and that night the tooting of railway whistles was the sweetest music in my ears. It was delightful to be ashore once more, and no schoolboy, I am sure, ever enjoyed his holidays more than we did those first days in Cape Town. To tread on solid ground was good, but it was still a greater joy to see the faces of a thronging crowd and to saunter through the streets of Cape Town: mingling again with our kind was very near the summit of our ambition for the time.

But we had to pay the penalty that all polar travellers have to pay on their return to civilisation: in a few days almost every one on board caught a very bad cold. That may seem to many rather a strange occurrence after our hardening in the south. But polar regions, in very virtue of their entire immunity from harmful germs, do not harden a man in his power of resisting germinal diseases such as colds are. His body has lost the art of throwing aside injurious bacteria through want of practice; and so, as soon as he returns to civilisation and the haunts of germs, he tends to fall an easy victim.

There can be few towns in the world that are able to boast of a finer situation than Cape Town circling half round Table Bay and spreading over all the lower slopes of Table Mountain, which rises majestically high above it, into its crown of cloud. But a closer acquaintance with the town is distinctly disappointing. In its many palatial buildings, very palaces of lavish expenditure, real architecture is markedly lacking: the streets are unimpressive, and instead of the glorious vistas of open sea or mountain-side they might command at either end, if planned with care, a sordid shed or rubbish-yard too often mars their terminal view. The whole city, in fact, gives one the impression that it has grown, and still grows spasmodically, reflecting the waves of prosperity and adversity that the colony has known. It is, in fact, a city increasing without a definite plan. The buildings have been designed and placed here or there but for the utilitarian purposes of the moment, the result being that the town as a whole is striking in its unharmonious contrasts. But its noble situation could save it yet; and could its inhabitants but pause a little in their delirium of money-making to develop the latent possibilities of their town, Cape Town might still become a "city beautiful."

It was an unfortunate time to see South Africa, but none the less instructive for all that. The colony—and one saw it very clearly as regards Cape Town—is paying the penalty for its recent war. Instead of a prosperous South Africa, open to the overcrowded peoples of Great Britain, it is a dejected, almost starving South Africa, that can barely support its own population, and from which all would-be emigrants are carefully warned off. South Africa may recover in time, for it undoubtedly has great agricultural possibilities, and when these are developed as they should be, it will fulfil all expectations; but as long as deluded and short-sighted men will think that wealth enduring is to be found in gold and diamonds, so long will South Africa remain a curse and a burden to itself and the Empire. When once individual fortunes can no longer be made, then will dawn the era of the colony's prosperity with the tilling of the soil and the settling on the land which in these future days will come. But Cape Town was certainly very kind to the *Scotia* and her crew, and in company with several of the local scientists we had many enjoyable excursions in the vicinity; nor must I omit to mention the very keen interest that the Governor of Cape Colony, His Excellency Sir Walter Hely-Hutchinson, G.C.M.G., displayed in the ship and her equipment during a whole afternoon which he spent on board. Dr Gilchrist and Mr J. Stuart Thomson of the Government Biological Laboratory, as also Mr Stewart of the Meteorological Commission, were assiduous in their attentions to the *Scotia's* scientists; and the former was good enough to procure for us a permit to land on some of the penguin islands up the coast. On these islands the birds (*Spheniscus demersus*) are a strict monopoly of the Government, who place a keeper on each island whose duty it is to keep off intruders, and, in the season, to collect the eggs: these are sent to Cape Town for sale, while the guano, too, yields a handsome profit. Mr Bruce, ever a keen collector, let no opportunity go by of adding to our stock of specimens; and, much to the delight of a small crowd, spent one Sunday morning chasing crabs among the piers of the coaling jetty, and pulling off molluscs and tunicates. On May 17 we said good-bye to Cape Town and steamed out of Table Bay. We had an additional inhabitant on board in the shape of a live West African monkey, gifted to the Expedition by the South African Museum. The reputation it brought with it was decidedly bad, and we were warned to treat it with a becoming and withal distant respect. I regret to say that the monkey more than answered to its description, as within two days it savagely attacked Cuthbertson, when he forgetfully gave it a chance, and inflicted a nasty wound on his leg. We determined then that the *Scotia* was too small for such a character, and it had to suffer the penalty of death.

Our course was northward along the coast of Africa, and by the next fore-noon we lay off Dassen Island. This is one of the preserved penguin islands; so, armed with our permit and collecting-gear, several of us put off in the whale-boat under the captaincy of Davidson to try and effect a landing. But a wild surf was breaking all around the rocky shores of the island, and skilled though our boat's crew were, they considered the project rather more risky than desirable, in view of the fact that several other islands lay ahead of us where landing should be easier, and where the same birds would be found. So after trawling in thirty fathoms and securing a haul, principally composed of small dog-fish, we pro-ceeded onwards towards Saldanha Bay.

Saldanha Bay, where we anchored the same evening, is a splendid sheltered bay about six miles north and south, and two and a half miles from mouth to head. It constitutes the only natural harbour of any extent on the west of Cape Colony. Were it not for the extreme scarcity of the fresh-water supply, it is a harbour that might long ago have superseded the exposed and dangerous Table Bay. Three or four sunken rocks lying in it might easily be removed, and the harbour is large enough to shelter a whole fleet. Several centuries ago, before South Africa was colonised, it used to be the calling-place of the Dutch East Indiamen who, on their outward journey, left letters here under a big flat boul-der, to be called for by homeward ships. At its mouth lie a couple of guano islands, Malagassen and Jutten Islands, but the swell broke even fiercer than at Dassen Island, and any hope of landing had to be abandoned. At the north-west end of Saldanha Bay, in a sheltered nook, lies the little fishing-village of Houtjes Bay, off which the *Scotia* lay at anchor, alongside a little coasting vessel and the bi-weekly mail-boat. The village has a population of some 400, of whom considerably over half are white men, while the rest are Kaffirs or half-breeds. English is the lan-guage one chiefly hears, but the faces are more Dutch than British, and the village serves as a shipping-port for the Dutch farms of the surrounding country. There is but one "street," with many whitewashed houses straggling for a mile along the beach and a few stores dealing in everything, several drinking-bars, and a little church. Landwards the virgin African veldt rolls away to the distance with an occasional massive farmhouse visible with its surrounding fields. We were just in time to see the fishing-boats return with their catches: the fish is at once cleaned by Kaffirs, and afterwards salted and dried preparatory to export to Mauritius, where the Catholics maintain a large demand for this commodity. At the other end of the bay is the much smaller and more primitive village of Langebaan—a mere collection of rush-and-mud huts dotted down indiscriminately above high-water mark. One of the few stone buildings is the tiny church, which is also used as a schoolhouse. Even it, however, has a floor of hard-trodden dung. At one end of the village is a large substantial stone building of Dutch appearance, which was evidently once a farmhouse, but now is the chief store of the district. A not exceptionally forlorn cottage rejoices in the name of Hotel Metropole, but, unprepossessing as its appearance might be, it afforded excellent laager beer, which was highly appreciated after a day spent wandering about under an almost tropical sun. The inhabitants of Langebaan are chiefly of mingled races, with a few whites, and some Kaffirs: some of the men seemed to have a decidedly Italian cast of features. When we walked through the village, the population turned out almost in a body to stare at us; but it was with difficulty we contrived to photograph them, and only after some coaxing. Langebaan is also a fishing-village, but on a smaller scale, and shallow water prevents shipping approaching. South of Langebaan the bay extends another two or three miles in the form of a shallow creek, with several branches running westward. These creaks and little bays are the haunts of many water-birds, especially gulls, shags, and flamingoes (*Phœnicopterus*). On a tiny island lying not far from Langebaan, Meuuw Island, were some very curious shags' nests. On low acacia bushes the shags one year build a platform of twigs and grass with perhaps a dozen nests on the same level, next year a second platform with new nests is built above the former one, and so on year by year, each successive series of nests covering the previous one, until one finds a stack, higher than a man, of ten to fifteen years' growth. Often, on pulling such a stack to pieces, deserted eggs of years ago may be discovered. Dainty little sugar-birds were visible at times to the observant, and were elusive enough to escape capture. Dry sandy plains, sparsely covered with low scrubby acacias and other thorny bushes, characterise the veldt which I spent a day in walking over.

Many plants show a succulent nature, their stems or leaves being swollen with stored-up water—a necessary provision in a country where rain is far from frequent, and whose porous and sandy soil drains the water away only too quickly. Euphorbias and mesembryanthemums were common, as well as many aloes, resplendent in their scarlet blossoms. These succulent plants are very characteristic of dry regions such as Cape Colony, especially in the west. I was much interested in a splendid collection of living succulents got together by Dr Marloth, who very kindly presented me with a few aloes and a stapelia to grow on board. To these I now added a few hardy succulents of the veldt, as well as a native

141

South African pelargonium (the common geranium of European gardens), and appropriated the port end of the navigating bridge as a botanic garden, as being one of the few places practically immune from sea-spray.

Small green lizards swarmed among the more stony parts of the veldt, and Wilton captured a beautiful specimen of the horned lizard. A most interesting find was a small West African tortoise (*Cinyxis homeana*), for which this latitude was almost a southern record. It throve on board for many weeks, and ate greedily of cabbage and potato-peel. During the voyage it laid an egg, but, as was only to be expected, the egg failed to hatch.

CHAPTER XIII

THE HOMEWARD VOYAGE

*QUICK RUNS—PLEASANT TIMES—ST HELENA—NAPOLEONIC
RELICS—EXCURSIONS—PRICKLY PEARS—AN EXTINCT FLORA—
SWARMS OF FISH—BIRDS ON BOARD—ASCENSION—A SHIP ON
SHORE—TURTLES—WIDEAWAKES—A DESERT LAND—GREEN
MOUNTAIN—WATER-SUPPLY—ROLLERS—TROPICAL HEAT—
FLYING FISH—PELAGIC ANIMALS—THE DOLDRUMS—LOOKING
FOR THE TRADE-WIND—CAPE VERDES AGAIN—GULF WEED—
ANOTHER EFFIGY—THE PRINCESS ALICE BANK—FAYAL—A
SMILING LAND—MORE TEMPERATE CLIMES—A BREEZE IN THE
BAY—TUSKER LIGHT AGAIN—A WILD MORNING—KINGSTOWN
HARBOUR—IRELAND'S WELCOME—IN THE CLYDE—HOME AT
LAST.*

AT length, on the evening of May 21, we said our final farewell to South Africa,
and under steam and sail, with a fine south-east trade-wind blowing, set out on
our homeward voyage. Deep sounding and trawling were now over: the former
was already done for these seas, and, while the latter still offered rich discoveries,
the nature of our trawling-gear, with the necessity of manual labour to work the
cable-drums, rendered a satisfactory trawling almost impossible in the heat of
the tropics. We had perforce to leave these untouched deep-sea treasures for
some future workers. There was, therefore, no cause for delay, and the Captain,
as indeed all of us, seemed to be seized with the desire to cover the distance as
speedily as possible; so for the next week the *Scotia* sped onwards with a full
spread of canvas, and often with the aid of steam, until she averaged seven to
eight knots an hour, and sometimes did over nine,—a wonderfully quick pace
for a vessel of her type. The trade-wind held fresh and favourable, with just enough
sea to make the ship pitch and roll a little and add to the glory of the motion.

In many ways this was the pleasantest part of the whole voyage. What trials and hardships we had had were over; storms and contrary winds were things of the past, and a large measure of our projected work was accomplished: before us was the prospect of tropical heat tempered with the cool trade-winds, of placid seas and pleasant out-of-the-world ocean islands, and, above all, the feeling that home was within measurable distance.

The days were still cool, for we were only on the verge of the tropics, and the wind blew fresh, but it was the grandeur of the nights that was particularly impressive. Light fleecy clouds scud across the almost full moon, the sea to the east is a blaze of light, to the west the horizon is lost in the purple black night, the ship seems to roll lazily onward, and, looking aloft, I see the quadruple tiers of swelling canvas motionlessly towering skyward, capped by the gilded mastheads dancing gaily against the stars. It is difficult to believe that we are really moving onwards, until my ear catches the swish of water as the eager ship parts the sea and sends to either bow a creamy wave of curling foam and spray, and then I know the *Scotia* is rushing northwards at the rate of eight knots an hour.

We sighted no ships, for we were rather off the track of any but an occasional steamer to or from St Helena. To one who has not sailed the seas it may seem inexplicable that vessels do not sight one another oftener, considering the numbers of ships and the multitude of trade routes. But the ocean is very vast, and a ship can rarely be seen more than some ten to twelve miles off, so that unless on the great trade-routes—for the minor ones are little frequented—a vessel does not expect to meet with others. Early on the forenoon of May 30 the loom of land could be discerned ahead, and by afternoon we were skirting the bleak and barren cliffs of St Helena, and a few hours later were anchored off the little town of Jamestown, nestling in its narrow ravine.

The town consists of one street, running from the sea up the valley. At its seaward end it has quite a tidy and prosperous appearance, where it broadens into the square and parade-ground. Here stands the fort of the East India Company, rebuilt in the early part of the eighteenth century, and now the Government offices. Adjoining the square is a small public garden and a little museum, started by the initiative of the late Governor, R. A. Sterndale, where, among many objects, not all worthy of it, is a beautiful collection of the ferns of the island. Farther up, past the hotel and barracks and market-place, the street becomes gradually more sordid, and at the same time more interesting. There one comes to the more purely negro quarter, with its white- or red-washed houses, or sometimes mere hovels, its scattered banana palms and other tropical plants, and its ever-animated population. The lower part of the town, with its old substantial stone houses and its dull quiet, reminded me strongly of many an old English market-town, now quietly falling into oblivion. The prosperous days of St Helena are, I fear, over. The opening of the Suez Canal and the development of the steamship robbed the island of the trade in fresh provisions which used to be carried on with homeward-bound sailing-ships, as many as a thousand of which visited the island in a year in former days. The Boer prisoners brought a slight revival, but at the time of our visit they had, of course, all left, and the staple industry of St Helena seemed to a casual observer to be the sale of Napoleon relics. I was told— but I will not vouch for the truth of it— that *five* legs of Napoleon's table are still on sale in Jamestown, and the table is in Paris with its original four legs perfectly intact!

We paid a visit to Longwood and to Napoleon's original tomb. Longwood is beautifully situated on a lofty ridge overlooking sea and island, but it strikes one with melancholy in its deserted and rather mournful rooms and neglected grounds, while, surely, it is an unnecessary insult to the memory of Napoleon to still quarter a company of English soldiers within a stone's-throw of his house. The only room still in use is that in which Napoleon died. There, on the site of his bed, is a little altar, and every Sunday the Catholic chaplain holds service for those of the troops who are of that faith. Napoleon's tomb at the head of his favourite Geranium valley is a delightful contrast to his gloomy house. The tomb, enclosed in an iron railing (doubtless as a protection against relic-hunters), stands amidst a trim lawn overshadowed by stately Norfolk island pines, while a babbling brook from the hillside breaks through the little enclosure, and runs on its course down the beautifully verdant valley, at whose end one catches a glimpse of the sea. Beside the railing around the tomb stands a miserable stunted and semi-leafless willow. That is the tree from which relic-dealers would have people believe that the thousands of articles they have on sale were manufactured. Tomb and house alike, each form a little French possession in the island, and are in charge of a French consul. Near Longwood we found a ramshackle little hut of wood and corrugated iron and mud, displaying the sign, "Neilson's Good Templar Café," and as the day was hot and dusty we went in to explore. The resources of the house were not great, but the company was interesting. Neilson himself was a Boer of Danish descent—a giant of strength and stature—who had been brought here a prisoner, and, not being a born Transvaaler, was refused permission to return at the close of the war. And so, having nowhere to go,—for he had left Denmark as a child, and had no prospect of getting work to suit him there,— he had remained in St Helena, and opened a little café near the encampment of British troops at Deadwood; and here we found him on the best of terms with his erstwhile enemies, but I could not help drawing a comparison between the stalwart Boer giant and the relatively puny British troops who were his customers.

Fortunately the *Scotia* was not so urgently pressed for time as to prevent us spending a few days at St Helena, and so, early next morning, Wilton, Pirie, and I landed for a walk through some of the western parts of the island. We started up the steep stairway known as Jacob's Ladder, of 700 steps—a far more formidable climb than its mention may imply, or even its appearance conveys. At the top of the Ladder are Ladder Hill fort and artillery barracks, which can also be reached by a winding road zigzagging up the mountain-side. Once up to this height we found ourselves on an undulating plain, cut here and there with ravines, and here and there rising into peaks, the most prominent of which is High Knoll Hill, surmounted by a commanding fort. The hillsides are generally very barren or overrun with that plague of tropical countries, the prickly pear (*Opuntia*), which, once established, it is almost impossible to exterminate, for the smallest fragment of a "leaf" will hardly fail to take root on even the most barren and inhospitable ground. Farther inland the landscape rapidly improved, and we crossed some beautiful grassy meadows and whin-covered slopes, and passed some delightful houses nestling among a wealth of flowers, and surrounded by great hedges of purple *Plumbago*. The roads we traversed, particularly those cut out of the sides of valleys, were excellent, and they are almost entirely due to the labours of the troops formerly quartered at St Helena to guard Napoleon. These troops spent much time and trouble in road-making throughout the island, for want, I take it, of other occupation, but with the result that St Helena can boast of far better roads than many a country not half so mountainous. St Helena at least must be ever indebted to Napoleon, if only for these splendid roads.

The native flora of St Helena has now almost entirely disappeared, and probably could scarcely be found in even the most isolated places in the island, but a rich introduced flora has replaced it. On the higher ground the vegetation has a more temperate aspect, and some of the lanes were quite homelike in appearance. The ordinary European whin (*Ulex europæus*) luxuriates and flowers in profusion. Scattered oak-trees are to be seen, and in places fir- trees (*Pinus sylvestris* and *P. pinaster*) grow in plenty, all curiously bent towards the northwest before the ever-blowing south-east trade-winds,—just as, for example, many trees on the east coast of Scotland growing along the sea-cliffs are bent before the easterly onshore gales. Everlasting flowers (*Helichrysum*), natives of South Africa, grow by every roadside as well as many familiar European weeds. Lower down in the more sheltered valleys the vegetation is almost tropical, and castor oil-plants (*Ricinus communis*) and many species of yuccas and agaves with tall twenty-feet flower-spikes flourish. I have seen these flower-spikes occasionally cut off and placed side by side, the lower ends sunk into the ground, the upper bound by interwoven willows to form the walls of a hut. Banana palms bear excellent fruit in the valleys, and beans, potatoes, cabbages, and yams are produced on the uplands. Our first experience with prickly pears did not tempt us to try again. The fruits are studded over with tiny bunches of hooked hairs which must be carefully removed, but I, all unsuspectingly, neglected to do this, and found my fingers, and tongue also, tingling with a hundred sharp little needles, which took several days to ultimately disappear. The natives scrape all the fruits before eating them, and so protect their mouths, but seem quite unconcerned over getting their fingers covered with the prickly hairs. The substance of the fruit is a sweet watery pulp, generally rendered tepid by the hot sun, and far from luscious at any time.

The present conditions of the climate and vegetation in St Helena are excellent examples of the disastrous effect of too greatly interfering with the original vegetation of a country. St Helena was at the time of its discovery, in 1501, clothed with a rich vegetation and forests of red wood and ebony (*Melhania melanoxylon*). Then some early visitors, in about 1513, with laudable intentions, introduced goats, believing they might prove a source of food to castaway sailors, but the experiment was one whose full unwisdom was not to be revealed till much later. The goats, as these animals always will do, wrought great havoc among the trees. In 1709 the forests were rapidly diminishing, and a century later they had totally disappeared, and in consequence the rainfall most materially diminished, and, what was as bad, became spasmodic, so that when rain did fall it swept in torrents, its course unchecked now by vegetation, down the hillsides, washing the soil with it and leaving great tracks of barren desert only fit for their present crop of prickly pears. Surely the case of this island might be an object-lesson to statesmen and land-owners in other countries. But it would appear that it is not, and criminal negligence allows the small short-sighted policy of the destruction of timber to be pursued with yearly increasing activity in Scotland.

The harbour of Jamestown is teeming with fish of all kinds, many of them gaily coloured in crimson and blue and gold, all easily discernible in the clear water. The St Helena fishermen pursue their calling with apparently very little difficulty. From a small boat anchored in the bay a boy catches multitudes of little fish by simply scooping them up in a basket; these he passes on to the fisherman, who baits his line with one, casts it, and almost instantaneously hauls on board a large bonito (*Thynnus pelamys*) There is no delay and no precariousness The fish seem to be there waiting for their captor. Unfortunately our large Monagask trap was lost in this bay—probably by falling off some ledge of rock into deep water,—so that our collections here were more limited than we wished. On the evening of June 2 we got under way, and steamed along the coast of St Helena. Across the mouths of the ravines adjoining Jamestown valley I noticed that high walls were built with a little guard-house beside each. This, doubtlessly, is a relic of Napoleon's day, when these walls were designed to prevent his possible escape. Jamestown similarly is cut off from the sea by fortifications, which, unlike most others on the island, are still guarded, and the gate is nightly closed to inhabitants at 9 P.M., apparently with the only effect of denying them the one walk—that along the sea-front—where they can get any fresh cool air, unless they climb to the heights above. Strangers, however, are allowed by the guard to pass through the gates at any hour to get on board their ships.

The weather now began to get appreciably warmer, but the trade-wind still held fresh, which was an important consideration for us, as our coal-supply, after lavish use, was diminishing all too quickly. Next morning we sighted away to the east, on her way to Ascension, the RM.S. *Goth*, from the Cape and St Helena to Southampton, and we knew she was taking news of our whereabouts to Britain, which would arrive many weeks before the *Scotia* herself put in an appearance.

The ship was now full of little bird-cages containing some thirty or forty canaries and red-beaks (or Napoleons), natives of St Helena, which the crew, with a sailor's love of pets, had purchased before we left. There was a keen competition for favourable places to keep the cages, and for days birds were the chief topic of conversation. Some of the canaries were good singers, and all seemed to prosper well on board. After a time some men tired of them, and were willing to barter their birds. The ever versatile cook now showed himself in a new light, and assiduously tried to "corner" the bird-market on board, and he certainly had a fair measure of success,—only, I fear, to sell them for a mere song at Gourock on our return. Among the scientists were several owners of birds: but though we all vigorously resisted the offers of the cook, Mr Bruce's specimens alone arrived home safely; the others escaped, and were either blown off the ship or fell victims to Russ's insatiable hunting propensities.

During the night of June 6 the *Scotia* lay under easy steam, and early next morning steamed up to the island of Ascension. Rounding the northern point of the most uninviting and desert wilderness I ever saw, we found ourselves in Clarence Bay off the little collection of white cottages and barracks known as Georgetown. A sloop of war lying at anchor in the bay seemed to look familiar, and we were delighted to find, on nearer approach, that she was our old friend H.M.S. *Beagle*, whose captain and officers had given us such a hearty welcome at the Falkland Islands last December.

There was no mistaking Surgeon Bowen as he waved a cheery welcome to us from the quarterdeck. After the harbour formalities had been gone through we rowed off in the whale-boat to pay a visit to our friends on the *Beagle*, and once more were made welcome in her hospitable ward-room. She was leaving the same day, homeward-bound, *viâ* Sierra Leone to be paid out of commission, so our visit was, of necessity, short, and before we had landed the *Beagle* was away under steam and sail for the coast of Africa.

We landed at the Tartar Stairs, which are steps cut in a rock jutting out into the bay, and passing by the dockyard stores and great heaps of coal, reached the barrack square. Here are situated the captain's office, the barracks, the canteen, the bakery, and the little church. Every building is painted white and looks very neat and clean and bears a label descriptive of its use. Captain R. M'Alpine, R.N., greeted us cordially, and gave us full permission as British subjects to go anywhere on the island and to photograph anything we chose. It appears that the German Antarctic explorers, when they landed here from the *Gauss* on their homeward voyage, had a somewhat different experience. They were promptly arrested on setting foot on shore and marched to the captain's office, for Ascension ranks as a fortress, and no foreigner is allowed to set foot upon it. However, on Dr Drygalski's explaining that their objects were not aggressive, and that they had no desire to spy out the forts, Captain M'Alpine allowed them to stay ashore, and kindly ordered a couple of marines to accompany them to point out the most interesting scenery! but no cameras were allowed. The whole island of Ascension is but a fort, and is governed, just as a ship, with a captain in command. The population consists of some 200 seamen and marines, and about 100 West African Kroomen. A few of the men have their wives and families, but there is no civilian population, for even the Eastern Telegraph Company's clerks are considered as naval men during their stay at Ascension, as practically the sole use of the cable is for Admiralty dispatches. Life in Georgetown—or, as it is more generally known, Garrison—certainly cannot be exciting, yet all its inhabitants whom I spoke to assured me that they would far rather serve on H M S *Ascension* than on any ship afloat. Routine seems to be much as it is on board ship, but no doubt lacks the danger and possible emergencies, and also, I should think, the compensating excitement of a life at sea. There is a clock on the church, but time is marked by the striking of bells, and sentries dutifully keep watch on the barrack square. I suppose the order of sea-life becomes so ingrained in sailors that even when put to govern an island the old habits assert themselves, and they subconsciously fall into their accustomed sea-routine. We were courteously made free during our stay of the Royal Naval Club—a true oasis in a desert of cinder and dust. Captain M'Alpine, himself a keen naturalist, has made the beginnings of a small museum in Georgetown, and is gathering a very representative collection of the local fauna and flora, and it was gratifying to see that this museum, unlike so many others where there is far less excuse, is less cumbered with the usual impedimenta in the way of odds and ends chaotically thrown together, and only too valueless.

In the canteen—where, by the way, we found almost any article we could wish for, and all very cheap—we witnessed the usual evening scene of distributing the beer rations. White men are allowed two pints a-day, and many take it away with them, but the Kroomen are only allowed one pint, which must be drunk within the canteen: this is a necessary precaution to prevent them trading it to one another or storing it up for a "feast," at which wild orgies of a surety would take place.

Adjoining the settlement of Georgetown are the turtle-ponds, which, lying close to the sea, have their water renewed at every tide. There were some fifty huge turtles (*Chelone mydas*) in the two ponds, not to mention many smaller ones, down to tiny creatures half the size of one's hand. Two of these Mr Bruce carefully abstracted and kept on board alive until we reached Scotland. The full-sized turtles measure about four feet across, and weigh upwards of 600 lb., though how many years they take to attain this size I cannot say, but the growth of all these reptiles is slow. The Governor of St Helena had in his garden a tortoise over four feet across, which history said was almost as big when it arrived on the island 126 years ago. These turtles are captured when they come ashore to lay their eggs in the sand in the early part of the year. Men are stationed at their favourite beaches, and as soon as they have laid their eggs in the sand, and are in the act of again taking to the water, they are skilfully turned on their backs, and, thus rendered quite helpless, are easily transported to the turtle-ponds. Here they are kept until required, and appear to thrive excellently on a most scanty fare. Every week one is generally killed for the garrison, and served out as rations for meat and soup: men-o'-war calling here usually have one presented to them, but the majority are shipped to England alive with only a daily dose of sea-water to sustain them on the way. The Lords of the Admiralty have the right to receive a certain number annually from whence to make the much-relished turtle soup, and it has been suggested that that privilege is one of the most weighty reasons with the British Government for retaining possession of Ascension.

The great sight of Ascension is the Wideawake Fair, which is the name given to the gathering of the tropical terns (*Sterna fuliginosa*), which arrive at Ascension in thousands to lay their eggs every year at more or less uncertain intervals. Our visit did not coincide with the fair, but we nevertheless made an excursion to its site. The way lay for some three miles to the south and east of Georgetown over an absolutely barren plain of cinder, piled with heaps of clinker and strewn with fragments of volcanic bombs. It was difficult at first to convince myself that I was on natural ground and not crossing the artificial slag-heaps around some factory. It gave a good impression of what a recently or still active volcanic region must look like. Here and there were a few struggling plants, but not until we reached the vicinity of Wideawake were they even plentiful enough to give a tinge of green to the landscape. The most conspicuous plants were the purslane (*Portulaca oleracea*)—a common weed on all tropical shores, and a widely spread tropical grass (*Setaria verticillata*). In addition were a few plants of a species of Cape gooseberry (*Physalis peruviana*), and half a dozen wonderfully thriving specimens of clematis. The euphorbia (*E. origanoides*), one of the very few native plants of Ascension, was not to be seen on this road, but scattered plants of it were not uncommon on the road to Green Mountain, all growing strong and vigorous as if the conditions exactly suited it. The Wideawake plain lies in a hollow surrounded by the usual cinder-heaps,—not beautiful, but still very interesting, especially from a geological point of view. Though the terns were not present, plentiful skeletons testified to an enormous mortality among the birds annually.

The following day with Wilton and Pirie I set out to climb Green Mountain —the summit of the island. The road, which is practically the only road in the island outside Georgetown, winds its way across the desert plains for some three or more miles past the usual cinder-heaps and several wonderfully well-preserved cinder cones. Vegetation, from being almost absent except for a few euphorbia and purslane plants, gradually becomes more evident as the mountain slope is approached. Cape gooseberries and Madagascar roses (*Vinca rosea*), as well as a few aloes and prickly pears, are to be seen. A few planted palms are met with here and there, but none appear vigorous, and most look as if their period of existence is nearly at an end. The water-pipes from Green Mountain, whence the island's water-supply is obtained, follow more or less the course of the road, and we passed two or three drinking-tanks on the way. The most attractive was one inscribed "God be thanked!" for there, in addition to a supply of passable though somewhat warm water, was the welcome shade of a few prickly-pear bushes, to say nothing of their fruit. At the foot of the mountain is a resting-place of two up-ended boats sunk half-way into the ground, and from this spot, known as the Two Boats, the ascent by the winding roadway known as the "Ramps" begins. The scenery now rapidly changes, and becomes more and more verdant in appearance as the top is approached. The road is skilfully cut out of the soft and friable ash, but the mountain is steep and the way makes many turns. This does not suit the swift-footed Kroomen, who have constructed short cuts between each turning, resulting in a path almost straight up the slope: running up or down this they seem equally at ease. As we got higher the cool trade-wind made itself felt in tempering the scorching sun, and at each turn of the road it came to cheer us with a bath of fresh invigorating air. Half-way up, the road branches to the sanatorium—a home for sailors invalided with fever from West Africa. As a recruiting-station for our sailors and soldiers (and why not civilians too?) whose health has been undermined by the damp, hot, fever-haunted climate of West Africa, Ascension is looked on, and rightly too, as a valuable possession. It is no better in this respect than St Helena; but it is nearer to the mainland and that is all important, and if alone for this reason it would be a pity to abandon the island, whose cost is, after all, proportionately small. But the use of Ascension as a sanatorium might surely be developed if—and that is the great difficulty—the water-supply could be increased. At present it is so limited that the population must be rigorously kept within certain numbers.

About 600 feet from the summit we came upon the island gardens. Here a supply of vegetables are grown, chiefly sweet potatoes, with some cabbages and beans, for the garrison, and a certain number of cattle reared, while gorgeous begonias and cassias were flowering in profusion at the time. The farm and gardens are in charge of a sergeant of marines, with about a dozen marines and some twenty Kroomen under him. These men live in barracks adjoining the gardens, and are generally chosen from the garrison as men of particular knowledge in farming, shepherding, or the like. They were certainly all dressed in some semblance of uniform, but discipline is apparently not carried to the same extent at the farm as it is in Garrison. As one of the marines said to me, "Going to sea is all right up here: no clean buttons, no church parade, and only an officer now and then, when he takes the trouble to come up"—sentiments that they all echoed. We found the sergeant very friendly and glad to see us, and, what was most welcome news to us, learnt he was willing to supply us with plentiful draughts of delightfully cool ale. We sat at his window enjoying this when we spied away down the road one member of the Expedition, who shall be nameless, sitting by the roadside mopping his brow and, we felt sure, muttering imprecations about the weather and Ascension in general. Wilton and I hailed him and raised a tankard of ale to his sight, and then drank deeply to his luck. That action had a wonderful effect on the weary scientist. He rose like a new man and ascended the hill with feverish energy, certainly never halting until he found himself within the sergeant's room in the barracks. Passing through a dark tunnel 200 yards long, cut through the rock, we reached the water-collecting tanks. Some four or five acres of the south-eastern hillside are covered with cement, with a view of catching every rain-shower. The water drains down to a tank below, and thence is carried by pipes to Georgetown. The springs that half a century ago yielded a fair supply are all more or less dry now, and the island has to depend on rain for its supply of water. Daily this is served out in rations of two gallons per head of the population, and in times of drought this small ration has to be reduced, so that the keen interest that is taken in the occasional cloud-cap of Green Mountain can be imagined. In Georgetown the rainfall is under 3 inches a-year, but on the mountain-top reaches nearly 17 inches. While Mr Bruce and the others ascended some 500 feet higher to the top and the artificial water-lily pond to be found there, I explored a fascinating pass which I discovered running right round the mountain, a distance of nearly three miles. The way was ever varied, leading five times through short tunnels coated with moss and fern; then hanging over the edge of a precipice or suddenly diving through a mass of beautiful vegetation, to shortly emerge again and unfold a view over half the island and the shimmering ocean beyond; again to plunge once more through a narrow rocky defile,—and so on with endless changes. It afforded at one time or another a view over the entire island, and showed to perfection the structure of the land with its numerous little craters still so complete as to almost convince one they were the work of yesterday, and not of bygone ages. Coming again to the farm, I found a monument to the effect that this was "Elliott's Pass, built in 1840," and named, I believe, after the officer then in command.

The descent in the cool of the evening was very different to the morning climb, and even Ascension seemed a very charming spot as we crossed the plains of cinders in the glory of the sunset; but our peace of mind was rather shaken when we met Captain M'Alpine, who told us that the dreaded "rollers" had set in, and that to get on board would be extremely difficult. I need not enter into a discussion of these rollers: every traveller to Ascension or St Helena has spoken of them, and all equally in vain have tried to account for them, and their origin, despite the many ingenious theories, is still a mystery. But certainly the explanation that the rollers are the waves produced at the floating off from the Antarctic glaciers of huge icebergs, can be dismissed as a perfectly groundless theory, even could the non-occurrence of similar rollers on many southern islands nearer to Antarctica be overlooked. After a long wait,—for Mr Bruce and Pirie had gone a roundabout way across country, under the guidance of one of the marines, to see the Devil's Riding-School crater,—we were ready to go aboard. The rollers by this time were worse, and were dashing wildly against the Tartar Stairs, or rolling majestically up the sandy beach on either side in great curling man-high waves of foam. It was now almost dark, but the attempt had to be made, and for half an hour the whale-boat under Fitchie's command had been lying off the landing-place with a picked crew. We found that between every two or three rollers there was a momentary lull—that was the time to take advantage of; and though it seemed a trifle rash to jump—I might almost say blindly—off the stairs towards a boat tossing madly six feet below one in a roaring sea, yet we all accomplished it without accident,—even Cuthbertson, who was still lame with wounds inflicted on him by our pet (?) monkey: but some of the collections suffered,—the plants got wet, and a few of Pirie's rocks missed the boat, and were never seen again.

On the morrow the rollers had moderated a good deal, and progress to and from the shore was relatively easy. The fact was, I suppose, that we were getting used to landing and embarking under practically any conditions in which a boat could live. The Antarctic had been a good training-ground.

Clarence Bay afforded many fish, and we caught with hook and line several splendid albacore (*Thynnus albicora*), one of which scaled 120 lb. Man-eating sharks were also to be seen hovering near the ship, and the cooks, ever keen fishermen, hooked several small ones. A sailor considers it nothing short of a duty to capture and kill every shark he is able to: sharks and sailors are sworn enemies, and the sailor for his part will never cease to wage the war. We trawled in the bay and caught over a hundred fish, including the hog- or coffer-fish (*Ostracion*), a porcupine fish, and many flat fish.

An interesting bird in the harbour was the frigate-bird (*Fregeta aquila*), which hovers high above the water, spying out its prey, and then suddenly, with a splash like a cannon-ball, drops straight down into the sea, to emerge in a few moments with a captured fish.

On June 10 the *Scotia* got under way on the next stage of her homeward journey. We were rapidly approaching the equator, but at that season of the year the south-east trade-winds generally hold to several degrees north of the line. The weather now began to get oppressively warm and damp, hardly an invigorating climate, and yet we had much to do. All the accumulated zoological specimens of the past eighteen months had to be overhauled. Pirie and I had out every individual bottle and renewed the preservative fluid in each, while, with the help of the piper, we sealed each one with a firmly secured bladder to make all ready for transportation to Edinburgh from our port of discharge. At the same time Wilton undertook the more laborious and less pleasant task of over-hauling the barrels and tanks of fish, and, when needed, of strengthening or renewing the spirit in which they were preserved. We all took our turns at the meteorological observations, which were now, however, only taken every four hours, and in the almost monotonously steady weather we experienced afforded little of interest and no excitement. Two or three times daily I cast my tow-net over, continuing my *plankton* collections. The catch was now markedly different to that in Antarctic waters. Instead of the then predominant diatoms, I now rarely got algæ: small crustaceans were commonest, but seldom was the catch large. Occasionally, if by shortening the line I allowed the net to skim the surface, one of those curious tropical insects (*Halobates*) was caught,—the only insect which, skimming always over the surface of the water, has its home on the open ocean. At noon Wilton regularly took a sample of ocean water to determine its specific gravity, and Ross was busy with his bird-skins, to say nothing of the floats which were thrown overboard day by day. Cuthbertson was always at his painting or his drawing, for we secured enough beasts to keep him more than busy; and Mr Bruce was every-where superintending.

Flying-fish (*Exocetus volitans*) became very plentiful, and shoals were to be seen continually rising out of the waves on either bow, skimming the water for twenty or thirty yards, and then plunging into another wave. I watched them carefully both on our outward journey and now, on our homeward, but despite what has been said in support of the theory, I cannot say that I ever saw them use their fins to propel themselves while in the air. Their "flight" is more in the nature of a spring from the water than a real flight, and though no doubt their pectoral fins buoy the fish to some extent when once they are in the air, I doubt exceedingly if they can in any sense be looked upon as functional wings.

Fleets of Portuguese men-o'-war (*Physalia atlantica*), and other characteristically tropical animals, continually passed, their "sails" set to the breeze. They seem to always go before the wind, and could not well do otherwise; but where, in this case, do they all come from, and whither do they all go? Delicate velellas, transparent blue creatures that seem all too fragile for an ocean home, floated by at frequent intervals.

On June 13 we crossed the equator after eighteen months in the southern hemisphere. The previous day the last Antarctic beard in the cabin disappeared. Did its owner anticipate a summary removal on crossing the line, or was its disappearance due to the proximity to home, which our passing into the northern hemisphere signified?

We were now on the verge of the belt of "dead" water between the easterly Guinea current and the westerly equatorial current. This part of the ocean is of great physical interest, and we spent several hours on three consecutive days taking water-samples with the Pettersen-Nansen water-bottle. The wind was getting lighter as we approached the "doldrums," and rain-showers began. They were welcome enough at first, but were decidedly unpleasant as they became heavier and more frequent, and one awoke in one's deck-hammock at night with a stream of chilly water pouring into it from the spanker sail. That meant a frantic rush below, and a more or less vain attempt to sleep on floor or cabin table for the remainder of the night—the bunks themselves were uninhabitable in that heat. In about 6° N. we were fairly in the equatorial calms. The last of the cheery south-east trade-wind had died away in a faint southerly air, leaving a calm oily sea rising in great northerly heaves of swell with no apparent force behind them, and around the black threatening sky or the mist of steady down-pour with the sudden random squalls from anywhere and everywhere, and through all the stifling stagnant heat. All contributed to a feeling of uncanniness that made me more than once think with longing of the belt of blazing sunshine and steady breezes to north and south. Fortunately we were not at the mercy of these capricious squalls as a "wind-jammer" would be, and our engines helped us northward; fortunately, too, at that particular season of the year the north- and south-east trade-winds come relatively near one another and leave a narrower belt of calms than usual, so the Captain hourly hoped to pick up a breeze. One night—he used now to sleep in a wigwam on the bridge—the Captain felt a breeze as he put his head out to have a look at the weather, and at once jumping to the conclusion it was the looked-for trade-wind, he gave the order to put the ship "by the wind." But it was only a variable "doldrum" breeze, and yet before he discovered his mistake we had gone W.N.W. and W. for some five or six hours.

Next day we picked up a breeze, but it was not easterly enough: probably we were too far to the east, for the farther west one goes the more easterly, and consequently more favourable for homeward-bound ships, is the north-east trade. The Captain held on, hoping to pass eastward of the Cape Verde Islands with the help of the westerly monsoon off the African coast, but somehow we never found that monsoon, and in 20° 30′ W. the only sure prospect we had was of passing altogether eastward of the trade-winds. So about went the *Scotia*, and under steam and sail we held to the westward in search of that elusive trade-wind. The sun was now hotter than ever, and bare feet burnt on the scorching decks; but the nights were cool and pleasant, and gradually the wind drew little by little towards the north-east. At noon on June 21, in sight on our starboard bow, was St Jago, one of the Cape Verde Islands, and soon after Fogo loomed up ahead. Time and the certainty of spending money prohibited us calling at Porta Praya, and we made sail to the westward to clear Brava before hauling up to the north-ward. Hazy weather spoilt the view, but Fogo's smoke was clearly visible as we passed.

The *Scotia* was getting very light with her diminished coal-supply, and was always close-hauled these days, so she heeled over at an angle of 10° to 20° when the breeze was fresh. For several days we held on as near the wind as possible, but always to the west of north, and never very quickly. We were now getting into the

Western Ocean, and gulf-weed (*Sargassum vulgare*) was plentiful, in fragments from the size of a plate to great floats many yards across. Angling for the gulf-weed provided a new interest, and the bulwarks seldom lacked some keen scientist or sailor armed with a long bamboo at whose end was a net or a set of shark-hooks. Many quaint animals shelter themselves among the weed, particularly lively little crabs and sometimes beautiful little fish (*Antennarius*) or shrimps: but since every beast that makes the weed its home is protectively coloured, they were difficult to pick out. A piece of gulf-weed in a sealed bottle was a curio added to most of the sailors' collections. A characteristic animal of these seas is the dainty reddish-brown jelly-fish (*Pelagia noctiluca*), which gives to the waters at night the curious effect of splotches of dull light.

The dog-watch in these days was always lively, sometimes with a concert, oftener with some form or other of mischief, and, if the latter, Murray was quite sure to take a leading part. Florence, the steward, held mock auctions on several evenings on the fo'c'sle head of odds and ends and surplus clothing from the cabin. Partly, I think, because our progress was too slow to suit the eagerness of the crew to be home, but largely, no doubt, as a mere diversion, an effigy of the chief engineer was one day prepared and in the dog-watch produced, solemnly convicted and condemned to be strung from the fore yard-arm and burnt—a sentence duly carried out.

Delightful weather favoured us as we passed beyond the trade-wind into the "horse latitudes," and as we steamed north-westward towards the Azores we overhauled more than one nearly be-calmed ship, who must have wondered at our speed until we had passed, and our funnel, abaft the mainsail, was revealed to view.

As a preparation for our return, all hands that could be spared were now busy painting the ship. The total want of taste exhibited by sailors is really most remarkable. All they seek for is brilliance, and congruity of colour would appear to be an idea utterly alien to the seafaring mind. Had not Mr Bruce been arbiter in the decoration of the ship, it would soon have borne a striking resemblance in colour to an Italian ice-cream shop. And, moreover, certain colours must, it appears, be used for certain parts, and these conventions are as firmly rooted in the sailors' belief as any canon of the social code might be in the mind of the average Britisher.

On July 3 the height of Pico, the loftiest of the Western Isles, was sighted, only to be shortly lost again in cloud. Mr Bruce was anxious to trawl on the Princess Alice Bank, a shoal of about 100 fathoms fifty miles south of Fayal. A day was spent in looking for it, and ultimately a trawling in 800 fathoms failed through the trawl jamming in the rocks, and the catch was nil.

On July 5 we dropped anchor off the town of Horta in Fayal. S.M.S. *Gazelle* of the German Navy, homeward bound from the West Indies, was on the point of leaving. Her anchor was up, and she was getting under way as the *Scotia* entered the harbour, but her captain very kindly sent on board at once to ask if he could take a mail to Europe for us. We gladly took advantage of his offer, and certainly letters would not otherwise have reached Scotland before us.

The Portuguese health officials were exceedingly angry that the Germans had boarded us before we were cleared, but the *Gazelle* was off by this time, and their anger had to waste itself away.

Near us in the harbour lay the American whaler, *Morning Star* of New Bedford, which had for many months pursued her trade in the South Atlantic, off the coast of Africa, and now had put in here to boil down blubber and refit.

The town of Horta is a typically southern town, with its square whitewashed houses and narrow streets, and a general appearance of easy-going good-natured content. No one seems to be in the least hurry or to have any work on hand, except a very few who struggle along with huge loads on their heads. The inhabitants are all natives or Portuguese: negroes are very rare. The quaint black scuttle bonnet of the Azorean women and the long black cloak seem to be a vanishing costume, for only the older women wear them now.

There is a fort commanding the harbour, but it has an air of dilapidation,— so much so, that the tired-looking and sleepy sentry outside is quite in keeping.

The youthful wander-thirst of the young men of Fayal used to find outlet in migration, for a few years in early manhood, to the United States, where the wages were relatively high, and enabled the wanderer to return in time with his savings to settle down in Fayal. In consequence of this English is commonly understood in parts of the island, particularly among the older people. A more direct connection between this island and the United States seems to be in contemplation by the latter country, which has lately shown some inclination to purchase the island of Fayal, doubtless as a coaling-station, and, one might almost fear, in some measure as an armed outlier thrown towards the Powers of Europe.

Accompanied by Captain Acuña, the British Consul, several of us went a drive through the island on the following day. Up on the ridge above Horta we got a view across the fertile island, all cut up into tiny fields, with white cottages dotted here and there. The higher ground is uncultivated and thinly populated, but all along the ridges windmills are to be seen. Descending, we drove through the sleepy little village which goes by the name of Flamingoes (so called after the earliest settlers, who were Flemish, a word corrupted into Flemings, and thence to its present form). The village streets are narrow and crooked, but paved, and often very well paved. The houses seemed deserted except for the children playing about the doors, and now and then a glimpse of a pretty face from behind a shutter, quickly withdrawn if one dared to look. The men and the older women were all at work in their fields, for in Fayal the peasants own their land, and though they are heavily taxed by Portugal, yet are left largely to themselves in other respects, and seem very happy. The whole population is agricultural, and grows chiefly maize, wheat, peaches, and oranges. Only the year before peaches had been so cheap that they were sold for over 200 a penny. Dairy produce is plentiful in Fayal; and I was told on good authority that a brisk trade in eggs is done with the stewards of the Portuguese mail-boats, who in their turn sell them at Madeira to the stewards of the Cape liners, and thence they find a market in poor starving Cape Town. The very name Horta means garden, and it is richly deserved, for the whole island is one beautiful garden. Fortunately we were there in time to see the exquisite pale-blue hydrangeas at their best: along the road we drove they were in league-long hedges, often ten feet high.

In the evening the *Scotia* was surrounded by scores of little boats conveying the beauties of Horta, who gazed on her with undisguised admiration, but who seemed a little startled when the piper broke forth upon his pipes.

I would gladly have spent longer at the Azores, but we had peremptory orders to be home; and so on July 6 we were off at nightfall, with our bunkers replenished and water-tanks filled. The neighbouring island of Pico was soon astern, and at daybreak Graciosa was fading away on the port-quarter, and Terceira, on the starboard beam, was quickly losing itself in mist. Shoals of porpoises accompanied us at times. When they are seriously fishing their movements are very quick: they jump right out of the water some two feet and in again, an animation quite foreign to their movements when they are lazily shifting ground.

After a few days of uncertainty the breeze drew more to the westward and freshened. The *Scotia* sped onward at some seven or eight knots under full sail, heading straight for Waterford. The weather was chilly now, and no more did a tropical sun scorch the deck. Fitchie, who always had a yarn ready when he liked, told me it reminded him of a sailor who, coming home after five years in the tropics, ran into a gale of wind in the Channel, and with great relish exclaimed, "This is more like it: none of your God-damned blue skies here!" And certainly it was homelike to see the soft rainclouds again. We ran across the Bay of Biscay with a full-sail breeze on the port-quarter. In the chops of the Channel it freshened and the sea rose a good deal, but the wind held fair and still we kept on our course. There was no stopping the good ship now: as the sailors put it, "The girls have got hold of the tow-rope!" Plenty of ships were sighted now in these busy seas. We passed close to a homeward-bound barque steering for the Channel under a full spread of canvas, and sighted near us to the east a four-masted basque outward-bound. On the 14th (Thursday) the breeze had freshened again, but the more the merrier, for land was only a day ahead. We passed many trawlers bound for the Biscayan fishing-grounds, struggling onward into the teeth of the gale, pitching madly into the sea, and ever and again lost in a cloud of sea and spray.

At 7.30 P.M. we sighted the light of Coningsby lightship, and almost at once picked up the Barrel lightship. A few minutes after the look-out man hailed the bridge with "Red light on the starboard bow," and all the cabin tumbled on deck to see the Tuskar Light.

The night closed in wild and thick, and shut out the Lucifer Shoal and Blackwater lightships. The tide ran with a phenomenal speed that upset all the mate's calculations, and, in consequence, at daybreak we were fairly at a loss to know what part of the Irish coast was nearest us, and how far from land we were; and this on the morning of our return. But the South Arklow lightship warned us off in time when we were running straight for the dangerous Arklow bank; and a friendly little schooner, with an unmistakably Irish skipper, whom the Captain hailed, put us right again, and at noon on July 15 the *Scotia* anchored in Kingstown Harbour.

At home, in Scotland, we had not been expected for a few days yet, for naturally no plans could have foreseen such a rapid run across the Atlantic as the *Scotia* had contrived to make from the Azores. In consequence we received most imperative orders not to show ourselves in the Clyde until the 21st, on which day a great reception had been prepared for us.

It was tantalising to have come from so far, and then after so long an absence to have to wait outside the very threshold of home, but there was no alternative. Our reception had already had its date changed once, and to do it again was impossible. Perhaps we would all of us have liked to quietly slip home and escape it, but thousands longed to give us a welcome, and the day was really theirs.

Our stay in Ireland was delightful, and its ever kind inhabitants vied with one another to accord us a royal triumph in Kingstown, Bangor, and Lame. But at last the day of home-coming came. We steamed across to Lamlash as the mists of morning rolled away, and there at length was the Scotland of our dreams before us in the purple hills of Arran. Mr James Coats, jun., was awaiting us there with a cheery welcome, and, escorted by his yachts *Triton* and *Gleniffer*, we proceeded up the Clyde towards Millport. Soon the little *Mermaid* of the Millport Marine Station met us and signalled she had a communication to deliver, which proved to be a telegram from the King to the Leader in the following words:—

> "I am commanded by the King to congratulate you and the officers and crew of the *Scotia* on your and their safe return, and on the completion of your important additions to the scientific knowledge and discoveries in the south-eastern part of the Weddell Sea.   KNOLLYS."

Almost at the same time a larger and crowded vessel bore down on us, and, with a piercing shriek of welcome, turned and joined our escort. Then from her bridge, where the form of that veteran world-traveller, Sir John Murray, was easily distinguishable, rang the cry, "Three cheers for the *Scotia*": to Ailsa Craig the echo of those cheers must have rung. It was the *Marchioness of Lorne* with the relatives and friends of these on board the *Scotia*, and many also of these patriotic Scotsmen who had sent us on our voyage. Half an hour later we landed opposite the Marine Station, and were received by Sir John Murray, K.C.B., and Dr J. F. Gemmill, President of the Station, amid the cheering of a vast crowd.

That night the *Scotia,* to the salvo of guns, the shrieking of fog-sirens, and the cheering of multitudes, proceeded up -stream and let go her anchor in Gourock Bay—the end of her 30,000 miles of wanderings. And of that little band of us, comrades for twenty-two long months, each went his separate way.

CHAPTER XIV

THE SECOND WINTER

DEPARTURE OF SCOTIA—HOUSE IMPROVEMENTS—SOUTH-EAST GALE—BUILDING A BREAKWATER—CAPTURE OF CUTTLE-FISH—ANOTHER SOUTH-EAST GALE—HOUSE IN DANGER—DAMAGE DONE—BUILDING OF NEW STORE-ROOM—INDEPENDENCE DAY—OPTICAL AND ATMOSPHERIC PHENOMENA—WINTER ROUTINE—A COLD SNAP—A REMARKABLE ICEBERG—SCIENTIFIC WORK IN WINTER.

ON Monday, February 22, at noon, the *Scotia* steamed out of Scotia Bay, and proceeding through Washington Strait into Jessie Bay, was last seen at 4.30 P.M. heading for Cape Dundas. The week succeeding her departure, as was to be expected, was one of great activity. There was much to be done in the way of arranging stores and putting things in order generally; but much was got through by the end of the month. The *personnel* consisted of Mr Szmula, who had already had considerable experience of meteorological work while in the service of the Argentine Meteorological Office; Mr Valette, naturalist to the Expedition, who had travelled extensively in Tierra del Fuego and Patagonia, and an Argentine youth named Acuña, whose profession it was difficult to define. Having come down armed with a post-office letter-stamp and a mail-bag containing books, we named him the P.M.G.—otherwise Postmaster-General; Smith, the house-steward, who had given every satisfaction during the stay of the summer party left here while the *Scotia* was absent at Buenos Aires, remained on in that capacity. The work to be undertaken for the Argentine Meteorological Office was—to continue the hourly meteorological observations commenced on the *Scotia's* arrival here on March 25, 1903, and also to obtain as complete a series of magnetic observations and natural history collections as circumstances would

161

permit of. The proposal to have the station continued until the end of 1904 originated with Mr Bruce, and was cordially supported by Mr Davis, the enterprising Director of the Argentine Meteorological Service, who sent me a very kind letter asking me to remain on and assist in the work. Although it was with considerable regret that I parted with Mr Bruce and my associates on the *Scotia*, still I felt that it was very desirable that I should remain at the South Orkneys. The meteorological work on the *Scotia* was in able hands, and my absence during the short time that would elapse until the arrival of the ship at Cape Town was unimportant. On the other hand, it was very necessary that there should be some one left behind who had experience in running a winter station, and was familiar with the dangers incidental to life in a region where glaciers and pack-ice offered innumerable traps for the unwary. It may be parenthetically observed that the scientific results to be obtained from the continuation of the meteorological observations until the end of 1904 would add very considerably to our scanty knowledge of the climatic vicissitudes in this part of the globe, the value of the work being much increased by the circumstance that for a part of the time the *Scotia* would be making simultaneous observations to the south and east, while to the west there was the French Expedition under Charcot. Thus, by combining these observations and co-ordinating them with observations taken on ships going round Cape Horn, daily synoptic charts for the Weddell quadrant could be prepared, the study of which would throw much light on the atmospheric phenomena of this portion of the South Atlantic and Antarctic seas. Much the same considerations applied to the magnetic work.

During the visit of the *Scotia* a number of improvements were made on the house. The roof was covered with wood, and a shed and coal-locker of the same material were erected,—the former along with the old whale-boat forming the store-room. A covered passage joining up the porch of the house with the store-room was also constructed, thus giving ready access to the stores and coal without having to dig away snow, which, in this particular portion of The Beach, drifted excessively owing to the proximity of high cliffs to the south-west.

Early in March migratory movements of birds began to take place. On the fifth I have an entry as follows: "Very few penguins have been seen for over a fortnight, and none of the black-throated species (adelia penguins) since February 11, when they were seen at the rookery. There are still a large number of ringed penguins and gentoos moulting on the north moraine, but they have practically deserted the south beach, their favourite resting-place. Cape pigeons, snowy petrels, and terns have been rarely observed, but skuas and nellies are still with us." A heavy snowstorm and strong south-east wind set in early on the morning of the 8th. At 7 A.M. I was awakened (having gone off night-watch at 4.30 A.M.) by hearing Smith shout "The boat," referring to the dinghy which was lying on a bank of snow in front of the house, and close to the sea, which was heavy. Large portions of the ice-foot continued to break away from time to time, and that on which the boat was placed gave way and was seen to be going, boat and all, into the water. Hurriedly putting on some clothes, I went out with some of the others and pulled the boat into a position of safety. Soon after the outer stone wall and path round the south and south-east side of the house got undermined by the waves and partly broken down. The house had thus been built too near the sea for safety. It must be remembered that when Mr Bruce and myself selected a site for the magnetic hut, meteorological station, and house, soon after the arrival of the *Scotia* in the Bay in March 1903, the whole beach was covered with a vast load of snow. The previous summer, that of 1902-3, must have been a very cold one, even for this inhospitable region, and it is very probable that the break-up of the ice in Scotia Bay took place but a few days before our arrival there on March 25, as there was a considerable ice-foot. Practically nothing of the south beach could be seen, consequently it was impossible to form any idea regarding the general configuration of the ground. The building was placed at a considerable distance from the water, so far as could be judged from tidal cracks in the ice, but the nearest of these cracks to the house was certainly not the "high-water mark." When the ice went out on November 23 it left a perpendicular ice-foot from six to twenty feet in height projecting into the sea beyond the low-water mark. This was gradually undercut, and, continuing to break away at intervals, it was well on in January before any idea of the general nature of the ground on which the house was built could be formed. Another point to be noted was that until March 8 we had never had a south-easterly gale of any consequence. The effect of a breeze from this quarter would of course depend on the quantity of ice in the ocean to the south, because, with a sea full of pack, the bay would fill up with ice and there would be no danger. The summer of 1903-4 must have been a very open one in the Weddell Sea: no pack was seen by us in the vicinity of the islands, and, as subsequently transpired, the *Scotia* on her voyage south did not encounter any until the Antarctic circle was reached.

The three weeks succeeding March 8 were devoted to building a breakwater in front of the house, the stones being brought from an adjacent scree-slope on sledges. Some very large ones were used,—one weighing considerably over a ton. This monster took the five of us seven hours' hard work with block and tackle to drag a distance of sixty-five yards. There were also several others, each weighing over half a ton. Altogether about forty tons of rock were used in building the breakwater. Work at this occupied us till the 29th. "We could labour at this indefinitely, but wish to see how it will stand before doing anything further at it. I hope, all the same, that it is not put to the test." On the 23rd a large cuttle-fish was caught in Scotia Bay. The creature, which was over six feet in length, had evidently been injured in conflict with a seal, as it was in a torpid state, with a deep wound about the centre of its body. There is no doubt that the Weddell seal preys upon this creature, as we frequently found the undigested beaks of cuttle-fish among the contents of their stomachs.

On the 22nd there were a considerable number of penguins (ringed and gentoo) on The Beach. "It is fully two months since there have been so many about." On the 27th a Ross seal—a rare variety here—was seen on the south beach close to the house. It was unfortunately too near the water, and, being disturbed, made its escape before there was time to fetch a rifle to shoot it. Numerous penguins were seen on the 28th, evidently on their way north, in which direction they were unable to proceed owing to the very heavy sea and surf beating on the north beach. A high tide and considerable sea on the 30th washed a great deal of rubble up on our sea-wall, making a more natural slope and tending to consolidate the whole.

By the end of the month the effects of the long summer thaw were apparent, imparting an appearance of ineffable dreariness to the prospect. "To the north a cold stormy sea dashes its clouds of semi-frozen spray against the iron-bound coast. To the south great bergs drift in silent procession past Ailsa Craig, which rises sharp and grim from the ice-cold waters. Everywhere ice and snow and crumbling tooth-shaped mountains covered with glaciers which descend into the sea, while ever and anon huge fragments break away, churning the waters into a chaos of foam. Above, a cold leaden sky covered with thick flying clouds, through which the pale disc of a lifeless sun can at times be dimly perceived through the whirling drift-snow. Is it to be wondered at that our minds reflect to a certain extent the gloom of the surroundings? How different is the scene in winter, when everything is draped in a mantle of virgin white, and when the pack covers the sea and extends the field of our peregrinations."

On April 2 another Ross seal was seen on the north beach, but, as on the former occasion, again escaped, much to the chagrin of our naturalist, who was anxious to secure a specimen. On the evening of the 3rd a very heavy south-east gale set in, the wind reaching a velocity of seventy miles per hour for the hour ending midnight, the barometer failing with great rapidity. I was on night-watch (11 P.M. to 4 A.M.), and before turning in at 5 A.M., went down to the water's edge to have a look at the sea, which was setting right into the bay, the south-east being the only direction in which it is exposed. I did not then apprehend any immediate danger. Valette, who was on morning-watch, reported that the 5 A.M. observation was taken without difficulty. At six o'clock the sea had risen to such a degree that he was caught by a wave when at the anemometer, and got soaked up to the waist. The path round the south side of the house as well as the sea-wall in front were at this hour intact. At seven things were looking serious,—the breakwater had been demolished, and of the path only a breadth of about eighteen inches was left. Seas at this time were sweeping past the house on both sides, while clouds of spray dashed over it. Again in taking the observation Valette got a soaking. At 7.30 the inmates were wakened, as the sea was now sweeping a long way over the spit, carrying boxes, barrels, &c., right over the highest ridge. Every wave we thought would give the finishing stroke, and to all appearance there was little hope of the southern half of the house standing. Everything was now water-logged with brine, the air-temperature at the time being 15°. After having a hurriedly-prepared breakfast we rapidly collected clothing, bedding, documents, and some other necessary articles, which were placed in the store-room, and vacated the building. The tents were taken over to the highest point of the north beach as a precautionary measure, but owing to the strong wind could not be pitched. Soon after eight o'clock we gathered together in the magnetic hut, where we awaited the apparently inevitable demolition of the southern half of the house with a composure due doubtless to the numbing effect of the unexpected situation. Every one was soaked to the skin, due to our previous exposure in getting the boat and some stores into a position of safety. Even the hut was not to be relied upon as a place of refuge; and as several seas swept past it, carrying small pieces of ice a distance of fifty feet beyond, we could not help thinking of our position should this go too. Part of the dry-stone wall round it was also washed away. A further source of danger was the large blocks of ice, some weighing several tons, which had been torn off the glacier to the north-east and carried by the sea into close proximity to the hut. One of considerable size was stranded in a line with it, while there was a large piece grounded thirty-four yards to the E. N. E., which was 17½ feet long, 4½ feet high, and 6 feet 8 inches broad. These storm-tossed blocks, which extended fully 100 yards from the shore, presented a magnificent and imposing spectacle, which we should have appreciated more had our position been less precarious, as had one of these pieces struck the hut it would have demolished it—such was the force and impetus of the seas. At 9 A.M. I went over to a piece of high ground to the south-west of the house and took two photographs, snap-shots, which show the building with waves sweeping past it. Large stones were carried away from the base of the cairn and from a heap surrounding the anemometer. From 8 to 10 A.M. was the critical time, and it was a miracle that the house stood. About ten Szmula and I returned to the house, although there was some risk in doing so. We were both chilled to the bone, and wanted to change our wet clothes. At this time the sea had fallen somewhat, but the wind still blew very hard. By 11.30 all immediate danger was past, and the rest of the party joined us. The fire fortunately had not gone out, so Smith made us some coffee, which was very acceptable. Everything inside, on and near the floor, was wet, a considerable quantity of water from the heavy seas having managed to get in. During the early forenoon the outer porch got undermined and collapsed, while the strong wind wrecked the covered passage leading from the porch to the store-room, into which an entrance was made by removing boxes from the lee side. The house now presented a truly deplorable appearance. The south corner, under the buttress and extending from the door to the E.S.E. window, was entirely gone, and the buttress itself for this distance was literally suspended in the air without support, and only kept from falling by a mass of frozen spray which glued the whole together. The north-east side of the building was in a less precarious condition. The whole beach for about twenty yards to the north of a line passing through the anemometer, cairn, and magnetic hut was strewn with seaweed and marine organisms in large numbers, not to mention boxes of stores. For example, a case of meat measuring about 5 feet by 21 by 12 inches was stranded ten yards due north of the anemometer. To the southwest and west of the house numerous boxes, barrels, sledges, and miscellaneous gear were firmly embedded (some covered) with frozen brine. In the afternoon both wind and sea moderated,—a most fortunate circumstance, as an evening tide and sea of the same height and impetus as that of the morning would undoubtedly have destroyed the house. As it was, in the late evening the sea came right up to the house, but as there was no great force behind it, no further damage was done. The exceptional features attending this gale were due to an unusual if not unprecedented combination of circumstances. The Weddell Sea was open to the south, the wind was of hurricane strength, and from the only quarter to which the bay was exposed. It was, further, the equinoctial tide, the moon being in perigee and nearly full. Further, the barometer was very low, which of itself alone would have raised the waters some twelve or eighteen inches above the normal. It is not unlikely that most of the damage was done by a tidal wave about the time of high-water.

The relief from this pressing danger, although in every way gratifying, gave no assurance of permanent security. Twice within a month we had seen the results of weeks of toil swept away by the sea in a few hours. It seemed futile to labour further at a sea-wall. At a moderate calculation some 150 tons of rocks would be required to build up to the buttress from a sufficiently broad base. This would mean at least forty days' work doing nothing else, and we were at the commencement of an Antarctic winter. Every exertion was now made to repair the damaged buttress. Empty barrels, boxes, and coal-sacks filled with rubble from the beach (on which part of the house now stood) were utilised, and as we all worked like niggers, good progress was made on the 5th and 6th. On the 7th, however, the sun came out strong, and underpinning had to be hurriedly done by shoving boxes of ship's biscuits, &c., under the buttress, which had started to thaw, and was in imminent danger of collapsing. Work in this direction was practically finished on the 11th. "Whether our efforts so far as we have gone will meet with permanent success remains to be seen, as no definite opinion can be formed at present, owing to the large patches of ice which still glue the whole together." A new store-room, which might possibly have to serve us as a living-room in the event of another Neptunian invasion, was now in process of construction, the walls being composed of boxes of stores, with a canvas roof covered with rubberite. This was surrounded by a dry-stone dyke, which was completed on the 22nd, about sixty tons of rock being used in its construction. The stones were sledged from an adjacent scree-slope, the work being greatly facilitated at first by fine weather. From the 19th to the 22nd it was, however, unpleasant work, there being much snow, while the stones had to be hacked out with picks, being frozen hard. On the 29th it blew another hard gale from the south-east, but as the sea continued quite moderate it was evident that there was ice to the south. At 2 A.M. on the 30th pack-ice was seen to the south-east; at 3 A.M. it was about Ailsa Craig, and by 11 A.M. Scotia Bay was full of it.

As regards animal life, in April a sea-elephant (*Macrorhinus leoninus*) came ashore on the 11th; I noted on the 19th that skuas had been scarce for some days, but that for a week large numbers of paddies were in the vicinity of the house, and had become remarkably tame. On the 20th hundreds of Cape pigeons and a few nellies were feeding on the surface of the water in front of the house. The Cape pigeons were probably in process of migration. Penguins were scarce, but on the 26th large numbers of the ringed species were on the beach. No black-throats (adelias) were seen during the month. Another Ross seal was seen on the 26th. Very good weather for this unsettled region characterised the month of May: from the 4th to the 31st there was not a day on which I did not get from two to three hours' exercise, which took the form of short excursions over the floe (which consolidated by the 11th) or up on the northern glacier. The 25th being "Independence Day" of the Argentine Republic, we treated it as a holiday, and had a special menu at lunch and dinner. The Argentine flag was flying from the cairn, on which Szmula stood in a striking attitude, like Ajax defying the lightning, in which position he was photographed by Valette. As opportunity presented itself we killed penguins for winter consumption, over 100 being ob-tained during the month. A welcome change of fare was also afforded by the capture of large numbers of fish resembling rock cod. They weighed on the aver-age a little over a pound, and proved excellent eating, tasting rather like whiting. Almost every day Acuña and Valette were out fishing, a hole being kept open in the ice through which lines or a trap were lowered.

During the month some exceptionally fine days were experienced. The 30th was one of the most glorious I have ever seen. In the afternoon I ascended to the crest of the ridge which overlooked Wilton Bay. The prospect was indescribably beautiful, the sky being cloudless, the horizon perfectly clear, and the air in-tensely transparent. No less than twenty-five icebergs were seen to the south. As the sun declined the numerous snow-clad peaks were tinged with innumerable irradiations,—indeed all the shades resulting from a combination of brilliant red, deep purple, yellow, and orange hues were at various times to be seen. One small dome-shaped peak coruscated for some time like an enormous fiery opal, exhibiting a phantasmagoria of kaleidoscopic effects. To the south on the hori-zon a curious purple cloud, or rather nebulosity, could be seen, while at the same time a brilliant shaft of red light, the last effort of the declining sun, streamed over the floe, illuminating the eastern extremity of a distant berg. After the sun set a deep purple overspread the landscape, and the sky to the north became of a rich carmine colour, shading into blue near the zenith. A bright star came out,

the moon rose to the south, the combined colour effect giving the scene an indescribable but ineffably beautiful character of silence, solitude, and peace. No
climate or region could have produced a finer day. During the month little snow
fell, there being still some portions of the beach visible at the close. Animal life,
except for penguins, was almost entirely absent One (black-throated) penguin
was seen on the 3rd, three were observed on the 7th, and two on the 8th. Gentoos
were seen on the 5th, 8th, 9th, 13th, 19th, and 21st, the greatest number being on
the 8th, when there were over 200 on the north beach, and on the 13th when
thirty were observed. The ringed species of penguin was not seen during the
month. Before the middle of the month skuas and other winged fowl had disappeared, but several paddies were in the vicinity of the house throughout, and a
Weddell seal was lying on the pack in Scotia Bay on the 16th.

June was a very uneventful month. We had settled down into a monotonous
winter routine, one day being to all intents and purposes the same as another.
The weather was well behaved on the whole, and there was little drift-snow,
which in some respects was rather a disadvantage, as the house continued very
cold.

On the other hand we were not troubled with much digging, which had to be
done after every snow-storm, owing to doors and windows getting blocked with
drift. During the month several interesting phenomena were from time to time
observed. On many occasions beautiful ice-crystals were deposited out of thick
fog at low temperatures. These take the form of small crystalline spicules of ice
of the feathery or cone-shaped type, and are deposited on every object exposed
to the drifting fog. The branches of the crystals lie at an angle of 30°, their primary axis pointing to windward. Their rate of growth varies with the thickness
of the fog and the velocity of the wind, and under normal conditions of moder-
ately thick fog and wind increased in length about half an inch every hour.

Fog bows, both solar and lunar, were also seen: these differ in no respect from
rainbows, except that they are pure white, the prismatic colours being entirely
absent. Several other interesting optical phenomena were observed, such as solar and lunar halos accompanied by mock suns and moons, also remarkable
mirage effects. On two occasions a curious phenomenon was seen at the mouth
of crevasses from which smoke appeared to be issuing. The temperature being
very low (from 40° to 50° of frost), the ice had opened up and thus liberated a
quantity of relatively warm air from the interior, which condensed on coming
into contact with the cold external atmosphere. These and other phenomena
peculiar to a polar region served to sustain our interest in life during the short
mid-winter days and long nights. Since the gale of April 4, ice for cooking and
domestic purposes was taken off the beach, where there was a large quantity.
This had to be melted on the stove; and as five people had to be provided for, it
was seldom that the pots were off the fire. A bath was a rare luxury seldom indulged in. Owing to the short days no long excursions could be taken, but Szmula

and myself always made a point of taking a couple of hours' exercise on ski or foot daily. We were well provided with winter clothing, so that we could exercise out of doors with comfort in all weathers. The only marked cold snap occurred on the 26th, when the thermometer fell to 26° below zero, the average for the whole day being 19° below zero. Animal life was scarce. An occasional snowy petrel, shag, orblack-backed gull was seen from time to time, and paddies continued to hang around the house. Two gentoo penguins were killed on the 21st, and a Weddell seal was observed on the 23rd lying on the ice which now covered the north bay. The general health of the small community continued good, but Smith and myself were beginning to feel the strain induced by a second winter in such a trying and inhospitable region. However, as soon as the days began to lengthen we rapidly improved, and so far as I was concerned I enjoyed excellent health during the spring and summer.

July was a very uneventful month, there being little to chronicle. The weather, speaking generally, was good, and drift-snow, the greatest curse of the place, was almost absent until the 23rd, when a snow-storm came on which lasted till the 26th. Up to the middle of the month there was very little snow on The Beach, except in the vicinity of the house. The scree-slopes were almost bare, and along the ridge, passing through the magnetic hut, anemometer, and house, there was at the outside less than a foot anywhere. As in June, excursions were on a restricted scale. On the 5th I visited Delta Island, which presented quite a different aspect from what it did at the same period of 1903. Deep ravines that were snow-covered last year were to be seen, and at Point Davis there was fully twenty feet less snow, which statement may help one to form an idea of the relative difference between the snow-fall of the two seasons. The ice in Uruguay Cove and a considerable part of Jessie Bay was bearing during most of the month, and swell was rarely observed, showing that there was much pack to the north. The 9th was another Argentine holiday, the anniversary of a great battle fought in 1816, so we had a special dinner, followed by cigars in the evening. These little breaks went a long way to dispel the monotony of the mid-winter days. Between the 9th and the 20th a considerable number of adelia penguins made their appearance, and we killed as many as we could for food. The greatest number seen was about 100 on the 19th. Where they came from and whither they were going were, of course, matters for conjecture, but there can be little doubt that the prime impetus was to get to open water to the northward, where they could obtain food, as the lanes among the floes to the south became frozen up by the increasing severity of the cold.

Life had now become very dull. The social atmosphere was by no means brilliant—a marked contrast to that on the *Scotia* the previous winter, when, what with sledge-parties coming and going and the hundred and one details associated with ship-work, there was always plenty to break the monotony of the situation. Smith alone was the only one of us who kept up an almost constant flow of good spirits, although even he at times summarised the situation in the words, "Life's too slow for a funeral." As our principal work consisted in taking hourly meteorological observations, the clock was the autocrat. There being four observers, the day was divided into as many watches of six hours each, and the watches changed every week. The morning observer rose at 4.30 A.M., when the man who had been on duty all night retired. At six o'clock the cook was wakened: breakfast, consisting of porridge, fish, or tinned meat and coffee, was partaken of at eight o'clock by every one except the night-watchman, who did not rise till twelve. After breakfast the two observers who were on day duty broke up a quantity of ice, which was then melted to replenish the water-supply kept in pots and a large copper. Then, if necessary, the store-room door and windows were dug out. The forenoon was spent in any odd jobs that cropped up, and the afternoon largely in exercise. Lunch was practically a repetition of breakfast, except that there was no porridge, and tea was substituted for coffee. Before dinner ice was sledged in either from the east glacier or from hummocks off the floe. Dinner at five o'clock consisted of tinned soup, penguin, and some form of pudding, and it was seldom that any one ate anything in the evening. Except between noon and 6 P.M. there was usually some one asleep, so that conversation as a rule had to be carried on in somewhat subdued tones.

A gentoo penguin was seen on the 27th, but none of the ringed species were observed. Birds were few and far between, and were restricted to snowy petrels, nellies, and black-backed gulls. Seals were remarkably scarce, in marked contrast to last winter. Only one or two single specimens (Weddell) were noticed.

August opened with a snow-storm and a high temperature, but on the 2nd the thermometer fell rapidly, until at midnight on the 3rd it registered the phenomenally low reading of 40° below zero or 72° below freezing-point. This was 13° lower than was experienced at any time during the winter of 1903. In the afternoon I went a walk to beyond Point Martin, and, in spite of a keen south-east and south wind, did not feel the cold much. On the 4th the temperature was again 40° below zero, the sky was absolutely cloudless, save for some low clouds at the northern horizon caused by "Barber," which is the name applied to the appearance of smoke occasioned by the condensation of vapour rising from a water-surface during extreme cold. This phenomenon was of somewhat common occurrence here during the winter, and has occasionally been observed at home, especially during the great frost of January 1814, when it was seen on the Forth above Queensferry, and on other rivers, which were covered with floating ice. Soon after 10 A.M. on the 4th I left on ski, climbing to the crest of the ridge overlooking Wilton Bay immediately to the south-west. The view was exquisite—nothing but pack-ice with about a score of small bergs. In spite of the cold I had to discard my pilot coat before beginning the ascent. This was the coldest day of the whole winter, the mean of the hourly temperature readings giving an average of 65° of frost. On the morning of the 8th we had the unusual phenomenon of a thunder-storm. On the 22nd I made an excursion to a remarkable iceberg of the cathedral form, which was aground some 2½ miles beyond Cape Burn Murdoch or about 5½ miles from the house. Near the mouth of Scotia Bay there was a pressure ridge, the ice being crushed up to fully fifteen feet in places. In the vicinity of the berg the ice was also much crushed and distorted, doubtless due to slight movements of the berg caused by tidal effects. The water here must have been very deep, as the portion of the berg *above* water was fully 160 feet. After taking some photographs of the iceberg and of Coronation Island, I sat down on an ice-block and had lunch, enjoying to the full the fine views of the surrounding country. The ice was very close and compact everywhere, and in excellent condition for sledging,—in marked contrast to the corresponding period of 1903, when the islands were surrounded by loose shifting pack, which greatly hindered Mr Bruce in his sledge-journeys, while the bad weather further impeded his survey work. This season all would have been different: the weather was remarkably fine for days together, and the survey of Coronation Island, an impossibility last winter owing to the disturbed ice conditions, would not only have been practicable but easy. On the 28th there was a "Föhn" wind, which raised the temperature to 40°. Animal life continued remarkably scarce. In spite of the numerous excursions taken by the different members of the Expedition, only three Weddell seals were seen during the month. On the 17th the snowy petrels returned to their nests in the cliffs near the house. Shags were also seen about this time, and a solitary adelia penguin observed travelling north on the 21st completes the record.

During the winter the routine of scientific work was continued without interruption. Personally I was much occupied with magnetic observations which were prosecuted under many difficulties, due to the disturbing effect of weather agencies, of which the principal one was the freezing up of the windows and shutters of the hut. Indeed on several occasions during a silver thaw (rain falling with a temperature below the freezing-point and congealing as it falls) it took me over an hour to get into the hut, which would be plastered on the weather side with solid ice over an inch thick. This had to be carefully cut away from the door so as to avoid injuring the woodwork. Inside the hut further difficulties had to be overcome, as the instrument would often be found incrusted with frost spicules requiring thawing out. This done, and everything in working order, the rattling of torrents of drift was at times so great that the beats of the chronometer about two feet off could not be heard, thus making it impossible to take the time of vibration, while in the deflection series the mirrors would become covered with frozen dew resulting from the moisture generated by the observer's breath. To get rid of this I have often opened the door of the hut and put the lamp out, taking the observation in temperatures ranging from 10° to 20° below zero. Frequently from one of these causes the first or second part of the observation could not be completed, thus invalidating the series. Troubles much of the same description accompanied the observations of magnetic dip; while as regards the declination, the principal source of annoyance was the snowing up of the distant mark to which the readings were referred. The hourly meteorological observations continued to be made with great regularity and devotion. No matter how bad the weather, it was considered a point of honour to get to the screens and anemometer somehow or other in spite of blinding drift, which was at times so severe that the observer could hardly keep his eyes open.

With regard to the general working of the instruments, in the main satisfactory results were obtained. As is usual on polar expeditions, there was a good deal of trouble with the wet bulb, which required much attention. At temperatures below 10° F. I found the best method was to do away with the muslin covering altogether, and merely use a film of ice, by painting water on with a camel-hair brush. The hair hygrographs at low temperatures gave better all-round results than the wet-bulb thermometer, but the traces were frequently imperfect owing to the blizzards that prevailed. So fine was the snow that the inside of the recording instruments was full of it; and even the anemometer got filled once or twice although protected by a glass cover. Most of the snow that fell was hard and granular, and large flakes—so common at home—were rarely seen. Silver thaw was of frequent occurrence, and gave much trouble owing to the frequency with which the screens became choked with icy incrustations. The instruments employed were those that experience had shown to give satisfactory results under the prevailing climatic conditions. The barometer of the Fortin pattern was hung in the living-room of the house as far from the stove as possible. There were also two large Richard barographs, one recording in millimetres, and the other in inches. The thermometer screens, four in number, were fixed on to two thick spars resting on cairns and securely anchored to the ground by stout cables. This precaution was necessary owing to the extreme violence of the squalls that occurred from time to time. In these screens were two thermographs, two hygrographs, two pairs of dry- and wet-bulb thermometers, and a maximum and minimum registering thermometer. Screwed to the side of one of the screens was a stand containing a black-bulb solar radiation maximum thermometer *in vacuo*. Close to the screens was a snow-gauge, while a little farther off was the Robinson anemometer, mounted on a post, with the cups about 74 feet above the ground. There were also two sunshine recorders—one a Jordan and the other a Campbell-Stokes instrument. A terrestrial minimum thermometer was occasionally in use, but, unfortunately, our low-scale instruments of this class got out of order and could not be employed just when their readings would have been of most interest.

CHAPTER XV

RETURNING SPRING

*WEDDELL SEALS—A LONG EXCURSION—A BLIZZARD—AN
UNPLEASANT MONTH—RETURN OF PENGUINS—A LONG-
CONTINUED SNOW-STORM—PENGUINS' EGGS OBTAINED—A
SUN-BATH—FANTASTIC BERGS—EXCURSION TO CAVES—A
YOUNG ROSS SEAL—BOLDNESS OF SKUAS—A BOATING TRIP—A
BUSY NATURALIST—A DULL CHRISTMAS—ARRIVAL OF RELIEF
SHIP.*

WITH the advent of September the inspiring effect of the lengthening days began to make itself felt. Excursions which for some time had been on a restricted scale were now extended, a source of interest being the return of the Weddell seals, which on the 2nd began to bring forth their young. On this day there were no less than thirty-two at the S.S.E. point, thirteen with young ones. The 3rd was a very fine day, so that I took advantage of the good weather to go and photograph the seals. One of them which had just pupped, on my approach turned on its offspring and killed it, shaking the poor little thing between its teeth as a terrier does a rat. Other seals with pups allowed us to approach without manifesting the slightest concern. After spending an hour and a half with the seals, I proceeded along the south coast for about two miles, obtaining a fine view of Washington Strait, Cape Bennett, and the distant peaks of Coronation Island. Large numbers of snowy petrels were seen, also black-backed gulls, paddies, and one or two nellies. On this day a penguin was seen by Smith, but owing to its being a long way off the species could not be determined. On the 5th I took a long walk on ski in an easterly direction, and after a march of four hours arrived at Graptolite Island, which was one of Mr Bruce's camps. The views here were in marked contrast. About N. N. W. were high towering mountains, while to the

173

eastward was the low flat penguin rookery (deserted at this season) and Cape Dundas. Some of the scenery between Cape Whitson and the island was very fine, notably a small but high glacier, which was splintered and crevassed to an extraordinary degree. Few seals were seen, not more than a dozen in all, and no other animal life except some shags. The weather was very favourable for the excursion,—hardly any wind, a temperature of 20°, and intermittent sunshine, while the snow could not have been in better condition for ski-ing. Only one short piece (about a quarter of a mile) of disturbed ice was met with, in marked contrast to last year, when the surface was very rough and hummocky. The return journey took me about half an hour longer than the outward, the total estimated distance traversed being about twenty-two miles. On reaching the house I found that during my absence Valette had fallen down a crevasse on the north glacier. He was ascending a steep slope on foot, and fortunately was carrying his ski, which he had taken off, one under each arm. These caught on either side of the crevasse, and Acuña, who was luckily with him, placed his ski crosswise, thus enabling Valette to raise himself up. Needless to say this spot was labelled "dangerous," and carefully avoided in future excursions. From the middle of the month much trouble and inconvenience were occasioned by the frequency and extent with which drift-snow accumulated on the front or south side of the house. The morning dig-out,—which devolved on the observers who were on day-duty,—instead of taking ten or fifteen minutes as formerly, on many occasions occupied nearly two hours. The labour was considerable, as the snow excavated had again to be shovelled away so as to avoid having a bank close to the building, which would simply have made the drifts unmanageable. Frequently the door had to be dug out every hour by night as well as by day, and as the drift literally boiled around this spot when it was blowing hard, the operation, needless to say, was usually an extremely unpleasant one. Much of this labour would have been spared us had the covered passage to the store-room survived the gale of April 4. On the 21st and 22nd there was a veritable blizzard from the south-east, the wind blowing from fifty to sixty miles an hour. On the afternoon of the 22nd, in order to get into the coal locker we had to break open the store-room door, as the interior was choke-full of snow, roof-high. So fine was the consistency of the snow that it had drifted in through a small orifice that had formed in the door through the wood warping. It took the four of us an hour working in short spells to shovel it out, as one could work but a brief time owing to the suffocating drift which poured in a stream right into the interior. The house during this storm was very cold, the temperature at times being under freezing-point, and this in spite of the fact that the stove was red-hot. This blizzard was succeeded by a spell of remarkably fine weather which lasted four days, during which time the sky was practically cloudless throughout. Walking was, however, somewhat difficult, as the surface of the whole floe was excavated by the wind into a mass of small pits called "sastrugi," some over two feet in depth. These ran approximately in a

S.S.E. and N.N.W. direction. In shape they resembled the inside of a mussel-shell, and one could even perceive concentric rings in their interior. I had a good opportunity of examining them on the 24th, when on an excursion to Cape Burn Murdoch. Penguins during the month were very scarce: one (species undetermined) was seen on the 3rd, and four gentoos travelling towards the south on the 16th. The paddies, which during the winter had hung about the house, left for the seal rookery at the beginning of the month. Although I have made one or two references to the coldness of the house, it must not be supposed that this was the normal condition. Indeed throughout the greater part of the year the internal temperature was high,— between 50° and 60°,—and except on rare occasions when it was blowing hard from the south and south-east, we did not suffer in any way from cold. In fact, at times during calm weather the house was on the hot side, and both inner and outer doors had to be left open in order to keep the temperature down.

October was a very unpleasant month, with much snow and drift, involving considerable labour to keep the porch and store-room clear. In spite of the prevailing bad weather I continued to take a great deal of outdoor exercise, and a day seldom passed without an excursion to one of the many spots of interest in the vicinity. Signs of migratory movements on the part of the penguins were visible early in the month. On the 8th I caught an adelia, and twelve gentoos were killed on the 10th. On the 11th we had a remarkably cold snap for the season, the average temperature for the day being 8°.5 below zero, while at midnight the thermometer had fallen to 25° below zero, or 57° of frost. On the 14th the first large arrival of penguins for the season took place. On that day there were several hundred adelias at the large rookery, but only four at the small rookery. Last year (1903) there were fifty at the large rookery on the 7th, and thousands arrived on the 9th. It is interesting to note that in both years the arrival of the penguins took place immediately after the last cold snap for the season. The first of the gentoos appeared on the 17th, but the detachment was small, only a score in all. On the 20th we had another thunder-storm, which is a rare phenomenon in this region. On the 21st four skua gulls were seen—the first of the season. From Tuesday the 18th to Sunday the 23rd inclusive we had a severe snow-storm, the prospect being limited to a quarter of a mile at the outside. Strong winds, terrific squalls, and blinding drift prevailed throughout, and the entrance to the porch had to be cleared of snow practically every hour during this period. At midnight on the 21st the observer's lamp went out, and, losing his bearings, he fell over a steep bank of snow which lay to the south of the house, and went in up to his neck in a snow-drift, sustaining a severe fright, and regaining the house with difficulty. The depressing effect of this prolonged spell of bad weather, the worst of the whole winter, was dispelled on the 24th, when we had no less than twelve hours' sunshine. All hands were engaged on this day for some hours clearing away the huge drifts that had accumulated round the building, and in digging out the boat, which latter operation had to be done, on the average, every three weeks during the winter. On the 27th the ice covering Uruguay Cove broke and went out, having been fast since the beginning of July. An ice-foot was left fully nine feet high in places, and not less than six feet in height anywhere, which, as the swell surged against it, presented to view a foaming line of breakers.

On the 31st I have an entry, "There are now a great many skuas always about the house. Paddies also hang around in considerable numbers. Cape pigeons, snowy petrels, and black-backed gulls are fairly numerous, and to-day I observed terns which were, however, reported by Valette some days ago. Glad to see the end of this month. We have had much bad weather, with heavy snow-storms and drift, but I expect our troubles in this direction are about over for the season.' The mean temperature of the month, 18°.4, is in marked contrast to last year, when the average was 27°.0 or 8°.6 higher."

November was on the whole a good month, and as the ice covering Scotia Bay remained unbroken throughout, ample opportunity was afforded for the excursions to the penguin rookeries and other spots of interest to students of natural history. The first penguins' eggs were obtained on the 2nd, at a small island near the large rookery. On the 3rd twenty-three were obtained, and every day an increasing number. On the 10th 1100 eggs were collected at the large rookery at Point Martin, and sledged in a distance of about 2¼ miles. Altogether about 1800 eggs were obtained, the change of fare being a welcome one. In the early morning of the 16th three-quarters of an inch of rain fell,—the largest daily fall we had yet had. In the forenoon the sun came out blazing hot, the solar radiation-thermometer rising to 158°.8, although the shade temperature at the time was only 37°.4. The day was so inviting that I lay down on a portion of the north beach that was clear of ice, and had a sun-bath. The heat in the sun's rays was really terrific, the heavy rain having rendered the air very diathermanous. The effect of the thaw was very noticeable. Miniature avalanches were sliding down the hillsides and over the rocks, which at a distance presented the appearance of waterfalls. Uruguay Cove and Jessie Bay beyond, as far as Saddle Island, were filled with heavy sea-worn pack, deeply excavated by the action of the water. Outside could be seen clouds of spray, and in the calm atmosphere the beating of the surf could be distinctly heard. We buried several boxes containing 800 eggs in the snow, which forms an excellent medium for purposes of preservation. So long as plenty snow is heaped on the top the eggs keep fresh, even although buried for months. The only danger is in winter, when they are apt to burst as the frost becomes keen. Water could now be obtained by making excavations in the snow in hollows, but our water-barrel was not available, as it was filled with rubble after the gale of April 4, and used to underpin the buttress. The surface of the floe covering Scotia Bay was rapidly getting covered with water through the excessive thaw and the rain.

The 19th was a superbly fine day with 14½ hours' sunshine, the greatest registered on any day since our arrival here on March 25 last year. The effect of the thaw was now very noticeable, as the general depth of the snow had decreased about two feet in the last week. A great many curious and fantastic bergs appeared in Jessie Bay. One resembled a Martello tower, with ramparts and bastions, whilst another was like a cathedral, with Gothic spires and arches. During the afternoon and evening there were again numerous cascades of *névé* falling from Mount Ramsay, and about 6 P.M. we witnessed a magnificent avalanche, which descended with a roar from the hanging glacier, raising a column of water some fifty feet high as it splashed into Uruguay Cove. About this time there were many beautiful ice-blocks aground on the west side of Uruguay Cove, on which penguins were wont to congregate. The first eggs of the gentoo penguins were laid on the 17th. A McCormick's skua (*Megalestris maccormicki*)—a rare variety here—was shot on the 11th. Wilson petrels and a ringed penguin were seen on the 12th. Eggs of the black-backed gull were got at Point Davis on the 23rd, of snowy petrels on the 25th, and those of terns, skuas, and ringed penguins on the 27th. The ice covering Wilton Bay went out on the 26th, on which date the ice in Scotia Bay was unbroken inside of a line joining Point Davis and the large rookery at Point Martin.

In December remarkably fine weather, though very cold (for the season), prevailed; there were no snow-storms of any consequence, and as the ice in Scotia Bay remained unbroken up to the end of the year, one could continue to take long excursions over the floe, there being few days in which I did not get four or five hours' healthful exercise. One could not help thinking how lucky the *Scotia* was in getting out last season (1903) on the 23rd of November. This year, had she been here, she would still have been fast, with fully two miles of ice from four to twenty or more feet thick to bar her way. It would not have been possible to have cut a canal from the outside, as there was always pack jammed against the fixed bay ice,—and altogether the situation would have seriously affected the prospects of the southern cruise during the summer. There can be no doubt that the South Orkney Islands are well within the area covered every year by polar pack, and that 1903 must be looked on as an early season for this region. During the month there was almost continuous frost, and the surface of the snow was in excellent condition for ski-ing throughout.

The general outlook continued very wintry, large quantities of pack-ice lay around the island, and on the 3rd there were no less than 117 icebergs in sight from the ridge overlooking Wilton Bay, a larger number than I had hitherto observed. All this ice did not look well for the relief ship's arrival. No doubt the *Scotia*, with Captain Robertson on board, would have been able to reach the islands; but, on the other hand, the commander of a relief ship not adapted for polar work might well be excused from entering the pack.

On the evening of 3rd, Smith, Valette, and Acuña left in the dinghy for the caves under Mount Ramsay, where so many eggs of the Cape pigeon and snowy petrel were obtained the previous summer. They could not, however, be entered, as the snow-bank which led up to them was not nearly high enough, and a ladder was necessary. The party then rowed across Uruguay Cove, and on the east side obtained the eggs of nine Cape pigeons, one snowy petrel, and some terns. The conditions were very favourable, no wind, sea practically smooth and no swell,—a rare combination, doubtless due to the large masses of pack-ice lying to the north.

On the 5th I clubbed a young Ross seal (probably about six weeks old) near Cape Burn Murdoch, and on the 6th Valette and Acuña went out and dragged it in a distance of fully three miles. The seal was probably born on the pack, as it was not known to breed at the Orkneys,—at least, we never saw any during the pupping season. After killing the seal I had the good fortune to find two tern's eggs, which I carefully wrapped in cotton-wool and placed in a bag. On reaching Point Martin I left the bag on the snow and proceeded to look over the rookery for young penguins. On returning I was much surprised to find that a skua had actually taken the eggs out of the bag and eaten them. The skuas of late had become very bold. On the 7th, when Valette was occupied in skinning a seal, he had no less than forty around him, and one, "Feathers" by name, who was noted for his excessive tameness, took food out of his hand; the others getting hold of considerable portions of the entrails of the seal, engaged in a miniature tug of war. On several occasions, when at the skuas' rookery for eggs, I was violently attacked by the birds; and on one visit, when they were very fierce, I had to beat them off with my ski stick. Swinging myself off my balance as the birds circled round me, I slipped on a steep ice-slope, landing on the floe some eighty feet below in a dazed but uninjured condition. On the 11th we again made an excursion by boat in search of Cape pigeons' eggs, but, unfortunately, could not land at their nesting-place. Inside the cove it was practically calm, but at the spot referred to furious squalls prevailed, and the boat was in great danger of being dashed against the rocks. Fortunately we had Smith with us, and his long experience as a boatman extricated us from a very unpleasant situation. The first newly-born adelia penguins were obtained on the 12th. From this time we began to keep a sharp look-out for the relief ship, which was promised "about the end of the year," although the general impression was that she would not come till the middle of January. The only one of us who was reconciled to the situation was Valette. A thorough naturalist, he simply revelled in the opportunities associated with the season, not only collecting numerous specimens daily, but making careful drawings of the same under the microscope. He also obtained skeletons and skins of the four species of seals, as well as specimens of all the birds known to breed in the islands. A good collection of eggs was also obtained, but we were unable to get those of nellies and shags, as our boat was too cranky a craft to risk the long boat journey to the breeding-place. During the winter Valette, along with Acuña, also made a map of Scotia Bay, Uruguay Cove, and some of the nearer small bays, supplementing this with about a hundred soundings, most of which involved cutting through the ice, which was three or four feet thick. Some of the work was done during very bad weather, and was not altogether free from danger, especially that part executed under the hanging ice-cap of Mount Ramsay, from which an avalanche might have fallen at any time. As for myself, I made a daily study of the state of the ice round the islands, frequently ascending to considerable heights in order to get an extended view. I also lent some small assistance in connection with the natural history work as I had opportunity. From about the beginning of August I made a point of keeping the snow-drifts down in the vicinity of the house, taking on the average about an hour of this excellent exercise daily. So far as social harmony was concerned there were no quarrels, but during the winter conversation flagged because there was nothing to talk about. The monotony, while bearable, was felt more than during the previous winter, as there was plenty life on board the *Scotia*.

Our Christmas dinner was a very dull affair, passing off very quietly: indeed no one spoke a word except the cook, who cursed his cooking in energetic terms.

For some weeks past I had made an excursion almost daily to the ridge overlooking Wilton Bay in order to get some idea of the distribution and extent of pack round the islands, and thus have some means of judging as to whether or not a ship could reach us. The wind had been blowing from the south or southwest all month, so that there was open water on the north side of the islands, but in every other direction heavy pack with the accompanying ice-blink was to be seen. On New Year's Eve I went off for my usual walk in the company of Smith, who left me at the small rookery, while I continued to ascend the steep snow-slopes leading to the col overlooking Wilton Bay, which I reached at 8 P.M. The evening was beautiful, the air calm and intensely transparent, while now and then a faint zephyr would play among the dark corries of the cliffs. The prospect to the south and south-west was, however, very wintry: nothing but heavy pack to be seen, with very few lanes of water among the floes. As usual, I crossed over to the east side of the glacier to get a view of the conditions to the north and east. On gaining the crest of the rocks just above Omond House, I saw a spectacle that was as agreeable as it was unexpected,—the long-looked-for relief-ship was in sight. This proved to be the Argentine gunboat *Uruguay*, which was already famous in Polar annals through having rescued the Swedish Antarctic Expedition the previous summer.

CHAPTER XVI

THE VOYAGE OF THE *URUGUAY*

*THE URUGUAY—VOYAGE TO THE SOUTH ORKNEYS—
DEPARTURE—A CRITICAL POSITION—SOUTH SHETLANDS—
DECEPTION ISLAND—GERLACHE STRAIT—WIENCKE ISLAND—
NO WORD OF CHARCOT—HEAVY GALE—RETURN JOURNEY—
ENCOUNTER WITH AN ICEBERG—CAPE HORN—HARBOURTOWN
—A HOSPITABLE FAMILY—FINE SCENERY—USHUAIA—BEAGLE
CHANNEL—ROSS HARBOUR—VILLARINO HARBOUR—STORM-
BOUND—MAGDALEN STRAIT—PUNTA ARENAS—TERMINATION
OF VOYAGE.*

THE Argentine gunboat *Uruguay,* under the command of Captain Don Ismael F. Galindez, left Buenos Aires on the 10th of December 1904. The ship had a twofold commission to execute: (1) To proceed to the South Orkney Islands and there take off the party left by the *Scotia* in February 1904. (2) After landing a new party of five with stores, coal, &c., the vessel was to proceed first to Deception Island, South Shetlands, and if necessary to Wiencke Island, Gerlache Strait, at both of which places Dr Charcot, in the Antarctic research-ship *Français,* had promised to leave despatches giving notice of the progress of his Expedition. This latter part of the programme was, however, to be undertaken at the discretion of the commander. The second in command was Lieutenant Jorge Yalour, who, the previous summer, accompanied the *Uruguay* during her memorable voyage to the relief of Nordenskjöld at Snow Hill. The other officers were Lieutenants Esquivel, Maveroff, and Caillet Bois, the last of whom was navigating-officer, while J. Gorrochategui, who had also taken part in the relief-expedition referred to, was doctor, and O. Pereira, chief engineer. There were also on board Señor Diebel and Mr Percy of the Cordoba Meteorological Office, who, along with other three men on board, formed the contingent sent out to continue the meteorological and magnetic work at the South Orkneys. (News has since been received that Señor Diebel died at the South Orkneys in September 1905.) The *Uruguay*, it may be mentioned, was an iron ship specially strengthened for ice-work, with a substantial sheathing of wood, but although everything that money could effect was done to render her suitable for navigation in ice-strewn waters, she was far from being a good Polar ship.

It had been intended to proceed to the South Orkneys under sail alone, taking advantage of the north-east winds, which were shown on the charts as the prevalent winds in the South Atlantic during the month of December; but continuous head winds from the southward being experienced, the *Uruguay* had to proceed under steam, thus necessitating a call at Ushuaia, the capital of Tierra del Fuego, for coal. This port being left on December 27, a course was steered for Saddle Island, South Orkneys. On the 30th, at 4 A.M., when in lat. 58° 30′ S., long. 51° 16′ W., the first iceberg was encountered. It was of triangular form and one mile in length, while that portion above the sea was estimated at 150 feet. Soon after the presence of pack was heralded by the characteristic ice-blink, and in the low latitude of 58° 40′ S. the pack-ice was entered. This was at first very dense, but in a short time gave place to streams of loose ice. For some hours the *Uruguay* coasted along the edge of two large unbroken ice-fields about thirty miles long. When approaching the 60th parallel of south latitude on the early morning of the 31st, very heavy pack was again met with,—and it says a great deal for the intrepidity of the Commander, who had no previous experience of ice navigation, that, undaunted by these obstacles, he proceeded on his voyage. The weather, fortunately, was exceptionally fine and clear, which greatly helped matters, so that the land could be seen at a great distance. The wind being from the south-west, the pack had been driven a few miles off-shore, leaving an expanse of open water several miles broad. In all other directions nothing but pack was to be seen, and an ice-blink on the sky all round showed that there was little water in any direction. The *Uruguay* dropped anchor in the North Bay, now called Uruguay Cove, at 9 P.M. on December 31, and soon after I went on board to make arrangements for our departure.

It had been the Commander's intention to remain a few days in order to help in the installation of the new party, but circumstances arose in the early morning of January 1 that necessitated an early departure. The weather, which had been exceptionally fine and clear, broke down, with thick mist and snow, and a north wind sprung up which threatened to fill the bay with heavy pack. Our embarkment and the landing of the new party had therefore to be hurriedly got through. Fortunately the sea in the bay was perfectly still, and as there was no swell the numerous packing-cases, sacks of coal, and general stores could be put ashore without difficulty and dragged up on the ice-foot. A new magnetic house for the self-registering instruments was in process of erection, and some additional lumber was also landed. Meanwhile our own party had been very busy packing their effects, the most bulky of which were Valette's natural history specimens. These were placed on sledges and dragged over to the north side of the beach some 250 yards off, whence they were transported to the *Uruguay*, which lay at anchor a quarter of a mile away. At 4 P.M. on January 1 we had a farewell dinner on board, and at 6 o'clock all communication with the shore was cut off.

It was not without some misgiving that I bade the new party farewell. I was at some pains to give them a very clear and definite idea of the effect of the gale of April 4 on the house, as they could form but little themselves owing to there being about ten feet of snow on the south side of the building, which concealed the repaired buttress. The great danger, of course, was to be expected from the sea; but at the time we left the ice covering Scotia Bay was unbroken,—great quantities of pack covered the surrounding ocean, and even when the ice did go out, an ice-foot about fifteen feet high would remain, which would, we hoped, protect the building during the few weeks that the Bay would remain open. One thing that would distract the new party from thinking too much was the amount of work before them. They had fifteen tons of coal and ten tons of general stores to sledge over from the north bay. The crew of the *Uruguay* were to have aided them in this, but there was no time, as an early departure was imperative. The *Uruguay* left at 10 P.M., during a temporary clearing of the weather, bound for the South Shetland Islands and Gerlache Strait, at which places despatches from Charcot's French expedition were expected. At first the pack gave little trouble, and from 4 to 8 P.M. on the 2nd the navigation was through open water. During the forenoon of the 3rd heavy ice was again entered, and about noon, the open sea being observed about five miles off, the ship's course was changed to north so as to get out of the ice as quickly as possible,—a measure all the more necessary as the vessel was not sufficiently strong to encounter heavy pack. During the five hours we were occupied in gaining the open we momentarily expected the propeller and rudder to be carried away. Much of the ice met with consisted of those large blocks called "growlers," so common at the edge of the pack. These had long deep tongues, which at times projected a far way under the vessel's stern. The pieces were so close together that there was no room to manoeuvre the ship, so that all hands were kept busy with poles and oars pushing them off the ship's sides. There was fortunately no swell, and by 5 P.M. we were in open water, much to every one's relief, as every now and then the screw and rudder would be struck by an ice-block. Some Weddell seals were observed lying in the pack. Soon after clearing the ice the sea rose, and during the next three days heavy seas were experienced.

About 10 A.M. on the 7th the South Shetlands were sighted, Cape Melville being passed at 6 the same evening. No pack-ice was visible, but close to Cape Melville no less than sixty-two icebergs were counted, many of them aground.

The South Shetlands presented an inexpressibly desolate and inhospitable appearance, being entirely covered with snow and glaciers, except in one or two places where there was bare rock. On the 7th Cape pigeons, Wilson petrels, and giant petrels continued to follow the ship, and many whales were seen.

On the early morning of the 8th we anchored in the crater-harbour of Deception Island (lat. 62° 56′ S., long. 60° 40′ W.) This island, or shell of an island, is certainly one of the most singular of nature's productions. Entrance to it is obtained on the south-east side through a narrow channel of only 550 feet across, which leads to a large elliptical basin of about five miles in diameter. The external shores form a perfect barrier or wall, thus affording the utmost security within. When the island was visited in 1829 by Captain Forster, in command of H.M.S. *Chanticleer,* numerous fumaroles were seen, from which hissing jets of steam escaped, and hot springs with a temperature of 190°.4 F. were met with near the shores of the basin. Smiley, the American sea-man who called at the island in February 1842, reported that the whole southern side was in full volcanic activity, there being no less than thirteen "active centres" of eruption. In November 1902 Captain Larsen of the *Antarctic,* then proceeding to the relief of Nordenskjöld, was prepared to land a party on Deception Island in order to investigate its condition; but as the narrow entrance to the basin was blocked by pack-ice, which also filled the interior, all idea of exploration had to be given up. As there were no reports available of the state of the island since Smiley's visit in 1842, it was with much interest that we entered on our reconnaissance.

The harbour of Pendulum Cove was found almost entirely filled with ice and ashes, and close to the observatory spot of Forster there was a small lake, probably due to the melting of snow from the heights in the vicinity. Owing to the quantity of detritus mixed with the water it was in a semi-liquid condition. The hot springs were in an active state, but I did not observe any signs of volcanic activity on land. From a comparison of Forster's soundings with those made by the *Uruguay,* it was found that in the seventy-six years that have elapsed since his visit there is a difference of forty-two feet, because where he got twenty-five fathoms of water there are now only eighteen. Whether this is due to a general elevation of the land or to a filling up of the basin by volcanic emanations is a matter of conjecture. Among the animal life observed in Deception Island were Weddell and Ross seals, gentoo and ringed penguins, black-backed gulls, and giant petrels. Numerous Cape pigeons were observed at the narrow entrance to the basin, so that it is very probable that this is one of their breeding-places.

No despatch from Dr Charcot being found at Pendulum Cove, a record was left on an adjacent height in a conspicuous position. There being a strong gale from the north-east, with heavy and continuous snow, we were detained in Deception Island till 6 P.M. of the 9th, when the weather cleared. Our destination was Wiencke Island, at the southern end of Gerlache Strait. During the early morning and forenoon of the 10th we passed through some very fine scenery.

Here could be seen the processes involved in the spawning of icebergs, the glaciers which formed the sides of the strait being much crevassed, and projecting
into the sea for a considerable distance. About 1 P.M. we reached the south end of
Wiencke Island, having coasted along its shores for two hours without seeing
any cairn or beacon in which Charcot might have left a despatch. We could not
examine the west side of the island, as the northern entrance to Neumayer Channel was closed with a line of icebergs. It was the Commander's intention to proceed
south-west into the Pacific, but progress in this direction was barred by heavy
pack-ice which completely filled the mouth of the strait from Cape Lancaster to
Cape Renard. For this reason we were unable to enter Neumayer Channel from
the south in order to complete the examination of Wiencke Island. Being now in
lat. 64° 57′ S., long. 63° 40′ W., we had to return the way we came owing to the
unfavourable ice-conditions to the south. In the early evening it began to snow
and blow hard from the north-east, with a rapidly falling barometer and a heavy
sea, so that, having reached the shelter of Two Hummocks Island at 10 P.M., we
lay-to for the night in a heavy snowstorm, with many rapidly moving icebergs
about. The gale moderating about mid-day of the 11th, the homeward voyage
was resumed. On the 12th we sighted Smith Island (lat. 62° 53′ S., long. 62° 35′
W.), but could not see much of it for fog. In the afternoon, during a thick fog, the
Uruguay encountered an iceberg of large dimensions. It was fortunately observed
when about a ship's length off, but so close were we that the yards barely cleared
its face as we swung past.

We now bade farewell to the regions of ice and snow. The stormy waters to
the south of Cape Horn were in an unusually propitious mood, and although
the good ship rolled considerably on the 13th and 14th, the weather experienced
was much better than the average for this region. We had come out safely from
the dangers inevitably associated with navigation in Polar waters, and a word of
praise must be accorded to Captain Galindez for the able manner in which he
had looked after the safety of the ship. Some of his spells on bridge-duty—
running from twenty to thirty-six hours on end—were particularly arduous,
and his efforts were ably seconded by Lieutenant Yalour and the other ship's
officers. In the forenoon of the 15th, when about sixty miles off Cape Horn, we
had remarkably fine weather: the sky was cloudless and the sea smooth, and the
air felt so mild that it was difficult to realise that we were passing through a
region notorious as having one of the worst climates in the world. In the afternoon, however, it began to blow hard with a heavy sea, but coming soon under
the lee of the land we could make light of the elemental strife. In the early evening
we entered the placid waters of the Beagle Channel in the south of Tierra del
Fuego, and anchored for the night at Harbourtown opposite the residence of the
Messrs Bridges, who visited the ship in the evening, bringing with them a welcome supply of fresh bread and vegetables, luxuries which we much appreciated.

In the morning of the 16th I had the pleasure of breakfasting with these gentlemen under surroundings to which I had long been a stranger. Their house was a large one of two storeys, with sheds and storehouses near by, while inside the mansion was replete with numerous luxuries which we could hardly have expected in such a remote situation. Rich articles of furniture, beautiful pictures, a fine library, and costly bric-a-brac, surrounded one on every hand. After breakfast the Messrs Bridges showed us round the estate, and one could see on every side proofs of their handiwork and energy. Such labour as was necessary was furnished by the Indians brought into a state approaching civilisation by the long-continued efforts of the late Rev. Thomas Bridges, the founder of the Mission at Ushuaia. Now the brothers Bridges are ranchmen with large flocks of sheep, herds of cattle, and numerous horses, which roam about in the ten square leagues lying along the Beagle Channel. In the vicinity of the house was a well-kept garden, in which I was surprised to find roses, pansies, and other flowers in full bloom. In the garden were also all sorts of vegetables, and such fruits as apples, strawberries, and gooseberries. The scenery here was very similar to that of the more mountainous parts of the west of Scotland. The higher slopes were covered with snow, while lower down were forests of beech and magnolia. On the 17th we arrived at Ushuaia, the capital of Tierra del Fuego, where we remained a week while the ship's boilers were being cleaned. This is a somewhat important place, being a penal settlement of the Argentine Republic, besides being a military port. The harbour is good and well-sheltered. At the back of the town one plunges all at once into a thick forest, above which rise glaciers and rugged snow-covered peaks.

Ushuaia was left in the early morning of January 24, and we proceeded on our way to Sandy Point through the north-west arm of the Beagle Channel and Darwin Sound. The scenery here is very grand. There are many mountains which rise to a height of from 3000 to 4000 feet, with one peak above 6000 feet. Glaciers descend right to sea-level, fragments of which are continually breaking off, floating away in miniature icebergs. From the high snow slopes descend numerous cascades, and one bit of landscape was quite unique, there being no less than eight waterfalls several hundred feet high in close proximity to each other. Specially interesting was another portion where a combined glacier and waterfall extended from the mountain-side to the water-edge. In the evening we anchored close to Londonderry Island in Ross Harbour. The following day the weather quite broke down, with mist obscuring the hills, and rain descending in torrents. The navigation was again very complicated, there being quite a labyrinth of small channels with numerous islands. In the evening we anchored at Villarino Harbour, under the lee of Barrow Island. Here we were detained till noon of the 28th by a south-west gale of almost hurricane strength, accompanied by a perfect deluge of rain. Proceeding through Cockburn Channel and Magdalen Strait, we saw little of the grand scenery for which this region is so celebrated. Mount Sarmiento (7000 feet), the highest mountain in Tierra del Fuego, was invisible, but we had an excellent view of the two magnificent glaciers which descend from it into the blue waters beneath. Every now and then an Indian canoe would appear: they are made of bark and skins stretched upon a wattle framework. Their occupants were ugly, repulsive-looking beings, ill-favoured and dirty. At 10 P.M. we arrived at Punta Arenas (Sandy Point), and were now within the pale of civilisation. The voyage through the Straits of Magellan was resumed on the 30th, and the commission of the *Uruguay* terminated at Buenos Aires on February 8, the total distance traversed being 6184 miles.

INDEX